QUMRAN INTERPRETATION
of the GENESIS FLOOD

QUMRAN INTERPRETATION
—— *of the* GENESIS FLOOD

JEREMY D. LYON

☙PICKWICK *Publications* • Eugene, Oregon

QUMRAN INTERPRETATION OF THE GENESIS FLOOD

Copyright © 2015 Jeremy D. Lyon. All rights reserved. Except for brief quotations in critical publications or reviews, no part of this book may be reproduced in any manner without prior written permission from the publisher. Write: Permissions. Wipf and Stock Publishers, 199 W. 8th Ave., Suite 3, Eugene, OR 97401.

Pickwick Publications
An Imprint of Wipf and Stock Publishers
199 W. 8th Ave., Suite 3
Eugene, OR 97401

www.wipfandstock.com

ISBN 13: 978-1-4982-2009-5

Cataloguing-in-Publication Data

Lyon, Jeremy D.

    Qumran interpretation of the Genesis flood / Jeremy D. Lyon.

    xii + 212 p. ; 23 cm. Includes bibliographical references.

    ISBN 13: 978-1-4982-2009-5

    1. Genesis Apocryphon. 2. Dead Sea scrolls. 4Q. 3. Bible. Genesis—Criticism, interpretation, etc., Jewish. I. Title.

BS1235.5 L95 2015

Manufactured in the U.S.A.   09/25/2015

This book is dedicated to the Lord, who sat enthroned over the Flood (Psalm 29:10).

יהוה למבול ישב וישב יהוה מלך לעולם

The Lord *sat enthroned at the Flood,
and the* Lord *sits as King forever.*

Contents

Acknowledgments | ix

Abbreviations | xi

1 Introduction | 1
2 Genesis Apocryphon (1QapGen) | 13
3 Commentary on Genesis (4Q252) | 69
4 An Admonition Based on the Flood (4Q370) | 95
5 Paraphrase of Genesis and Exodus (4Q422) | 120
6 Conclusion | 141

Appendix A: Text and Translation of Columns 0–XII of Genesis Apocryphon (1QapGen) | 151

Appendix B: Text and Translation of Columns I–II:5 of Commentary on Genesis (4Q252) | 175

Appendix C: Text and Translation of An Admonition Based on the Flood (4Q370) | 181

Appendix D: Text and Translation of Paraphrase of Genesis and Exodus (4Q422) | 187

Bibliography | 193

Index of Scripture and Second Temple Period Literature | 203

Acknowledgments

A NUMBER OF PEOPLE have been instrumental in helping me bring this research to fruition. I would like to thank Dr. Robert Cole and Dr. Mark Rooker, who mentored me in Hebrew Bible/Old Testament studies and provided helpful feedback during the process of this writing. Also, I am grateful to Dr. Stephen Stout, who read through this, offering helpful suggestions and encouragement. I want to thank my colleagues at Southern California Seminary, who encouraged and supported me in various ways during the writing of this work. I would also like to thank Dr. Stephen Pfann and Claire Pfann at the University of the Holy Land for their generosity and hospitality toward my family in the months we spent in Jerusalem studying the Dead Sea Scrolls. Concerning various scroll images provided for this publication, I would like to thank James E. Trever, the Israel Antiquities Authority, and Dr. Marilyn Lundberg and Dr. Bruce Zuckerman at West Semitic Research.

My family has always been such a wonderful support for me over the years. I would like to thank my beautiful wife Ashley, who endured many days and nights, never wavering in her support, while I was researching and writing. I would also like to thank my precious children, Isaiah and Hadassah, for allowing daddy to get work done and for always bringing such joy into my life. I am truly blessed and thank the Lord for my wife and kids. I would like to thank my mom, Kim Young, who taught me God's Word through word and deed. No person has taught me more. I thank my dad, Charlie Lyon, for modeling such a strong work ethic. Also, with great fondness, I am grateful to my grandpa, Bill Lyon, who is now with the Lord. His prayers and letters of encouragement have made a profound impact.

Most of all, I thank the Lord Jesus Christ, who called me to this work and enabled me to complete it. May He get the glory.

Abbreviations

1 En	1 Enoch
1Q19	Book of Noah
1QapGen	Genesis Apocryphon
1QH^a	Hodayot
1QpHab	Habakkuk Pesher
1QS	Community Rule
3 Macc	3 Maccabees
4Q176	Tanhumim
4Q244	Pseudo-Daniel
4Q252	Commentary on Genesis A
4Q253	Commentary on Genesis B
4Q254	Commentary on Genesis C
4Q254a	Commentary on Genesis D
4Q370	An Admonition Based on the Flood
4Q422	Paraphrase of Genesis and Exodus
4Q464	A Narrative Based on Genesis and Exodus
4Q504	The Words of the Heavenly Lights
4Q508	Prayers for Festivals
4Q534–36	Book of Noah
4Q577	eight fragments containing allusions to the Flood story
5Q13	small fragment quoting 1QS

ABBREVIATIONS

CD	*Damascus Document*
DJD	*Discoveries in the Judaean Desert*
Jub	*Jubilees*
LXX	Septuagint
MT	Masoretic Text
NT	New Testament
OT	Old Testament
PAM	Palestine Archaeological Museum
Sib Or	*Sibylline Oracles*
Sir	*Wisdom of Ben Sirach*
SP	Samaritan Pentateuch
Wis	*Wisdom of Solomon*

CHAPTER ONE

INTRODUCTION

IN 1947, A BEDOUIN stumbled upon some ancient scrolls when he tossed a rock into a cave opening and heard pottery shatter. This discovery would turn out to be one of the greatest archaeological finds in history, leading to the search for more scrolls. Between 1947 and 1956 some nine hundred manuscripts, dated 250 B.C.–A.D. 68, were discovered in eleven caves around Qumran, along the northwestern shore of the Dead Sea. Among these manuscripts were Jewish sectarian writings, pseudepigraphal and apocryphal writings, and biblical books. These largely fragmentary manuscripts, collectively known as the Dead Sea Scrolls, have transformed our understanding of Second Temple Judaism and have shed ancient light on the formation, preservation, translation, and interpretation of the Hebrew Bible.

This book focuses on the particular impact of the Dead Sea Scrolls for understanding biblical interpretation during the Second Temple period.[1] In particular, these Qumran scrolls contain the most ancient surviving interpretations of the Genesis Flood, dating to the first-century B.C.[2] Several non-biblical texts from Qumran refer to Noah and the Flood, revealing how certain ancient Jews understood and employed the Flood material.

---

1. The Second Temple period generally refers to the period of Jewish history beginning with the dedication of the Second Temple around 516 B.C. and ending with the destruction of the Second Temple by the Romans in A.D. 70. Some scholars begin this period as early as the return of Jews from Babylon to Jerusalem around 539 B.C. and end it as late as the conclusion of the Bar Kokhba revolt against the Romans in A.D. 135. The Dead Sea Scrolls date to the latter half of the Second Temple period.

2. Flood texts included here are 1QapGen (30 B.C.–A.D. 30), 4Q252 (50–51 B.C.), 4Q370 (50–25 B.C.), and 4Q422 (100–50 B.C.).

Some of these references are very brief and somewhat obscure, while other manuscripts preserve more detailed references for serious examination of Qumran Flood interpretation. These texts contain, among other things, commentary, paraphrase, and admonition, which provide additional value in seeking to understand how they viewed the biblical text.

Four scrolls, in particular, have drawn significant attention from scholars concerning Qumran interpretations of the Genesis Flood. The *Genesis Apocryphon* (1QapGen) is a large, but badly damaged manuscript, preserving twenty-three columns of Aramaic text. Several fragmentary columns preserve a retelling and expansion upon the Genesis Noah/Flood narrative which includes a first-person account from Noah. The *Commentary on Genesis* (4Q252) is a fragmentary text which gives significant attention to the chronology of the events during the Flood. The *Admonition Based on the Flood* (4Q370) is a fragment, containing two columns of text. The first column contains a retelling of the Flood, which leads into an exhortation found in the second column. The *Paraphrase of Genesis and Exodus* (4Q422) is also fragmentary, preserving portions of three columns of text, of which the second provides a paraphrase of the Flood. But what do these texts mean as a collective whole and what are the implications?

Since the discovery and publication of 1QapGen, 4Q252, 4Q370, and 4Q422, there has been renewed interest in scholarly investigation concerning ancient interpretations of the Genesis Flood narrative. Numerous studies have been published on these individual Qumran Flood texts since their discoveries.

Notable Research on Noah and the Flood in the Dead Sea Scrolls

From the time of the discoveries between 1947 and 1956, considerable time had lapsed before the official publications of many of the scrolls. Hence, the scholarly examination of the individual Flood texts was delayed. 1QapGen was an exception among these Flood texts as it was published (in part) in an official edition in 1956, opening up study of this manuscript. However, even scholarship of 1QapGen has been a developing process as this manuscript presents its own issues. Once all of the manuscripts were made available for scholarship, these Flood texts began to be scrutinized. However, it was not until the 1990s when the study of these Flood texts began to flourish.

Since the 1990s the individual Qumran Flood texts have received attention from scholars in official editions of the text, articles, segments of chapters, whole chapters, and monographs. While considerable work has been done on the individual texts since the 1990s, what about studies on the Qumran Flood texts as a whole? To date, there have been several notable contributions to investigating the Flood texts as a whole, and thus, working towards a fuller understanding of the various aspects of Qumran interpretation of the Genesis Flood.

Jack P. Lewis (1968)

In 1968, Brill published Jack P. Lewis's 1962 dissertation, *A Study of the Interpretation of Noah and the Flood in Jewish and Christian Literature*, which was written prior to the publication of a number of relevant Flood texts from Qumran. Lewis provided a comprehensive compilation of the interpretation of Noah and the Flood in Jewish and Christian literature, which included apocryphal and pseudepigraphal works, Hellenistic-Jewish writings, the Greek and Aramaic versions, and early Christian and rabbinic interpretations. While Lewis made a foundational contribution to research on the interpretation of Noah and the Flood in ancient Jewish and Christian literature, this 1968 work preceded the rise of studies on Qumran Flood interpretation. The only noteworthy discussion in his work dealing with the Qumran corpus was on the *Genesis Apocryphon*.[3]

If this topic were published today, one would expect at least a full chapter devoted to Flood interpretation in the Dead Sea Scrolls. However, at that time Lewis could not devote more space to Qumran interpretation since many of the Dead Sea Scrolls had not yet been published. Lewis could only note his awareness of the existence of other fragmentary texts relating to Noah and the Flood stating that, "Starcky has reported that Cave IV has two fairly large fragments relating to Noah literature...."[4] Though these texts had been discovered, they had not been published yet for scholars to examine.

Further, Lewis dealt with the *Genesis Apocryphon* at an earlier stage of its history in scholarly publication and research, which affected his coverage of this material. He noted, "Since the scroll is as yet unpublished in its entirety, one is completely dependent upon the preliminary report...."[5] Thus, Lewis's treatment of 1QapGen was limited.

3. Lewis, *A Study of the Interpretation of Noah and the Flood*, 14–17.
4. Ibid., 15.
5. Ibid., 14. The preliminary report referred to by Lewis was *A Genesis Apocryphon*, by Nahman Avigad and Yigael Yadin (1956).

While in many ways Lewis's study has contributed much to the general study of the interpretation of Noah and the Flood in ancient Jewish and Christian literature, in other ways his work was before its time, especially in regard to Qumran interpretation. With the publication of other Flood texts (4Q252, 4Q370, and 4Q422), which were not available to Lewis at the time, a comprehensive study is now possible.

Florentino García Martínez (1998)

In a 1998 work, titled *Interpretations of the Flood*, Florentino García Martínez produced a chapter titled, "Interpretations of the Flood in the Dead Sea Scrolls." The stated purpose of this 23-page chapter was ". . . to provide a rather summary overview of all the allusions to the Flood narrative found in the Dead Sea Scrolls, and to present in greater detail the two best preserved fragments dealing with this narrative, 4Q252 and 4Q370."[6]

In his first major section of the chapter García Martínez summarizes the brief references or allusions made to Noah and the Flood in the non-biblical Qumran texts. The manuscripts in this initial summary include: the *Damascus Document* (CD), the *Genesis Apocryphon* (1QapGen), 1Q19, 4Q176, 4Q244, 4Q253, 4Q254, 4Q422, 4Q504, 4Q508, 4Q534-36, and 5Q13. In general, most of these texts contain very little Flood content or are obscure references which do not contribute much to the understanding of Qumran interpretation of the Flood. Thus, in the next two major sections he only expounds on 4Q252 and 4Q370.

García Martínez provides certain reasons why he did not expound on the *Genesis Apocryphon* (1QapGen) and the *Paraphrase of Genesis and Exodus* (4Q422) for this chapter. Concerning 1QapGen, brief mention is made of some of the extant scroll's content such as the birth of Noah and "the book of the words of Noah." He does not mention other significant elements of the text dealing with Noah and the Flood though. His reason for not including 1QapGen in fuller treatment is that ". . . the manuscript is so badly preserved that in most of its columns very few lines, or even sentences or words, can be read with any certainty; in addition, its precise relationship to *Jubilees* is so unclear and disputed that it would require a study of its own. Therefore the study of its interpretation of the Flood . . . must be left for another occasion."[7] Since there are recognizable difficulties

---

6. García Martínez, "Interpretations of the Flood," 87.

7. Ibid., 89.

with this manuscript, it is understandable that 1QapGen was not included for further examination in his summary-style chapter. This omission of detailed study of 1QapGen leaves the opportunity for this current investigation to provide the occasion for detailed examination of 1QapGen as part of a comprehensive study on Qumran Flood interpretation.

García Martínez says very little concerning 4Q422, only stating the basic subject matter of the three fragmentary columns. He does not provide warrant for further examination, noting that ". . . very little can be concluded about the content of the fragments, about their relationship to the biblical text, or about the interpretation of the Flood narrative offered by its author."[8] However, Torleif Elgvin[9] and Ariel Feldman[10] have demonstrated the value of examining 4Q422 for understanding Qumran Flood interpretation. Though 4Q422 is fragmentary, the extant text certainly appears to warrant detailed investigation for this current study.

García Martínez has made a noteworthy contribution towards investigating the Qumran Flood texts as a whole. However, due to the brevity of being a single chapter, it was limited to summarizing without being able to go in-depth. Further, the only two manuscripts that received any significant attention were 4Q252 and 4Q370, omitting other noteworthy manuscripts for this discussion. The more detailed presentation of 4Q252 and 4Q370 in the chapter was also limited in scope due to space. Nonetheless, his chapter serves as a good brief survey to the Qumran Flood texts available for further study. García Martínez has laid part of the foundation for more detailed research on Qumran Flood interpretation.

Moshe Bernstein (1999)

Moshe Bernstein contributed a chapter titled, "Noah and the Flood at Qumran," in the 1999 Brill publication, *The Provo International Conference on the Dead Sea Scrolls: Technological Innovations, New Texts, and Reformulated Issues*.[11] Bernstein's purpose was ". . . to focus more closely on two aspects of a single unit from Genesis: the man Noah, and the event the Flood, in an attempt to evaluate comparatively the ways in which this

---

8. Ibid., 93.

9. Elgvin, "The Genesis Section of 4Q422 (4QParaGenExod)," 180–96.

10. Feldman, "The Story of the Flood in 4Q422," 57–77.

11. Bernstein, "Noah and the Flood at Qumran," 199–231. This is from a publication on the 1996 Provo International Conference on the Dead Sea Scrolls.

unit is employed in Qumran literature."[12] In other words, Bernstein is not so much providing *what* the Qumran community believed concerning the Flood, but *how* they employed the Flood texts in the Qumran literature. This is an important interrelated aspect in the discussion of Qumran Flood interpretation.

Bernstein provided a more detailed summary of the Qumran Flood material than García Martínez and he also elaborated on the approaches used in the Qumran literature. Bernstein mentions several minor references to Noah and the Flood from the Qumran corpus and discusses in most detail 1QapGen, 4Q252, 4Q370, and 4Q422. Bernstein's discussion on these four texts was summarizing and selective in nature, focusing on how these texts treated the Noah/Flood narrative. He concluded, "We did not expect to find a single conception or treatment of either Noah or the flood pericope in the texts which survive from Qumran, and our expectations were vindicated."[13]

Bernstein's chapter has contributed significantly to the research of Qumran Flood interpretation, examining the literature as a whole and adding an important element to the discussion–*how* the Qumran literature employed the Noah/Flood material. His work, however, does not elaborate on many details of the individual texts and is necessarily selective due to limited space. He does, however, deal with some of these Flood texts in more detail in other separate works.[14] While Bernstein's chapter provides an invaluable study on the "how," it does not discuss in detail the "what" of Qumran Flood interpretation. This current research seeks to provide full-length chapters for each of the individual Flood texts (1QapGen, 4Q252, 4Q370, and 4Q422). This study also seeks to provide a comprehensive understanding of not only *how* the Qumran literature employs the Flood material, but *what* the Qumran community believed concerning the Flood.

---

12. Ibid., 199.

13. Ibid., 223.

14. Bernstein, "4Q252: From Re-Written Bible to Biblical Commentary," 1–27; "4Q252: Method and Context, Genre and Sources," 61–79; "4Q252 i 2 באדם רוחי ידור לא לעולם: Biblical Text or Biblical Interpretation?" 421–27; "Contours of Genesis Interpretation at Qumran," 57–85; "Divine Titles and Epithets," 291–310; "From the Watchers to the Flood," 39–63; "Is the Genesis Apocryphon a Unity?" 107–34.

Ariel Feldman (2007)

Ariel Feldman made a significant contribution to the study of Qumran Flood interpretation with his 2007 dissertation, "פרשת המבול המקראית במגילות קומראן (1Q19, 4Q370, 4Q422, 4Q464 and 4Q577)."[15] Feldman's purpose was to examine the biblical exegesis in the texts, along with the interpretation methods and strategies employed while reworking the biblical text. He provided new editions of the five texts he examined (1Q19, 4Q370, 4Q422, 4Q464, and 4Q577), and provided detailed commentary and discussion of these texts. Feldman's dissertation research has been translated into English and published in a work, edited by Devorah Dimant, titled, *Scripture and Interpretation: Qumran Texts that Rework the Bible*.[16] While Feldman's work will likely become a standard in studies on Qumran Flood interpretation, his research differs from this current study in several ways.

While Feldman's study addresses some of the same Flood texts as this current study (4Q370 and 4Q422), he also selected three other texts (1Q19, 4Q464 and 4Q577) for his study which are not included in this study. Further, Feldman does not include 1QapGen and 4Q252, which are included in this current study. Overall, Feldman's research emphasizes the exegetical and interpretive methods employed in these texts. Thus, Feldman's research differs from this study in its focus and scope. This current research will also address exegetical methods and how the Flood narrative was employed, but will focus more on developing the various aspects of Flood interpretation (*what* was believed concerning different aspects of the Flood) within the various literary contexts of 1QapGen, 4Q252, 4Q370, and 4Q422.

Dorothy Peters (2008)

In 2008, Dorothy M. Peters published an intriguing study of Noah in the Qumran texts in a work titled *Noah Traditions in the Dead Sea Scrolls: Conversations and Controversies of Antiquity*. Peters explored all the Qumran manuscripts which included the figure Noah in a text-by-text fashion providing a full-length analysis of the interpretation of Noah in the Dead Sea Scrolls.

Peters's work has made an invaluable contribution to understanding the Noah traditions in the Dead Sea Scrolls and, in general, the Second

---

15. Feldman's research was conducted at the University of Haifa.
16. Dimant (ed.), *Scripture and Interpretation*, 14–158.

Qumran Interpretation of the Genesis Flood

Temple period. However, Peters's work focuses on Noah traditions specifically, not Flood interpretation at Qumran. For example, Peters notes several background questions guiding her research: "First, How and to what extent is Noah portrayed as an archetype for a particular interpretation of what it meant to be Jewish? Second, What does God reveal to Noah and how does he do it? Finally, To what extent is Noah claimed as a 'distinctly Jewish' ancestor, or alternatively, claimed as a common ancestor shared with Gentiles?"[17]

The study of both, Noah and the Flood, is generally understood as being interrelated, but they are not the same study. Peters's focus on Noah in 1QapGen, 4Q252, 4Q370, and 4Q422 is different than studying these texts to understand specifically Qumran Flood interpretation.[18] Further, these texts necessarily receive less treatment in Peters's work as they constitute only a part of her text-by-text analysis of a larger corpus of literature, whereas 1QapGen, 4Q252, 4Q370, and 4Q422 constitute the full scope of this treatment on Qumran Flood interpretation.

This current study is specifically concerned with how the Qumran community understood the Flood narrative itself. Since Noah is the central figure in the Flood narrative, this study will examine Noah only as specifically related to the Flood, recognizing the necessity of studying Noah as a part of the larger scope of Qumran Flood interpretation. Thus, there will be some significant points of contact between Peters's work and this current study where her work addresses the relevant Flood texts. While Peters's work differs in its focus, it nonetheless provides a foundational understanding of Noah traditions in the Dead Sea Scrolls and thus, valuable insight for this research.

Contribution of Current Research

Lewis, García Martínez, Bernstein, Feldman, and Peters have all laid foundational work for this research in various ways. Jack Lewis set forth a comprehensive compilation of the Noah and Flood traditions in ancient Jewish and Christian literature, including 1QapGen in his study. Florentino

---

17. Peters, *Noah Traditions in the Dead Sea Scrolls*, 2.

18. For example, Peters focuses on Noah in 4Q252, a text that highlights Flood chronology. Peters addresses chronology, but only as it relates to Noah specifically. This current research focuses primarily on Flood interpretation at Qumran and addresses the figure Noah secondarily.

INTRODUCTION

García Martínez provided a chapter summary overview of references to the Flood in the Dead Sea Scrolls corpus. Moshe Bernstein laid out a more detailed summary chapter on the Noah and Flood texts at Qumran, giving more attention to 1QapGen, 4Q252, 4Q370, and 4Q422. He further dealt with the various ways the Qumran literature employed the Flood narrative. Ariel Feldman presented a *tour de force* on exegetical and interpretive methods employed in various Flood texts. Dorothy Peters's comprehensive text-by-text analysis of the Noah traditions in the Dead Sea Scrolls was a watershed study for Noah studies and set a precedent for the task of this current research concerning Flood interpretation in the Dead Sea Scrolls. Furthermore, Peters's textual analyses of the Flood texts are invaluable for dealing with Noah in this current study.

Nonetheless, the necessity for a more detailed treatment of the multifaceted aspects of Qumran Flood interpretation remains. Lewis's 1968 work only included significant discussion on 1QapGen as the other relevant Qumran texts had not yet been made available for scholarly study. García Martínez provided only a short chapter summary of Flood references in the Dead Sea Scrolls, expounding only on 4Q252 and 4Q370. Bernstein provided more discussion on 1QapGen, 4Q252, 4Q370, and 4Q422 in his brief chapter, but much remains to be expounded upon. Feldman's comprehensive study of Flood texts differs from this current study in its focus and scope. Peters's full-fledged study focused on Noah traditions, not Flood interpretation in the Qumran literature. Thus, there is both the need and the occasion now to build on these foundational contributions. These individual Flood texts need to be fleshed out and examined as a whole corpus in a full-length single-volume work. The purpose of this research is to provide a text-by-text, literary analysis of the Qumran Flood texts (1QapGen, 4Q252, 4Q370, and 4Q422), in order to understand the meaning of the individual texts and set forth a more comprehensive understanding of Qumran interpretation of the Genesis Flood. The goal of this work could also be thought of as developing a more comprehensive Qumran Flood theology.

Which Scrolls to Study? Narrowing the Scope of Research

Which scrolls *should* comprise the focus of a comprehensive examination of Flood interpretations at Qumran? While a rather sizable amount of references or allusions are made to Noah and/or the Flood in the Qumran material (1Q19, 1QapGen, 4Q176, 4Q244, 4Q252, 4Q370, 4Q422,

4Q464, 4Q504, 4Q508, 4Q534–536, 4Q577, 5Q13), not all references are relevant for providing a significant contribution to this endeavor. This lack of relevance for some of the material is due to the obscurity of these small and often fragmentary references. For example, García Martínez noted a number of these small and quite fragmentary references to Noah and the Flood which he provided in his brief overview. However, he did not include such small and fragmentary texts in any detailed study due to the inability to glean anything significant from these particular references.[19] Thus, the small and obscure references or allusions to the Flood found in the small and fragmentary texts will only be addressed when found relevant to a particular discussion on the four primary texts examined in this research.

While García Martínez selected only 4Q252 and 4Q370 for a more detailed discussion, Bernstein's chapter, "Noah and the Flood at Qumran," provided more detailed treatment on 1QapGen, 4Q252, 4Q370, and 4Q422.[20] Indeed, these four texts contribute significant insight into Qumran interpretation of the Genesis Flood and will be the primary focus of this research.

Why examine these four texts? 1QapGen perhaps could be seen as primarily consisting of a "Noah narrative" and an "Abram narrative." Further, the narrative portion of the actual Flood event itself has not been preserved in this extremely fragmentary section of 1QapGen, only picking up the Flood narrative in column X, line 12, with the ark landing on "one of the mountains of Hurarat (Ararat)." Nonetheless, through the interrelated Noah content, 1QapGen provides significant insight into different ways the Flood was understood. The text reveals belief regarding the cause of the Flood, the landing of the ark, and the Flood as an archetype of eschatological judgment.

The extant texts of 4Q252, 4Q370, and 4Q422 deal more specifically with the Flood narrative. 4Q252, though fragmentary, is the best preserved Qumran Flood text which gives significant attention to the chronology of the events during the Flood. The "120 years" referred to in Genesis 6:3 is dealt with, along with the landing of the ark. 4Q370 does not mention Noah or the ark, focusing on the Flood as divine judgment on human sin, rather than as deliverance of the righteous. In addition, 4Q370 addresses the cause of the Flood and presents the Flood as an archetype of eschatological judgment. Though fragmentary, 4Q422 addresses several aspects

---

19. García Martínez, "Interpretations of the Flood," 86–108.
20. Bernstein, "Noah and the Flood at Qumran," 199–231.

of Flood interpretation, including the focus on judgment, the Flood as a reversal and renewal of creation, and the purpose of the Flood.

Each of these texts selected for this study contribute different aspects of Qumran interpretation of the Flood and different ways in which the Genesis Flood material was employed by the Qumran community. In other words, these texts reveal not only *what* the Qumran community believed concerning the Flood, but they also provide examples of *how* the Flood story was employed. Together, these four texts reveal, quite uniquely, an overall picture of Qumran interpretation. In order to develop this Qumran Flood theology, how will these texts be studied?

Research Methodology

This research is not just a survey of Qumran manuscripts dealing with (or alluding to) the Flood, nor is the primary purpose to examine only the exegetical and interpretive methods employed in these texts, though the methods will be discussed. Rather, this research, through literary analysis, seeks to understand the different aspects of Flood interpretation in the Qumran literature (1QapGen, 4Q252, 4Q370, and 4Q422), with the goal of developing a more comprehensive Qumran Flood theology.

Each manuscript will be analyzed individually in consecutive chapters. Due to the fragmentary nature of the texts, the investigation of these manuscripts will commence with a physical description, as the reading of the extant text could be affected. Physical analysis will also include paleography and dating of the manuscripts.[21] Three manuscripts (1QapGen, 4Q370, and 4Q422) will include a section on provenance and the legitimacy of studying

21. Paleography studies the development of ancient scripts based on the presupposition that handwriting changes over time. Cf. Naveh, *Early History of the Alphabet*. Naveh notes the nature and significance of paleography for the study of ancient manuscripts: "Paleography is . . . the study of ancient scripts which traces the development of letter forms so that documents (both inscriptions and manuscripts) may be read correctly and, if necessary, dated" (p. 6). Hence, paleography ensures a more faithful reading of an ancient text and allows one, theoretically, to date the manuscript to a certain period based upon the styles and shapes of the letters. Qumran scholars have employed this technique for dating the Dead Sea Scrolls from early on. Frank M. Cross designated three major paleographical periods for the scrolls: Archaic (250–150 B.C.), Hasmonean (150–30 B.C.), Herodian (30 B.C.–A.D. 68). Cf. Cross, "The Development of Jewish Scripts," 133–202; VanderKam, *The Dead Sea Scrolls Today*, 35.

The reliability of paleography for dating the scrolls was confirmed by carbon-14 testing of several scrolls in the 1990s. Cf. Bonani et al., "Radiocarbon Dating of Fourteen Dead Sea Scrolls," 843–49; Jull et al., "Radiocarbon Dating of Scrolls," 11–19.

these texts for *Qumran* interpretation. A review of modern research, occurring since the discovery of these individual texts, will follow, setting the stage for the literary analysis of these Qumran texts.

The literary analysis will begin with the composition of the material in the text as a whole (literary composition), in order to gain a "big picture" understanding of each text (as much as possible), which provides the necessary context for studying the parts (words, phrases, lines, columns). Matters such as literary genre, structure, compositional features, general content, and thematic outlines will provide the literary context in which to understand how the authors understood and employed different aspects of the Flood story. Then, analysis (e.g., grammatical, lexical, and thematic investigation) will largely proceed in a phrase-by-phrase, line-by-line manner through the relevant portion of text, dealing with the various aspects of Flood interpretation.

In the concluding chapter, the findings from the literary analysis of the individual Flood texts will be synthesized in summary form. The goal is to develop a more comprehensive understanding of Qumran interpretation of the Genesis Flood.

Qumran Flood Interpretation: Ancient Light for Modern Readers

What is the value of gaining a comprehensive understanding of Qumran interpretation of the Genesis Flood? The history of Flood interpretation carries some weight in regard to modern questions on the interpretation of the biblical Flood narrative. The history of interpretation of the Genesis account provides historical precedent for understanding the text today in lieu of modern tendencies. The nature of these Qumran Flood texts, as the oldest existing *Jewish* interpretations of the Flood, adds weight to their contribution to the discussion of biblical interpretation.

CHAPTER TWO
GENESIS APOCRYPHON
(1QapGen)

Discovery of 1QapGen

THE *GENESIS APOCRYPHON* (1QAPGEN) is one of the original seven scrolls discovered by Bedouin in 1947 in what later became known as Cave 1. 1QapGen would be part of a clandestine and adventurous journey that literally took it around the world. This manuscript, along with others from Cave 1, was brought by the Bedouin to antiquities dealer Kando (Khalil Iskandar Shahin) who was a member of the Syrian Orthodox Church. A meeting was set up with Athanasius Yeshua Samuel, a metropolitan associated with St. Mark's Monastery in Jerusalem, who purchased four of the original seven scrolls from Cave 1, which included the *Genesis Apocryphon* (1QapGen). The other three scrolls were purchased later that year by Hebrew University professor and archaeologist Eleazar Sukenik.[1] In 1948, Metropolitan Samuel moved his four scrolls from Jerusalem to Lebanon, eventually bringing them to the United States where he attempted to sell them. He even placed an ad in the *Wall Street Journal* on June 1, 1954, which was brought to the attention of Israeli archaeologist Yigael Yadin, who was in New York at the time. Yadin, through a middle-man, arranged

---

1. The original seven scrolls were thus split into two groups. Metropolitan Samuel purchased four scrolls: the Great Isaiah Scroll (1QIsa^a), the Community Rule (1QS), the Habakkuk Pesher (1QpHab), and the Genesis Apocryphon (1QapGen). Eleazar Sukenik purchased three scrolls: the War Scroll (1QM), Hodayot (1QH), and a second Isaiah Scroll (1QIsa^b).

for the four scrolls to be purchased for $250,000 and presented them to the state of Israel where they were reunited with the other three scrolls. The Shrine of the Book was constructed to house these original seven scrolls at the Israel Museum in Jerusalem where they remain today.[2] 1QapGen was officially published in 1956 by Nahman Avigad and Yigael Yadin in a work titled *A Genesis Apocryphon*.

Qumran Cave 1 (Photograph by Jeremy D. Lyon)

2. The story of the discovery of the Dead Sea Scrolls has been well documented in numerous general introductions. For example, see VanderKam and Flint, *The Meaning of the Dead Sea Scrolls* (2002).

The Shrine of the Book (Photograph by Jeremy D. Lyon)

Physical Description of 1QapGen

1QapGen is a badly damaged and fragmentary manuscript containing parts of twenty-three columns of an Aramaic text that covers narratives from Genesis 5 to 15.[3] Due to its deteriorated state, it was the last of the original seven scrolls to be unrolled. It was poorly preserved and stuck together so that it could not be unrolled without delicate treatment and certain expertise. After James Biberkraut opened the scroll in Jerusalem, scholars recognized that the beginning and end of the manuscript was missing. This manuscript was once thought to contain the remains of twenty-two columns.[4] However, in the early 1990s Bruce Zuckerman and Michael Wise provided a new reconstruction of the manuscript, and it is now generally accepted that some fragments from a column before the first preserved column (col. I) have also survived and consequently been labeled "column

---

3. Fitzmyer, "Genesis Apocryphon," 302.

4. For example, see Geza Vermes, *The Complete Dead Sea Scrolls in English*, rev. ed., 480.

o."[5] Of the twenty-three columns, only three columns (XX–XXII) are, for the most part, completely preserved while several others still contain a significant amount of text (col. II, XII, and XIX). The rest of the columns are much more fragmentary, preserving in some cases only a few words or lines of text.[6] Also, the text of column XVIII is not preserved.

The Genesis Apocryphon (1QapGen) as found in Cave 1, before it was carefully unrolled (© John C. Trever, PhD, digital image by James E. Trever)

The missing text at the beginning of the manuscript raises some questions. Where did the manuscript begin, how much of the beginning is missing, and where does the preserved portion of text fragments fit? The preserved manuscript may provide a possible solution. Various Qumran

5. Eshel, "Genesis Apocryphon," 664.
6. Fitzmyer, "Genesis Apocryphon," 302.

manuscripts are made up of multiple "sheets" of treated leather (parchment), each containing multiple columns of text, which make up the whole scroll. Interestingly, the sheet beginning with column V is numbered by the Hebrew letter פ, the seventeenth letter of the Hebrew alphabet. Further, the sheet beginning with column X is numbered by צ and the sheet beginning with column XVII is marked by ק, respectively the eighteenth and nineteenth letters. Thus, it possible the extant text was originally preceded by sixteen sheets of text.[7] This would result in the original composition of 1QapGen being a very large manuscript. After this discovery of letters in the top right-hand margin, Matthew Morgenstern argued the original scroll of 1QapGen could have had 70 to 105 more columns of text.[8] If this is so, the length of the original 1QapGen scroll could have rivaled the largest manuscripts from Qumran, such as the Temple Scroll (11QT[a]) and the Great Isaiah Scroll (1QIsa[a]).[9]

However, many scholars still do not support this idea of such a lengthy original of 1QapGen. Moshe Bernstein views Morgenstern's claims, based on the letter-numbers on the extant sheets, as "hard to imagine." He also questions if there is any guarantee that all these proposed sheets, numbered א–ע, were used for 1QapGen in particular.[10] Daniel Machiela, in his 2009 edition of 1QapGen, notes that Morgenstern's proposal ". . . has not been widely accepted, and the letters might be better explained as part of the leather preparation process (and, therefore, having nothing to do with the content of the scroll)."[11] Sidnie White Crawford added, concerning Morgenstern's proposal, ". . . other than the slim evidence he cites, there is no indication that that much material was missing from the beginning of the Scroll."[12] In fact, the extant text of 1QapGen begins with the story of the Watchers which is common in Second Temple period literature. Thus, while the original beginning of 1QapGen cannot be stated with complete certainty, the beginning of the extant text (columns 0-I) appears to represent the beginning of the work.

---

7. Vermes, *The Complete Dead Sea Scrolls in English*, rev. ed., 480.

8. Morgenstern, "A New Clue to the Original Length of the Genesis Apocryphon," 345–47.

9. Bernasconi, "A Literary Analysis of the *Genesis Apocryphon*," 141–42.

10. Bernstein, "From the Watchers to the Flood," 44.

11. Machiela, *The Dead Sea Genesis Apocryphon*, 29.

12. Crawford, *Rewriting Scripture in Second Temple Times*, 108.

Qumran Interpretation of the Genesis Flood

The extant 1QapGen manuscript consists of four leather sheets containing 23 columns of text, ranging from well preserved columns (II, XX–XXII) to very fragmentary in nature. The leather appears to have been prepared for writing in a similar manner to other Qumran scrolls. In many places the leather has been completely eaten away along the lines of text due to the erosive nature of the ink used in writing.[13]

Column II, one of the well-preserved columns of 1QapGen; part of column I is also visible to the right in fragmentary form with the "Trever fragment" at the bottom (© John C. Trever, PhD, digital image by James E. Trever)

Horizontal lines were also ruled on the sheets of leather with a sharp instrument and, like other Qumran scrolls, the script was written "hanging" down from the lines as opposed to being written on the lines. The

---

13. Fitzmyer, *The Genesis Apocryphon of Qumran Cave 1 (1Q20)*, 14.

number of lines for each sheet varies from 34 to 37 lines.[14] According to Avigad and Yadin the total length of the preserved scroll is 2.83 m. with a height of 31 cm.[15]

Date of Manuscript 1QapGen

Based on the archaeology of Khirbet Qumran and the caves in which the scrolls were found it is generally believed that the scrolls were placed in the caves prior to the Roman destruction of the Qumran site in A.D. 68. Thus, according to the archaeological evidence the *terminus ad quem* for the dating of 1QapGen is A.D. 68. Paleography, however, has been the chief means by which the scrolls have been dated more precisely.

Paleography

1QapGen is written in Aramaic script and, from early on, has been dated by a number of scholars using paleography. In their original publication of *A Genesis Apocryphon*, Avigad and Yadin noted that the script of the scroll indicated the date of this copy was the end of the first century B.C. or the first part of the first century A.D.[16] E. Y. Kutscher followed up a year later in 1957 with a linguistic study of 1QapGen, stating that ". . . the scroll can be dated in this manner and that it comes from about the first century C.E., possibly even the first century B.C.E."[17] Others such as J. T. Milik, Frank M. Cross, and Joseph Fitzmyer confirm this paleographical date. For example, Cross dated 1QapGen to 30 B.C.–A.D. 70,[18] and Fitzmyer affirmed "this copy is dated paleographically to 25 B.C.E. through 50 C.E."[19] It can be concluded that there is general consensus concerning the paleographical dating of 1QapGen from the end of the first century B.C. to the beginning of the first century A.D.

---

14. Avigad and Yadin, *A Genesis Apocryphon*, 14.
15. Ibid., 15.
16. Ibid., 38.
17. Kutscher, "Dating the Language of the Genesis Apocryphon," 288.
18. Cross, "The Development of Jewish Scripts," 133–202.
19. Fitzmyer, "Genesis Apocryphon," 302.

Radiocarbon Dating

The reliability of the paleographical dating of 1QapGen was put to the test in 1991 as several manuscripts, including 1QapGen, were subjected to radiocarbon dating at the Institut für Mittelenergiephysik in Zürich, Switzerland. The radiocarbon dating of 1QapGen became possible due to the new technique called Accelerator Mass Spectroscopy in which tiny samples containing 0.5-1.0 mg of carbon could be tested. The AMS result for the age of 1QapGen was 2013 ± 32 (BP),[20] which is calibrated to 73 B.C.–A.D. 14.[21] The authors who published the results noted: "Good agreement between radiocarbon and paleographic dates exist."[22] Concerning the radiocarbon dating of the manuscript, Daniel Machiela noted, "When combined with the paleographic dates assigned to the scroll, a date around the late first cent. BCE for this copy emerges as most tenable."[23] Thus, it is generally accepted that the paleographical dating of 1QapGen has been confirmed by radiocarbon dating. The date of the 1QapGen manuscript, however, is a different question than the date of its composition. Is this only copy of 1QapGen discovered the original? Was it composed at an earlier time in the Second Temple period? Is it even a Qumran composition?

Date of Composition of 1QapGen

A number of scholars, such as Joseph Fitzmyer[24] and Sidnie White Crawford,[25] have pointed out the possibility that this extant 1QapGen manuscript could possibly be the autograph since it is the only copy discovered to date. However, for various reasons scholars generally view the extant 1QapGen manuscript as a *copy* of an earlier composition from the second or first century B.C. The relationship between *Jubilees* and 1QapGen is debated among scholars and affects one's view of the date of the original composition of 1QapGen. Regardless of the various views of the relationship between 1QapGen and *Jubilees*, the original composition of

---

20. BP stands for "before present." In other words, the age of the dated sample was 2013 ± 32 years at the present time of testing in 1991.

21. Bonani et al., "Radiocarbon Dating of Fourteen Dead Sea Scrolls," 845.

22. Ibid., 847.

23. Machiela, *The Dead Sea Genesis Apocryphon*, 137.

24. Fitzmyer, "Genesis Apocryphon," 302.

25. Crawford, *Rewriting Scripture in Second Temple Times*, 106.

this work is generally dated by scholars to the second or first century B.C. Esther Eshel notes that a third century B.C. date should not be ruled out either.[26] Discussions continue and questions still plague scholars on the date of composition. However, it appears safe to state in general terms that the composition of 1QapGen is sometime between the third century B.C. and the end of the first century B.C.

1QapGen: A Qumran Composition?

Is 1QapGen a Qumran sectarian composition? If this text is not a Qumran composition, should it be part of a study of *Qumran* interpretation of the Flood? The standard dating of the extant 1QapGen manuscript is the late first century B.C., which places it during the period of sectarian writing at Qumran. Several scholars have noted that since this is the only copy ever found of 1QapGen, it could possibly be an autograph. However, this cannot be definitively determined one way or the other. Early on, some scrolls scholars viewed 1QapGen as being a Qumran sectarian composition. However, that view has subsequently been jettisoned by most scholars.

Several considerations point toward 1QapGen not being a Qumran sectarian composition. Fitzmyer, among others, has pointed out that 1QapGen is written in Aramaic, while the Qumran sectarian literature was written in Hebrew.[27] Thus, it is unlikely this manuscript was composed by the Essenes. Second, he argues, "There is nothing in this text that clearly links it with any of the known beliefs or customs of the Qumran sect. There is practically no Essene theology in this work . . . ."[28] For example, 1QapGen does not contain the dualistic theology or calendrical teachings that are prominent in the Qumran sectarian literature such as the *Community Rule* (1QS), *War Scroll* (1QM), the *pesharim*, and other texts.

There are, however, a number of other noteworthy observations that help clarify the relationship of 1QapGen and the Essenes at Qumran. Machiela astutely observed that just because a composition did not originate with the group responsible for the sectarian literature at Qumran, this does not necessarily mean that it is not an Essene composition.[29] The

---

26. Eshel, "Genesis Apocryphon," 664.
27. Fitzmyer, "Genesis Apocryphon," 303.
28. Fitzmyer, *The Genesis Apocryphon of Qumran Cave 1 (1Q20)*, 23.
29. Machiela, *The Dead Sea Genesis Apocryphon*, 135.

Essenes were apparently a larger sectarian movement of which only a group of celibate males called the יחד (*yahad*) dwelt at Qumran.

There are several indicators that point toward 1QapGen being composed in Judea. Machiela has pointed out the geographical knowledge of Judea apparent in this manuscript.[30] A number of scholars, including Fitzmyer, have recognized that the Aramaic language employed in 1QapGen indicates it was composed in Judea during the Second Temple period.[31] Further, the fact that the manuscript itself was discovered in the Qumran caves in the Judean wilderness solidifies 1QapGen as a Judean composition.

While 1QapGen was likely not composed by the Qumran community (יחד), it was certainly composed by Jews and found acceptable for study and use at Qumran. The relationship of 1QapGen to *Jubilees* and *1 Enoch*, popular books at Qumran, helps to explain why it appealed to the Qumran community. The theological teaching itself found in the text, though not blatantly sectarian, does upon closer examination fit nicely with Qumran thought. Another important fact is that 1QapGen was among the original scrolls found in Cave 1 in 1947 along with other Qumran sectarian texts such as the *Community Rule* (1QS) and others. The contents of this cave were that of the Qumran sectarian community. Fitzmyer noted that 1QapGen was ". . . a text composed by Jews, which was found acceptable for reading and study in the Qumran community."[32] Sidnie White Crawford affirmed that 1QapGen ". . . was congenial to the Qumran community but not its product."[33] Machiela also recognized that even though 1QapGen was not composed at Qumran, "it was certainly read and used there."[34] Thus, it appears that 1QapGen was not a Qumran composition, but was accepted by the Essenes and was part of this sectarian library at Qumran. Hence, the inclusion of this manuscript for understanding Qumran interpretation of the Flood is more than justified.

History of Research on 1QapGen

The *Genesis Apocryphon* has a long and rich history of research which includes initial publications of the manuscript, articles, books, and more.

30. Ibid., 134–35.
31. Fitzmyer, *The Genesis Apocryphon of Qumran Cave 1 (1Q20)*, 36.
32. Fitzmyer, "Genesis Apocryphon," 303.
33. Crawford, *Rewriting Scripture in Second Temple Times*, 106.
34. Machiela, *The Dead Sea Genesis Apocryphon*, 135.

Many of these works deal with a wide range of issues relating to this scroll. However, what is particularly relevant to this research is the history of research as it relates to the Flood section of 1QapGen. Thus, the history of research given here is necessarily select.

Nahman Avigad and Yigael Yadin

In 1956, Nahman Avigad and Yigael Yadin produced the preliminary edition of 1QapGen, titled *A Genesis Apocryphon*. This edition includes introductory sections on the scroll's physical description, contents, paleography and date, the Aramaic text and English translation. However, in this edition only several columns were published. Avigad and Yadin noted the extremely poor state of preservation for most of the columns and, consequently, the long process of deciphering those fragmentary columns as sufficient reason not to include them in their edition.[35] They did, at least, provide a summary of the contents of these columns that were not published. Avigad and Yadin justified their preliminary publication noting, "The scroll has, however, aroused so much interest and is actually of such importance that it was decided to publish this preliminary survey."[36] Their edition included the publication of the five more well preserved columns, II and XIX–XXII. Considering the length of time that had already elapsed from the scroll's discovery in 1947, the preliminary publication of these five columns of text was an accomplishment which opened up scholarly examination of this important manuscript.

Avigad and Yadin's work is relevant for this current study for several reasons. First, while columns XIX–XXII deal with the Abram narrative and are not directly relevant to this current study, column II contains discussion concerning Lamech, the birth of Noah, and the Watchers, which is relevant to the current discussion of Flood interpretation. Avigad and Yadin's edition was not focused on discussion of the Flood narrative, but it is a standard work on 1QapGen in general that provided a foundation for the research that would follow. Second, their edition provided a published physical description of the text and discussion of the content of the scroll. Third, Fitzmyer noted, "For all five of these columns the editors appended excellent, but brief notes on the reading and sense of the text."[37]

---

35. Avigad and Yadin, *A Genesis Apocryphon*, 8.
36. Ibid.
37. Fitzmyer, *The Genesis Apocryphon of Qumran Cave 1 (1Q20)*, 5.

Joseph A. Fitzmyer

A major advancement in the scholarly study of 1QapGen appeared in Joseph Fitzmyer's commentary on 1QapGen in 1966, with the second edition in 1971. Over thirty years later, due to more columns of the fragmentary text being read by scholars and made available to the public, there was a need for a new edition.[38] Fitzmyer published his third edition, titled *The Genesis Apocryphon of Qumran Cave 1 (1Q20): A Commentary*, in 2004. This work provides a nice introduction to the manuscript. But the major contribution is the publication of every column of 1QapGen in Aramaic with an English translation and an extensive commentary on the complete text. Fitzmyer's work is a standard in the study of 1QapGen, and this current research will necessarily interact with Fitzmyer's commentary in discussion of the text relevant to Flood interpretation.

Dorothy M. Peters

In 2008, Dorothy Peters published her comprehensive study of Noah in the Qumran literature in a work titled *Noah Traditions in the Dead Sea Scrolls: Conversations and Controversies of Antiquity*. In her full-length analysis, Peters includes an excellent section in which she discusses interpretation of Noah in 1QapGen.[39] Her literary analysis of the Noah portion of 1QapGen is tremendously helpful for this current study as it relates to Flood interpretation. Thus, this chapter is indebted to Peters's literary treatment of the Noah section of 1QapGen.

Moshe J. Bernstein

Moshe Bernstein has made multiple contributions to discussion of Noah and the Flood in 1QapGen. In the 1999 publication of *The Provo International Conference on the Dead Sea Scrolls*, Bernstein contributed a chapter, "Noah and the Flood at Qumran," in which he discussed Noah and the Flood in 1QapGen.[40] A few years later in 2002, Bernstein presented a paper entitled "From the Watchers to the Flood: Story and Exegesis in the Early Columns of the *Genesis Apocryphon*," which was published in 2005 as a

---

38. Ibid.
39. Peters, *Noah Traditions in the Dead Sea Scrolls*, 106–27.
40. Bernstein, "Noah and the Flood at Qumran," 206–10.

chapter in *Reworking the Bible: Apocryphal and Related Texts at Qumran*.[41] Further, in 2010, Bernstein published an article titled "Is the Genesis Apocryphon a Unity? What Sort of Unity Were You Looking For?"[42] This study is informative and relevant to this current study as it addresses how 1QapGen can be treated "as an integral literary artifact."[43] This issue must be addressed in seeking to understand if the Noah narrative is to be understood in tandem with the Abram narrative.

Daniel Machiela

In 2009, Daniel Machiela contributed a new edition of 1QapGen with the publication of *The Dead Sea Genesis Apocryphon*. Machiela's edition of 1QapGen included the Aramaic transcription of the text based on Michael Wise and Bruce Zuckerman's generally accepted reconstruction.[44] An English translation and textual notes are provided in this edition as well as a significant introduction to 1QapGen in general and the text in particular. Machiela also includes special treatment of columns XIII–XVII that are not the focus of this current research. He then provides conclusions on a number of relevant issues raised in the introductory chapters. Machiela's edition also provides photographic plates of the entire manuscript, including "column 0." His edition is thus an indispensable tool for any study regarding 1QapGen. While Machiela's edition does not focus on the question of Flood interpretation, this current research will necessarily interact with Machiela's edition concerning the text of the manuscript itself. Especially helpful are the textual notes, the photographic plates, and his introductory and concluding chapters.

Rocco Bernasconi

In 2011, Rocco Bernasconi added to the discussion of literary analysis of 1QapGen as a whole in his publication of "A Literary Analysis of the

---

41. Bernstein, "From the Watchers to the Flood," 39–63.
42. Bernstein, "Is the Genesis Apocryphon a Unity?" 107–34.
43. Ibid., 107.
44. In the early 1990s Bruce Zuckerman and Michael Wise arranged the 1Q20 fragments and the Trever fragment into a new order. J. T. Milik's 1Q20 was dubbed "column 0" and the Trever fragment was inserted into column I.

Genesis Apocryphon" in *Aramaic Studies*.[45] Bernasconi determined that literary analysis of a fragmentary and incomplete text could be done which would involve "a number of assumptions and speculations."[46] Since much of the original 1QapGen text is no longer extant, literary analysis of the original overall structure is beyond reach. Bernasconi notes, "However, a careful and systematic analysis of the literary structure of the extant parts of the Genesis Apocryphon may shed some light on that overall structure and hence on its genre."[47]

Bernasconi's study is relevant for this research in several ways. He sets forth a literary analysis in which he claims ". . . the original Genesis Apocryphon is compatible with three distinct text types: narrative, thematic discourse, or an aggregate of juxtaposed part-texts not explicitly connected to each other."[48] He further provides a topical outline, structural outline, and a literary analysis of what he refers to as the three independent part-texts (Lamech, Noah, and Abram sections). Bernasconi's analysis of the text as a whole and its structural parts is helpful as this current research is interested in the "Noah section" and, in particular, how it deals with the Flood. In order to understand fully the interpretations of the Flood in 1QapGen, it is essential to have an understanding of the literary structure of the whole text and how it may (or may not) affect the question of how the Flood was understood by the scroll's author.

Literary Genre of 1QapGen

The examination of literary genre and structure are interconnected and are thus generally discussed together. In this case an attempt is made to discuss preliminarily the genre of 1QapGen before investigating the multifaceted issues concerning literary structure. The question of literary genre for 1QapGen has proven to be problematic as numerous scholars differ in their attempt to define it. The genre of 1QapGen has been variously labeled as Targum, Midrash, parabiblical text, rewritten Bible, and even apocalyptic text.

In the 1956 preliminary edition, Avigad and Yadin concluded their study of the content, structure, and style of 1QapGen by stating:

---

45. Bernasconi, "A Literary Analysis of the *Genesis Apocryphon*," 139–62.
46. Ibid., 140.
47. Ibid.
48. Ibid.

All that has been said above about the contents, structure and style of the scroll, leads to the definite conclusion that it is actually a sort of apocryphal version of stories from *Genesis*, faithful, for the most part, to the order of the chapters in Scripture. Some chapters of the scroll begin and end precisely as the comparable chapters of *Genesis* do, though the narrative in the scroll is in large part couched in the first person.[49]

Based upon this conclusion the editors supplied their title, *Genesis Apocryphon*, for the scroll. However, many scholars have not been content with Avigad and Yadin's conclusions and have tried to determine more precisely the literary genre of 1QapGen.

Joseph Fitzmyer has noted that the ". . . conventional title, Genesis Apocryphon, assigned by the original editors, is a misnomer; it says nothing about the literary form of the writing."[50] Fitzmyer recognizes that 1QapGen depends on the Genesis text and contains elements or traits of Targum and Midrash. However, he does not see 1QapGen as either Targum or Midrash, but as a ". . . free reworking of the Genesis stories, a re-telling of the tales of the patriarchs (Lamech, Noah, Abram)."[51] This scroll is an example of Second Temple period Jewish narrative writing based on the Genesis stories of the patriarchs, but with imaginative additions. 1QapGen is more doctrinal and literary than midrashic literature and does not directly quote Genesis.[52] Fitzmyer states that 1QapGen ". . . is a form of parabiblical literature, resembling *Jubilees* (on which it depends); part of *1 Enoch*, and Pseudo-Philo's *Biblical Antiquities*."[53] Thus, while targumic and midrashic elements are involved, 1QapGen is not viewed as Targum or Midrash, but as a form of parabiblical literature. Fitzmyer then proposes what he sees as a more appropriate title for the scroll, כתב אבהתא (The Book of the Patriarchs).[54]

Sidnie White Crawford views 1QapGen as an example of "Rewritten Scripture." Since 1QapGen is written in Aramaic, not Hebrew, it is far removed from the biblical text, and its readers would not have mistaken this manuscript for the biblical text of Genesis itself. Crawford recognizes that

---

49. Avigad and Yadin, *A Genesis Apocryphon*, 38.
50. Fitzmyer, "Genesis Apocryphon," 302.
51. Fitzmyer, *The Genesis Apocryphon of Qumran Cave 1 (1Q20)*, 20.
52. Ibid.
53. Fitzmyer, "Genesis Apocryphon," 302. Fitzmyer also concluded in his commentary on 1QapGen (2004): "This [parabiblical literature] is the designation that I prefer to use in describing the literary genre of the *Genesis Apocryphon*."
54. Ibid., 302. See *The Genesis Apocryphon of Qumran Cave 1 (1Q20)*, 18n19.

while 1QapGen is an imaginative retelling of the biblical account joined with other traditions (*1 Enoch* and *Jubilees*), the author is not simply retelling or translating the story of Genesis.[55] The author of 1QapGen uses literary techniques of ". . . addition, omission, harmonization, re-arrangement, and anticipation to create a new, unique narrative that is unlike any other retelling of Genesis from antiquity."[56] Thus, in essence, Crawford sees 1QapGen as a unique re-telling of Genesis 5–15 in narrative form.

Moshe Bernstein has proposed describing 1QapGen not as a single genre, but as a "multigeneric text." That is, the text of 1QapGen as a whole is not sufficiently understood when viewed as a single genre, but as employing multiple genres. Bernstein has concluded ". . . that we can speak of the genre of Part I of the Apocryphon (columns 0–17) as 'parabiblical' and Part II (columns 19–22) as 'rewritten Bible'" and that there was "no convenient generic term for the whole."[57] Thus, Bernstein recognizes two distinct genres incorporated into a narrative unity, in which the story of Noah (col. 0–XVII) is written as parabiblical literature and the story of Abram (col. XIX–XXII) is more closely tied to the biblical text as rewritten Scripture.

Daniel Machiela also agreed with Fitzmyer, noting that 1QapGen as a whole could not be labeled as targum since most of the text, especially the Noah section, is more expansionistic than any known targum.[58] Machiela also noted the label "midrash" was helpful only to a degree in understanding the interpretive process employed in 1QapGen. While the term "midrash" can be understood in broad terms with Jewish biblical interpretation, it is often understood to refer to a specific rabbinic methodology of interpretation.[59] The genre labels "Rewritten Bible," "parabiblical text," "midrash," and "reworked Scripture" have become more popular over the years. However, Machiela shows that some confusion has arisen due to the "interchangeable and conflicting use" of these genre labels to "describe ancient Jewish texts that interpret Scripture."[60] Machiela concludes:

> The Genesis Apocryphon's status as Rewritten Bible is valid only when viewing the scroll in its entirety. Were we to possess only the first few columns, we would probably not consider this text

---

55. Crawford, *Rewriting Scripture in Second Temple Times*, 105–7.
56. Ibid., 107
57. Bernstein, "Is the Genesis Apocryphon a Unity?" 108.
58. Machiela, *The Dead Sea Genesis Apocryphon*, 2.
59. Ibid., 3.
60. Ibid.

rewritten Bible, but an Enochic writing. If, on the other hand, we had only column 22 it could legitimately be considered a targum.[61]

Machiela's observations of labeling the literary genre of 1QapGen further illustrate the difficulty in labeling the literary genre of 1QapGen as a whole.

In 2011, Rocco Bernasconi argued that none of these genre labels are satisfactory and that the generic, general, and uninformative nature of genre labels for 1QapGen showed the difficulty in defining the genre of 1QapGen. Bernasconi provided two reasons for the difficulty in classifying the genre. First, the "loose stylistic and narrative uniformity" defies a straightforward genre classification. Second, the decisive reason for this difficulty is due to the fragmentary, incomplete nature of the text.[62] He then argued that, based on some assumptions, the original 1QapGen is compatible with three distinct text types: narrative, thematic discourse, and an aggregate of juxtaposed "part-texts" not explicitly related.[63]

Reaching a consensus label for the literary genre of 1QapGen has proven very difficult. However, several recurring terms used in describing the literary genre are discerned: "parabiblical," "rewritten Bible," and "narrative." The Noah section (columns 0–XVII) is a form of parabiblical literature that is much freer and expansionistic from the biblical text while the Abram section (columns XVIII–XXII) is a form of rewritten Bible which is much less expansionistic and follows the biblical text more closely. The Noah section, in particular, has so much extra-biblical material that the canonical Genesis narrative itself is nearly absent. The extensive extra-biblical material in the Noah section reflects that at the time 1QapGen was written there were well developed traditions attached to this patriarch.[64] Further, an underlying observation is that the text as a whole is written in narrative form, including first person narrative. Thus, the author of 1QapGen is, in narrative form, retelling the Noah and Abram narratives in a very unique way in antiquity which employs more expansionistic "parabiblical" material (Noah section) and "rewritten Bible" material (Abram section) more closely tied to the biblical text.

Having gained a general sense of the literary genre, an examination of the literary structure of the text as a whole should provide a better sense of the literary context in which Noah and the Flood are discussed in 1QapGen.

61. Ibid., 5.
62. Bernasconi, "A Literary Analysis of the *Genesis Apocryphon*," 139.
63. Ibid., 140, 149.
64. Machiela, *The Dead Sea Genesis Apocryphon*, 131.

The way the author structures the content of the text can reveal much about the meaning of the text.

Literary Structure and Content of 1QapGen

Before narrowing this study, on the question of Flood interpretation in 1QapGen, it is beneficial to understand the literary context as a whole. While the manuscript is fragmentary and presents a barrier to discerning the original literary structure, there are still great insights that can be gleaned from a literary analysis of the complete extant text. The division and outline of the extant text's content have varied slightly among scholars. In general, however, the text uniquely retells Genesis 5–15 and is divided into two major thematic sections with an underlying literary structure constituting three sections.

Joseph Fitzmyer divides the text into two major sections: the story of Noah (Col. 0–XVII) and the story of Abram (Col. XVIII?–XXII). Fitzmyer's structural outline includes column "0" and he supplies question marks where there is uncertainty as to the exact start or end of a section due to the fragmentary nature of portions of the manuscript. Fitzymer's outline is helpful in describing the general layout of the content for the reader and is summarized here:[65]

I. The Story of Noah (columns 0:?–XVII:?)

    A. Depravity of humanity and Noah's birth (0–I:28)

    B. Lamech's anxiety about the conception of Noah (II:1–V:?)

    C. Noah and the Flood (VI:?–X:?)

    D. God's Covenant with Noah and Noah's vision (XI:?–XV:?)

    E. Noah divides the earth among his sons (XVI:?–XVII?)

II. The Story of Abram (columns XVIII:?–XXII:34)

    A. Abram in Ur and Haran (XVIII:?–?)

    B. Abram in Canaan (XVIII:?–XIX:10a)

    C. Abram in Egypt (XIX:10b–XX:33a)

---

65. Fitzmyer, "Genesis Apocryphon," 302–3; *The Genesis Apocryphon*, 46. The outline provided here is an adaptive summary of Fitzmyer's outlines set forth in both of these works.

D. Abram in the Promised Land (XX:33b–XXI:22)

E. Abram's defeat of the four invading kings (XXI:23–XXII:26)

F. Abram's vision: God promises him an heir (XXII:27–?)

Rocco Bernasconi recognizes that the topical and chronological framework of 1QapGen parallels with Genesis 5–15 and also sees the text of 1QapGen in two main parts: the story of Noah (0–XVII) and the story of Abram (XVIII–XXII). While Bernasconi subdivides the Abram section (XVIII–XXII) slightly different than Fitzmyer, the general subdivisions outlining the Noah section (0–XVII) are identical. Bernasconi thus recognizes essentially the same "topical" outline as Fitzmyer. Bernasconi also notes that dialogues, dreams, and visions are found throughout the sequence of events narrated in the text.[66] While a topical outline is provided, Bernasconi also recognizes another element to the structure of the text.

Bernasconi identifies an underlying *structural* outline by which the thematic content is told by three different "I-narrators": Lamech (0–V:28), Noah (V:29–XVII), and Abram (XVIII:? – XXII).[67] The narratives are moved along by the phrases "I, Lamech," "I, Noah," and "I, Abram" in each respective section. Noah and Abram are also the main characters of the whole work while Lamech is not. Even in the Lamech section, which addresses the conception and birth of Noah, the main character is Noah.

Scholars before Bernasconi, such as Sidnie White Crawford, had already recognized that the text of 1QapGen is divided into three literary sections, which she labeled: birth of Noah (0–V:28), Noah (V:29–XVII), and Abram (XVIII?–XXII).[68] Crawford recognized the same "I-narrative" features differentiating the respective sections and that column V ended with a blank space in line 28, indicating the end of the first section. Crawford also noted the phrase [פרשגן] כתב מלי נוח ([a copy of] the book of the words of Noah) in V:29 which marks the beginning of the Noah "I-narrative" section.[69] Esther Eshel noted that ". . . the central character in each section narrates in the first person, a storytelling technique that contributes to the vividness of the narrative."[70]

---

66. Bernasconi, "A Literary Analysis of the *Genesis Apocryphon*," 145.

67. Ibid., 146.

68. Crawford, *Rewriting Scripture in Second Temple Times*, 107–26.

69. Ibid., 110.

70. Eshel, "Genesis Apocryphon," 664.

Bernasconi argues that the extant shape of the text does not have a "higher order voice" in the material linking these three I-narratives together as there is ". . . no introductory or end framework unifying the whole text and transitions between the sections are not managed."[71] Since there is no higher order voice in the text linking the "I-narratives" Bernasconi then argues that "from a literary point of view, those three sections may not be seen as constructing a single text." He then labels the Lamech, Noah, and Abram sections as "part-texts," not "text parts."[72]

However, Bernasconi recognizes that due to the incompleteness of the extant text one cannot rule out that the original text did provide the text transitions.[73] One possible example of a text transition in the text is in column V, line 29, which ends the Lamech section and begins the Noah section with the phrase [פרשגן] כתב מלי נוח ([a copy of] the book of the words of Noah). It is possible, though there is no direct evidence, that a similar phrase like "a copy of the book of the words of Noah" at the beginning of the Noah section was also present in the original text at the beginning of each of the three sections. While V:29 may possibly hold a clue to the original literary structure the extant text does not provide definitive evidence. This raises the issue as to whether the three "I-narratives" should be read separately as three independent "part-texts" or together as "text parts" of a larger unified narrative.

Moshe Bernstein has argued that there is a lack of *compositional* unity in 1QapGen, but that there is a *narrative* unity, in which the author intended the text to be read as a literary whole. Bernstein views the text in two major sections: the story of Noah (0–XVIII) as "parabiblical" and the story of Abram (XIX–XXII) as "rewritten Bible." Bernstein provides three main arguments against a compositional unity of 1QapGen. First, the physical markers in the text indicate it is made up of parts.[74] For example, in column V, line 29, the phrase [פרשגן] כתב מלי נוח ([a copy of] the book of the words of Noah) marks a transition from the first literary section dubbed 'Lamech-Enoch' material to the Noah material. There is also a substantial *vacat* in the text of the illegible column XVIII which may also indicate a transition from the Noah material to the Abram material.[75] It is widely recognized that there are

71. Bernasconi, "A Literary Analysis of the *Genesis Apocryphon*," 146.
72. Ibid., 146–47.
73. Ibid., 146.
74. Bernstein, "Is the Genesis Apocryphon a Unity?" 110–12, 117.
75. Ibid., 110.

three major literary sections in the text. Second, Bernstein notes the very different approaches of the two major sections to the biblical text in retelling the biblical narrative. Part one (0–XVII) is more expansionistic while part two (XIX–XXII) is tied more closely to the biblical text. Third, he notes the divergent ways in which the different sections refer to God.[76]

Does 1QapGen possess a unity? While Bernstein argues that 1Qap-Gen lacks compositional unity, he recognizes a clear narrative unity in the text. He noted, "The very fact that it presents a sequential and unbroken narrative treatment of the stories of Genesis 5 through 15 is a very strong indication that its author considered it to be a whole, and intended it to be read that way."[77]

Bernstein provides several other textual evidences for the narrative unity of 1QapGen. Several are relevant and worth mentioning here. The first-person narrative is an important unifier. The major stylistic feature of 1QapGen is that most of the story is told in first-person by the leading character in the different sections. This style links the three literary sections together and indicates it is possibly the result of the final composer of 1QapGen.[78] Also, pertinent to this research, are the literary links between Noah and Abram in 1QapGen which indicate a narrative unity.

General Content of 1QapGen

The first section (columns 0–V:28) of the Noah story deals primarily with the birth of Noah. Columns 0–I are fragmentary and apparently deal with the pre-Flood wickedness of humanity and the cohabitation of the Watchers with women. Columns II–V:28 contain a fairly long narrative pertaining to the birth of Noah in which Lamech is concerned that the conception of Noah is due to the union of his own wife, Bitenosh, and one of the Watchers. Enoch reveals that Noah is, in truth (בקושט), the seed (זרעא) of Lamech and not one of the Watchers.

The first section ends at the bottom of column V with the second section (columns VI–XVII) beginning with the phrase פרשגן] כתב מלי נוח) ([a

---

76. Ibid. 115–17.

77. Ibid., 109.

78. Numerous scholars have noted the different sources used in writing 1QapGen which include: the Book of Genesis, *1 Enoch, Jubilees,* and arguably the "book of Noah." It appears that these sources were not simply "patched together," but composed as a unified narrative by the author of 1QapGen.

copy of] the book of the words of Noah) (V:29) which serves as a heading. This section deals generally with Noah, the Flood, the landing of the ark, Noah's sacrifice, visions, and division of the earth among his sons. Columns VI–VII deals with the righteousness of Noah leading up to the Flood event. Unfortunately, very little remains of columns VIII–IX which contain the narrative of the Flood event itself. The extant narrative resumes in column X, line 12, with the landing of the ark on the mountains of Ararat. Due to the largely missing columns of text directly dealing with the Flood event, the study of 1QapGen will, in some ways, be limited. However, there is still much to be gleaned from the extant text concerning certain aspects of the author's understanding and use of the Genesis Flood text.

The final section (columns XIX–XXII) deals with the patriarch Abram and is much more closely tied to the biblical text. This well preserved section parallels Genesis 12–15. Columns XIX–XX elaborately retell the exploits of Abram and Sarai in Egypt. In columns XXI–XXII Abram returns to Canaan and the battle with the invading kings is retold, paralleling Genesis 14. The text of column XXII ends with Abram's vision and God's promise of an heir. The 1QapGen text breaks off while retelling Genesis 15:4.

Conclusion: Literary Structure and Content of 1QapGen

Several factors provide major challenges to determining the genre and literary structure of 1QapGen. The primary difficulty is the incomplete, fragmentary nature of the text. This makes any discussion of the genre and literary structure tentative. The different styles of genre employed also add to the difficulty. There are, however, several clear observations that begin to emerge and provide a framework for understanding the content and literary structure. 1QapGen is a unique retelling of Genesis 5–15 in narrative form with two major thematic sections: the story of Noah (0–XVII) as parabiblical literature and the story of Abram (XIX–XXII) as rewritten Bible. The Noah section was more extensive than the Abram section in the original text as much of the text has since been lost. Another unique literary feature of 1QapGen is the "I-narratives" that break the text into three literary sections. Provided below is a general summary outline of 1QapGen:

Literary Genre	Topical/Thematic Outline		Literary Outline
N A R R A T I V E	Parabiblical (expansionistic)	Noah Story (0–XVII)	• Wickedness of man and birth of Noah (0–I:28)	Lamech Section Intro. (0?)
			• Lamech's concern about conception of Noah (II:1–V:?)	"I-Narrator": Lamech Main Character: Noah
			• Noah and the Flood (VI:?–X:?)	Noah Section Intro. "the book of the words of Noah" (V:29)
			• God's covenant with Noah (XI:?–XV:?)	"I-Narrator": Noah Main Character: Noah
			• Noah divides the earth among his sons (XVI:?–XVII:?)	
		MISSING TEXT (XVIII)		Abram Section Intro. (XVIII?)
	Rewritten Bible (more closely tied to the biblical text)	Abram Story (XIX–XXII)	• Abram in Ur and Haran (XVIII:?–?)	"I-Narrator": Abram Main Character: Abram
			• Abram in Canaan (XVIII:?–XIX:10)	
			• Abram in Egypt (XIX:10–XX:33)	
			• Abram in the Promised Land (XX:33–XXI:22)	
			• Abram's battle with invading kings (XXI:23–XXII:26)	
			• Abram's vision and God promises Abram an heir (XXII:27–?)	
		END OF TEXT MISSING		

Qumran Interpretation of the Genesis Flood

The text of 1QapGen contains separate stories (Noah and Abram) with apparently distinct genres (parabiblical and rewritten Bible) which form compositional distinctions. However, the narrative unity seems apparent as 1QapGen retells Genesis 5–15 in parallel fashion to the biblical text, all three sections are linked by "I-narrators," and there are literary links between the Noah and Abram stories. The literary links between Noah and Abram are particularly noteworthy as they may possibly shed light on how the author of 1QapGen understood and employed the Noah/Flood material. Thus, this research will focus on the portions of text directly relevant to understanding Flood interpretation in 1QapGen and will examine any relevant literary links between the Noah and Abram narratives that may affect the research goal of understanding how the author of 1QapGen interpreted and employed the Genesis Flood.

The Purpose of 1QapGen

One final observation, which concerns the purpose of 1QapGen, should be noted before embarking on this journey of Flood interpretation. The text of 1QapGen consists of the Noah story and Abram story which retells Genesis 5–15 in a very unique way. It is not simply a retelling or some sort of Aramaic translation of the Genesis text. Rather, 1QapGen adds many details not included in the biblical text, particularly in the Noah section. It becomes rather apparent that the author's focus is to narrate, in expanded form, the story of two biblical patriarchs: Noah and Abram. For what purpose does the author present these two patriarchs though?

The Noah and Abram stories in 1QapGen point to a "well-constructed narrative" with specific aims.[79] In particular, the numerous lexical and thematic links between these sections indicate an intentional literary unity.[80]

---

79. Peters, *Noah Traditions in the Dead Sea Scrolls*, 119.

80. Ibid., 119–20. Peters provides a comparative list of the lexical and thematic links between the Noah and Abram narratives. A few of Peters's examples are provided here: 1) God obliterates (מחה) in the day of His wrath (0:12, 15); the invading kings kill and threaten to obliterate (מחה). Abram defeats the kings (XXI:23–XXII:11). 2) Sexual misalliances between women and the Watchers (0–I). Noah was not the seed of sexual misalliance (II–V); sexual misalliance between Pharaoh and Sarai threatened but not consummated (XX:8–31). 3) Deliverance from primordial Flood destruction of the righteous one. Deliverance from eschatological destruction anticipated; deliverance from Egypt of the righteous. Deliverance of "Israel out of Egypt" anticipated (XX:31–33). 4) Noah's legitimate birth confirmed by Enoch (V:2–4); Abram appeals to the Book of the words of Enoch (XIX:25). 5) Noah's righteousness and wisdom (VI:4); Abram's

Dorothy Peters observed that ". . . some deliberate choices were made especially with respect to aligning the Noah narrative with that of Abram, so that both represented righteous archetypes who were delivered from outside threats, behaved as priests, and inherited the land."[81] Thus, 1QapGen uniquely retells the biblical stories of two paragons of righteousness, Noah and Abram, for a specific purpose.

A primary focus of the author's intended purpose is to present Noah and Abram as righteous archetypes who were delivered, behaved as priests, and inherited the land. The Flood event itself may not be primary and, furthermore, is mostly not preserved in the extant text. However, the inseparable connection between Noah and the Flood is indispensable for this study. There are several notable observations that can be gleaned from 1QapGen concerning the author's understanding of the Genesis Flood.

The Story of the Watchers and the Cause of the Flood

The biblical text provides few textual clues as to the cause(s) of the Flood (cf. Gen. 6:1–4, 5–8, 11–13), and Jewish exegetes during the Second Temple period sought to provide a more comprehensive explanation. Second Temple period literature generally attributes the cause(s), or reason(s), for the Flood to one or more of the following: 1) the wickedness of the "sons of God" (cf. Gen. 6:1–4), often interpreted as fallen angels called "Watchers"; 2) the wickedness of humans (cf. Gen. 6:5–7, 11–13); 3) a combination of both, the Watchers and corrupt humanity.[82]

The Watchers are portrayed as the primary reason for the Flood in two other popular books found at Qumran: *1 Enoch* (5–11; 54; 65–67;

---

righteousness and wisdom (XIX:25). 6) Noah sacrifices and atones for the land (X:13–17; XII:16–17); Abram builds altar and sacrifices (XIX:7; XXI:21–22). 7) Noah walks around mountaintop, Eden-like land with temple parallels (XI:11–12); "holy mountain" (XIX:8). 8) Noah is a cedar (XIV:9); Abram is a cedar (XIX:14). 9) Noah walks about (הלך) the length (אורך) and breadth (פותי) of the mountaintop land (XI:11) and Noah's sons receive the land as everlasting inheritance (ירת) (XVI:12, 14); Abram surveys the Promised Land and is told to walk (הלך) the length (אורך) and breadth (פותי) of the land. God promises that Abram's seed (זרעא) would inherit (ירת) the land (XXI:8–14). 10) The Noah section ends with a description of the everlasting inheritance (ירת) which belongs to Noah's sons (XVI:8–XVII:19); The Abram section ends with God's promise that Abram's legitimate heir would inherit (ירת) (XXII:34).

81. Ibid., 121.
82. Machiela, "Flood," 645.

83–84; 86–89; 106–107) and *Jubilees* (4:22; 5:6–20; 7:20–25).[83] Humanity is, nonetheless, depicted as being corrupt alongside the Watchers. While the Watchers were primarily responsible for the Flood, this judgment was specifically reserved for humanity, animals, and the earth (cf. Gen. 6:7, 13, 17; *1 Enoch* 10:1–3). The Watchers would be reserved for the later judgment by fire (cf. Jude 6–7).[84] Concerning 1QapGen, *1 Enoch* and *Jubilees* are also generally understood to be literary sources for the author/composer of 1QapGen. So what does the author of 1QapGen understand the cause(s) of the Flood to be?

Columns 0–I

Columns 0–I are very fragmentary, containing material that deals with the period before the Flood.[85] These columns contain material that appears to refer to the story of the Watchers in *1 Enoch*, based on Genesis 6:1–4, describing the wickedness of humanity before the Flood and the illicit relationships between human women and the Watchers.[86] Interestingly, according to *1 Enoch*, the Watchers taught humanity all kinds of wickedness.[87] Columns 0–I of 1QapGen also appear to elaborate on the text of Genesis 6:5: "Then the LORD saw that the wickedness of man was great in the earth, and that every intent of the thoughts of his heart was only evil continually." These columns seem to have provided the author's own version of the wickedness of humanity and God's response to it.[88]

If columns 0–I are truly the beginning of the scroll then they serve as an introduction to the whole work. As far as the author of 1QapGen was concerned, Crawford noted that "the important events of human history begin with the descent of the Watchers" which is "characteristic of Second Temple Jewish literature."[89] Thus the story of the Watchers appears to be primary concerning the wickedness on the earth which would be washed away in the Flood.

83. Ibid.
84. Ibid., 646.
85. Wise et al., *The Dead Sea Scrolls: A New Translation*, 90.
86. Crawford, *Rewriting Scripture in Second Temple Times*, 108.
87. Wise et al., *The Dead Sea Scrolls: A New Translation*, 90.
88. Fitzmyer, *The Genesis Apocryphon of Qumran Cave 1 (1Q20)*, 117.
89. Crawford, *Rewriting Scripture in Second Temple Times*, 108.

GENESIS APOCRYPHON

The fragmentary column 0, which was reconstructed by Bruce Zuckerman and Michael Wise, appears to deal with God's anger toward human wickedness prior to the Flood. Line 4 reads [כו[ל די חמ]ד], translated "[al]l that he de[sired]." This could allude to the statement in Genesis 6:5: "every intent of the thoughts of his heart was only evil continually." The term רגזך, meaning "your anger/wrath," appears four times in the extant text of lines 5–11. The term appears in lines 5 and 6: "5. [ ]*m* You will intensify (תתקף) Your anger (רגזך) and will be sustained. But who is there 6. [who can withstand]*m* the heat of Your anger (רגזך)." The first phrase of line 5 literally reads "your anger you will make strong" and appears to refer to God's anger. רגזך also appears in lines 10 and 11: "10. Your anger (רגזך) will dest[roy] 11. [ ]in Your anger (ברגזך) . . . from the time that we go to the house of *ns*[ ] the great [Ho]ly One." Due to the fragmentary nature of the text it is difficult to state with complete certainty whose anger is referred to. However, the literary context indicates רגזך is probably a reference to God's anger.

Several indicators point toward column 0 dealing with God's angry response toward the wickedness of humanity and the Watchers. First, the context of רגזך includes judgment language such as "who is there [who can withstand]*m* the heat (חמת) of Your anger" (0:5b–6), "Your anger will destroy (ישחט)" (0:10), "And now Your hand is near to strike (לממחה)" (0:12), and "fire (נור) which is seen" (0:13). Second, this column uses this language along with references to "the Great Holy One" (קדישא רבא) (0:11) and "the Eternal Lord" (מרה עלמא) (0:18), further indicating the angry response toward wickedness belonged to God. Third, the first five columns of 1QapGen, dealing with the story of the Watchers and Noah's birth, provide further literary context in which to understand column 0 as dealing with God's angry response to the wickedness of humanity and the Watchers prior to the Flood.[90] Last, the use of *1 Enoch* as a source for the Noah narrative in 1QapGen provides additional validation to this understanding.

In column 0, who is speaking concerning God's anger? Moshe Bernstein has suggested that the references to "Your anger" (רגזך) are probably addressed to God by the Watchers (sons of God or fallen angels) who have been imprisoned.[91] Column 0, line 8, reads [ ]וכען הא אנחנא אסירין,

---

90. In columns II–V the extended narrative of Noah's birth is directly linked to the story of the Watchers (columns 0–I) as Noah is presented as not being the seed of the Watchers. The text then moves the reader toward the judgment of the wicked and deliverance of righteous Noah (columns VI–XVII).

91. Bernstein, "From the Watchers to the Flood," 44–45.

Qumran Interpretation of the Genesis Flood

translated "[ ]and now, look, we are prisoners."[92] The theme of the fallen angels (Watchers) being bound is found in *1 Enoch* and *Jubilees*, sources for the author of 1QapGen, further indicating that the Watchers were likely speaking at this point in the text.

Column 0, line 17, is difficult to read and different readings of this line of text have been offered. Joseph Fitzmyer reads the text as [ ]אן מתחתנין ו...ן ... למא, which he translates as "[ ]'*n* that they would not ally themselves by marriage *w . . . n . . .* "[93] If this reading is correct, then this text would seem to be a clear allusion to the illicit relationships between the "daughters of men" and the "sons of God" (cf. Gen. 6:1–4). However, in Daniel Machiela's 2009 edition of the 1QapGen text, a different reading of this line is provided. Machiela reads it as מתחנניןו .... מן מרה עלמא ין.[ ], which he translates as ". . . seeking favor and . . . from the Lord of Eternity."[94] The readings of Fitzmyer and Machiela are apparently significantly different based on a few very difficult letters to read. Even with an enlargement of the electronic image of this scroll fragment, it is still difficult to determine one way or the other.

---

92. אסירין, in column 0, line 8, is understood variously as either a noun (prisoners) or a verb (are bound). Fitzmyer and Machiela render אנחנא אסירין as "we are prisoners," while Bernstein translates it as "we are bound."

93. Fitzmyer, *The Genesis Apocryphon of Qumran Cave 1 (1Q20)*, 117.

94. Machiela, *The Dead Sea Genesis Apocryphon*, 32.

GENESIS APOCRYPHON

Column o fragment containing line 17 (Photograph by Bruce and Kenneth Zuckerman, West Semitic Research. Courtesy Department of Antiquities, Jordan)

The first reading under question here is read by Fitzmyer as מתחתני and Machiela as מתחנני. There is agreement with the first three letters. Machiela notes that the end of this word is written compactly which adds to the difficulty of determining the fourth and fifth letters.[95] The fourth letter is rendered as ת (Fitzmyer) or נ (Machiela). The vertical crack in the fragment running through (at least partially) the third letter adds to the difficulty. Is the vertical line on the left edge of the vertical crack the left down stroke of the ח or the beginning of a ת? If the fourth letter is a ת, it is difficult to determine with certainty the top horizontal stroke of the letter. If the vertical line on the left edge of the vertical crack is the left down stroke of the ח (the third letter), then the fourth letter would appear to be a נ. Due to the compactness of the latter part of the word, the fourth and fifth letters appear to touch. The fifth letter could possibly be a ג, with the bottom of its vertical stroke being covered by (or overlapping) the bottom horizontal stroke of the fourth letter (either ת or נ), or it could be a נ. This fifth letter is

---

95. Ibid.

41

Qumran Interpretation of the Genesis Flood

generally understood to be a ב. At this point it remains difficult to state with certainty if the reading is מתחתנין or מתחנגין.

The reading of the last part of line 17 is also difficult to determine with certainty as Fitzmyer reads only למא ... ו...ן, while Machiela reads ו.... מן מרה עלמא. With an enlargement of the image, Machiela's reading is certainly plausible, but not certain. At this point the reading of line 17 remains uncertain. However, Bruce Zuckerman has developed Reflectance Transformation Imaging (RTI) which could be of great value in determining with more certainty the reading of column 0, line 17.[96] Thus, there is still further work which can be done on enhancing imaging (and readings) of 1QapGen.

Column I, line 1 contains extant text which reads הוו] א[נחת]י[ן ועם נקבתא, translated "[wer]e descend[in]g, and with the women."[97] This line of text fits nicely with the stories during that period of the illicit relationships between the "sons of God" and the "daughters of men" recorded in Genesis 6:1–4, *1 Enoch* 6–7, and *Jubilees* 4–6.[98] Column I mentions "women" נקבתא (I:1), along with wickedness/evil רשעא (I:2) and the phrase "as a curse on all flesh" (ולקלל לכול בשרא) (I:25).[99] Dorothy Peters recognized that "the language of 'women,' the ones who are 'bound,' and the presence of evil and wickedness evoke the context within which Noah is introduced both in Genesis and in the *Book of Watchers*."[100]

---

96. Zuckerman, "The Dynamics of Change" 69–88. Dr. Zuckerman has produced a revised and enlarged version of this chapter as an article available at www.usc.edu/dept/LAS/wsrp/DSSv10a.pdf (dated October 1, 2010). Zuckerman is also the director of two research entities at the University of Southern California which provide thousands of images of ancient texts and artifacts: the West Semitic Research Project (www.usc.edu/dept/LAS/wsrp/) and the Inscriptifact Project (www.inscriptifact.com).

97. Machiela's reading differs from Fitzmyer (2004) who only read ועם נחו.ן ...א [ ] נקבתא, translated "[ ] . . . .*n* and with the women," for column I, line 1. However, based on electronic imaging, Machiela's reading seems to be preferred.

98. Machiela, *The Dead Sea Genesis Apocryphon*, 32.

99. Fitzmyer renders this as part of "line 25" while Machiela renders it as part of "line 24."

100. Peters, *Noah Traditions in the Dead Sea Scrolls*, 107.

The Trever fragment containing part of Column I
(© John C. Trever, PhD, digital image by James E. Trever)

It appears evident that columns 0–I refer to God's angry response toward the wickedness of humanity and the story of the illicit relationships between the "Watchers" and the "daughters of men" prior to the Flood. The extant text and the relationship to sources such as Genesis and *1 Enoch* point in this direction also. Joseph Fitzmyer noted that "the fragmentary lines of columns 0 and 1 must have been devoted to a description of the depraved state of humanity before the flood as a result of the conduct of 'the daughters of men' and 'the sons of God' (Gen 6:2–4)."[101] Thus, in 1QapGen the story of the "Watchers" is primary concerning the wickedness on the earth which would be judged by God in the Flood.

Columns II–V

The biblical text provides only a brief statement regarding the birth of Noah in Genesis 5:28–29: "Lamech lived one hundred and eighty-two years, and had a son. And he called his name Noah, saying, 'This one will comfort us concerning our work and the toil of our hands, because of the ground

---

101. Fitzmyer, *The Genesis Apocryphon of Qumran Cave 1 (1Q20)*, 117.

Qumran Interpretation of the Genesis Flood

which the LORD has cursed." Columns II–V of 1QapGen contain a narrative concerning Noah's birth which expounds upon Genesis 5:28–29. The author presents a much longer story, not found in the biblical account, which deals with Lamech's concern about the legitimate conception of the wondrous child Noah and his connection to the story of the Watchers.

Column II begins in the midst of Lamech's dialogue with his wife, Bitenosh, concerning the conception of the child born to her. Lamech is troubled by this wondrous child and is concerned whether his son Noah is truly his seed or the seed of one of the Watchers:

> 1. Behold then, I thought in my heart that the conception was from the Watchers and the seed from the Holy Ones, and to Nephil[im] 2. And my heart within me was upset because of this child. 3. Then I, Lamech, was frightened, and I went to Bitenosh, my wi[fe and said to her, . . .] 4. [Behold, I adjure you by the Most High, by the Majestic Lord, by the King of all A[ges] 5. [with one of] the sons of heaven, that in truth you make everything known to me, whether [ ] 6. [in truth] you must tell me and without lies whether this [. . . swear by the Most High, the Majestic Lord] 7. By the King of all Ages that you are speaking to me in truth and without lies [ ]. (column II, lines 1–7)

Column II opens with Lamech's concern that the child's conception was not from him but from the Watchers (עירין), and the seed from the Holy Ones (קדישין), and to Nephil[im] ([ין]ולנפיל)" (II:1). This same situation is also found in *1 Enoch* 106–107. Lamech approaches his wife and adjures her to speak "in truth" concerning the conception of this child with one of "the sons of heaven" (בני שמין) (II:5). The "sons of heaven" are also synonymous with the "sons of God" (בני האלהים) in Genesis 6:2–4 and are known from *1 Enoch*. The author of 1QapGen appears to use "Watchers," "Holy Ones," Nephilim," and "sons of heaven" synonymously throughout 1QapGen. In lines 8–18 Bitenosh responds to Lamech that the child is, in truth, his seed and not the seed of the Watchers (or sons of heaven). After the protest of Bitenosh, Lamech went to Methuselah to ask him to get clarity from Enoch (lines 19–26).

Column III begins Enoch's speech to Methuselah concerning the matter. According to Bernstein the reply from Enoch is prophetic and is "linked to the corruption of the Watchers and the impending destruction of the earth."[102] Lines 1–13 state:

---

102. Bernstein, "From the Watchers to the Flood," 47.

> [ ] not 2. [ ] all . . . and not for the length 3. [ ] for in the days of Jared my father 4. [ ] . . . the sons of 5. [heaven] dwelling [ ] 6. [ ] . . . until the day of 7. [ ] . . . and they will be for you 8. [ ] . . . the houses of manki[nd] . . . [ ] and upon 9. will be over all the earth 10. [ ] . . . in my land to that sea 11. [ ] . . . he will place all of it as one fruit. The earth 12. [ ] . . . the earth . . . he called his people. Now go 13. [ ] . . . truthfully that without lies (column III, lines 1–13)[103]

The extant text of lines 9–12 employ the term ארעא (earth) four times in the nineteen Aramaic words (or partial words) preserved. Bernstein surmises that ". . . we may very easily reconstruct a scene wherein Enoch tells Methuselah that there will be water or rain on the whole earth and perhaps the earth will become sea."[104] Crawford also sees in column III that Enoch predicts the Flood.[105] Bernstein and Crawford's understanding is very likely and seems to be deduced from context. However, the fragmentary nature of this column still prevents any conclusive statements concerning the original material.

Column IV is very fragmentary but several lines are relevant to this discussion. Line 11 begins with חזית למעבד דין ומ[שפט] על, translated "I have seen fit to exercise judgment and ju[stice] upon. . . ." Line 12 reads די ק[ד]ישא רבא וקץ ... מן אנפי ארעא, translated "of the great H[o]ly One, and an end . . . from the face of the earth." Again, the language reflects God's response to the wickedness on the earth in which He brings judgment upon the earth. Thus, this fragmentary column seems to connect judgment with the story of the Watchers.

Column V begins with Enoch speaking to his son Methuselah and telling him that the child Noah is ל[א] מן בני שמין להן מן למך ברך (not from the sons of heaven, but from Lamech your son) (V:3-4). Enoch then tells Methuselah to tell his son, Lamech, that "the child is truly from you and not from the sons of heaven" (V:10). Lines 12–13 then provide a description of the wondrous child Noah which matches descriptions given in other sources such as *1 Enoch* 106. The speech by Enoch then addresses the wickedness of humanity or the Watchers in lines 16–19:

> 16. Then they will be ensnared and destroyed [ ] 17. Forever, giving according to their impurity to . . . [ ] 18. Doing much violence,

---

103. The translation is from Machiela's 2009 edition due to the improvement in imaging of this column and hence, his reading of column III.

104. Ibid., 48.

105. Crawford, *Rewriting Scripture in Second Temple Times*, 110.

they will act thus until [ ] 19. They will boil over and every path of violence . . . from . . . (column V, lines 16–19)

In these lines the wickedness and violence of the antediluvian period is addressed by Enoch in context with the story of the Watchers. Unfortunately there is not enough extant textual evidence to determine conclusively if his speech is referring specifically to humans or the Watchers.

In summary, columns II–V expound on the birth of Noah, which deals with Lamech's concern about the legitimate conception of the wondrous child Noah and his connection to the story of the Watchers. Columns III–V contain Enoch's speech which addresses the child Noah as truly being Lamech's seed, not the seed of the Watchers. Language of wickedness, violence, and pending judgment is also employed throughout these columns which already anticipate the Flood. Thus, the birth of Noah, the righteous seed who would be delivered from the coming Flood judgment, is introduced and expounded upon in connection to the story of the Watchers.

The story of the birth of Noah ends with a full-line *vacat* in V:28. The phrase פרשגן] כתב מלי נוח ([a copy of] the book of the words of Noah) (V:29), serves as a heading for the next literary section in which the setting has shifted. Now, the author narrates the adult Noah speaking in first person.

Columns VI–VII

Column VI begins with establishing the righteousness of Noah. In the Genesis account the righteousness of Noah is briefly stated (in contrast to the prevalent wickedness) in third person narrative: "But Noah found grace (חן) in the eyes of the LORD. This is the genealogy of Noah. Noah was a just/righteous (צדיק) man, perfect in his generations" (Genesis 6:8–9). In the 1QapGen narrative, however, Noah recounts in first person concerning his righteousness (קושט):

> 1. from iniquity; and in the womb of her who bore me I came forth for truth/uprightness (קושט); and when I came forth from my mother's womb, I was planted for truth/uprightness (קושט). 2. And all my days I have practiced truth/uprightness (קושט) and I have been walking along the paths of eternal truth; and with me [the] Holy One [ ] 3. in my paths truth/uprightness (קושט) was settled, and to warn me against the path of falsehood which leads to everlasting darkness and to consider whether 4. I would . . . the Lord. And I girded my loins in a vision of truth/uprightness

(קושטא) and wisdom. In a robe of supplication and ... 5. [ ] ... [ ] ... all the paths of violence. 6. T[h]e[n] I, Noah, became a man and I clung to truth/righteousness (קושטא) and strengthened myself in wisdom [ ] (column VI, lines 1–6)

Column VI develops themes already found in the Noah birth narrative. For example the term קושט was used in earlier columns relating to the birth of Noah being, "in truth," the righteous seed of Lamech and not the seed of the Watchers. Now, in column VI the meaning seems to have shifted to "righteousness." The life of "righteous" Noah is now presented in contrast to the "path of falsehood," "everlasting darkness," and "paths of violence."

Further, and importantly, concerning the law of marriage, Noah behaved "... according to the law of the eternal statutes [which] the [Lo]rd of eternity [gave] to the sons of man" (כדת חוק עלמא [די יהב מ]רה עלמא לבני אנשא) (VI:8–9). This is in stark contrast to the illicit relationships between the "daughters of men" and the "Watchers" presented in the previous columns of 1QapGen (cf. also Gen 6:1–4 and *1 En*). Thus, this text provides further clues in determining the cause(s) of the Flood judgment. The illicit relationships of the human women and the Watchers were in violation of "the law of eternal statutes which the Lord of eternity gave to the sons of man." It is at this point in the narrative that the coming Flood judgment is announced to righteous Noah.

Columns VI:11 to VII:5 contain a narrative of a vision Noah receives concerning the Watchers (VI:11–22) and the Flood judgment (VI:25–26), which will ensue due to their conduct.[106]

11. [and the Lord of] heaven [appeared to me] in a vision. I looked and was shown and informed about the work/conduct of the sons of heaven, and how all 12. [ ] heaven. I hid this mystery in my heart, and did not make it known to anyone. *vacat* 13. [ ] ... to me, and the great Watcher to me by a messenger and by an emissary of the great Holy One to me[ ] 14. [ ] he re[ve]aled and he spoke with me in a vision. He stood before me and said loudly, "To you, O No[ah]". . . 15. [And through an em]issary of the great Holy One to me a voice proclaimed,[107] "To you they are speaking, O Noah" ... (column VI, lines 11–15)

---

106. The narrative of Noah's vision ends in column VII, line 5. There is a *vacat* in the next line which further indicates the end of this section and the beginning of another section with the ensuing line.

107. I am following Machiela's translation in this line as he takes קל אשמע as a subject, followed by a 3ms *aphel* of שמע.

Qumran Interpretation of the Genesis Flood

Line 11 introduces this section wherein Noah receives a vision in which he was informed about the conduct of the "sons of heaven" (the Watchers or fallen angels). This is another allusion to Genesis 6:2–4. In line 12 Noah states, "I hid this mystery (רז) in my heart." This mystery refers to the content of the vision he received. Further, the term "mystery" (רזא), used in the vision (VI:12), recalls column I, lines 2–3, which speak of the "mystery of wickedness" (רז רשעא) in the context of God's angry response to the wickedness of humanity and the Watchers prior to the Flood. Lines 13–14 mention "the great Watcher," "a messenger," and "an emissary" from the "great Holy One," which spoke to Noah in the vision. Here, Noah is directly addressed by an angelic being. In the phrase, "and he spoke with me in a vision" (VI:14), the verb מלל (he spoke) refers to the "messenger" or "Watcher" of line 13.[108] Interestingly, in *1 Enoch* 10:1–3, an angel (Watcher) is sent to warn Noah of the coming Flood in order that his seed would be delivered.[109]

In column VI, line 16, Noah states, "I considered all the conduct of the sons of the earth (בני ארעא)." This line provides a reference to the conduct of humans (בני ארעא) as opposed to the "sons of heaven" (בני שמין). In lines 19–20 the vision then bears witness to "the blood that the Nephilim (נפיליא) had poured out" (VI:19) and speaks of "the holy ones (קדישין), who with the daughters of me[n] . . . " (VI:20). The "holy ones" (קדישין) are the fallen angels or "sons of heaven" (בני שמין) (see II:5). The reference to the "sons of heaven" with the "daughters of men" is another allusion to Genesis 6:2–4. Thus, according to the vision, the conduct of humanity is revealed and the sins of the Watchers (fallen angels) include both murder and sexual immorality.[110]

The narrative then contrasts God's angry response toward the wickedness of humanity and the Watchers with God's favorable response to righteous Noah as line 23 states, "I, Noah f[ou]nd grace, prominence, and justification/uprightness in the eye[s] of [the] L[ord]." This reflects Genesis 6:8: "But Noah found grace in in the eyes of the Lord." At this point, lines 25–26 then appear to provide a reference to the coming Flood judgment: ". . . unto the gates of heaven, which the Kin[g] of a[l]l [Ages] . . . to humans and to cattle and to animals and to birds and[ ]."

---

108. Fitzmyer, *The Genesis Apocryphon of Qumran Cave 1 (1Q20)*, 149.

109. Bernstein, "Noah and the Flood at Qumran," 204; Crawford, *Rewriting Scripture in Second Temple Times*, 112.

110. Bernstein, "From the Watchers to the Flood," 55.

To summarize, columns VI–VII continue the story of the Watchers, providing important clues in determining the cause(s) of the Flood judgment. Noah's righteousness is established in contrast to the illicit relationships of the "daughters of men" and the "Watchers" which were in violation of "the law of eternal statutes which the Lord of eternity gave to the sons of man" (VI:8–9). Noah then received a vision in which an angelic emissary showed him all the wicked conduct of the "sons of heaven" (Watchers) (VI:11–VII:5) which would result in the Flood. Numerous allusions to Genesis 6:2–4 are found throughout the vision and the story of the Watchers is central in the vision. By this point in the 1QapGen narrative the cause(s) of the Flood is apparent.

The Cause(s) of the Flood: Conclusion

Second Temple period literature generally portrayed the cause(s) of the Flood as being due to one or more of the following: 1) the wickedness of the Watchers, 2) the wickedness of humanity, or 3) a combination of both, the wickedness of humanity and the Watchers. Does 1QapGen portray the cause of the Flood as the wickedness of humanity, the Watchers, or both? The text of 1QapGen does not disappoint in this regard.

1QapGen does not present a singular cause to the Flood, but rather, multiple intertwining issues connected to a common story. First, 1QapGen portrays God's angry response to the wickedness and violence of humanity and the Watchers in the antediluvian world. Second, the illicit relationships between the daughters of men and the Watchers are a violation of the law of eternal statutes which the Lord gave to humanity. Thus, the cause(s) of the Flood in 1QapGen is attributed to both, wicked humanity and the Watchers, in which the story of the Watchers is primary.

The Flood as an Archetype of Eschatological Judgment

Another contribution of Jewish exegesis in Second Temple period literature is the connection between the Flood judgment and the eschatological fiery judgment. The *Sibylline Oracles*, *1 Enoch* (90; 108), the New Testament (Matthew 24:37–39; 2 Peter 3:3–7), and Josephus (*Antiquities* 1.70–71) attest to this Second Temple period understanding of the Flood as an archetype of

Qumran Interpretation of the Genesis Flood

eschatological judgment.[111] Devorah Dimant observed: "The catastrophic nature of the flood, and its function as a punishment for wickedness, made it an ideal prototype for the last generation and the cataclysmic punishment at the End of Days."[112] But how does the author of 1QapGen treat this issue?

Columns 0–I

The early columns of 1QapGen provide themes which are developed in the author's presentation of the Flood as an archetype of eschatological judgment. Columns 0–I, which deal with God's anger (רגזך) toward human wickedness prior to the Flood, appear to anticipate an eschatological fiery judgment.

> 5. [ ]*m* You will intensify (תתקף) Your anger (רגזך) and will be unrelenting. And who is there 6. [who can withstand]*m* the heat (חמת) of Your anger (רגזך). *vacat* 7. [ ] the [sim]ple and the humble and the lowly ones are trembling and quivering 8. [ ] And now, we are bound (אסירין) 9. [ ] ... this 10. and [to] relent from Your anger (רגזך) [ ] *vacat* 11. [ ] in Your anger (רגזך) ... from the time that we go to the house of [ ] the great [H]oly One 12. And now, Your hand (ידך) is near to strike (לממחה) ... [ ] and to remove all 13. Because he ceased his words at the [time] of our imprisonment [ ] ... a fire (נור) which is seen. (column 0, lines 5–13)

These lines contain multiple occurrences of רגזך (Your anger; cf. lines 5–6, 10–11), in reference to God's anger/wrath toward the wickedness of the antediluvian world. There is also mention of a coming destruction/obliteration in which God's hand is near "to strike/wipe out" (לממחה) and "to remove all" in judgment. The use of "heat" (חמת) and "fire" (נור) anticipate an eschatological fiery judgment. This destruction is also echoed in Noah's eschatological vision: [עיא]פשׁ כול נורא על ורמי (and He [the Mighty Lord] threw all the wicked/rebellious ones onto the fire) (XV:10–12).[113]

The use of תקף in column 0 becomes a recurring theme in 1QapGen. This term is employed in both, the Noah and Abram narratives.[114] In particular, this root (תקף) appears in columns 0–I, Noah's first vision preceding the Flood judgment (VI), Noah's second vision concerning

---

111. Machiela, "Flood," 646.
112. Dimant, "Noah in Early Jewish Literature," 135.
113. Peters, *Noah Traditions in the Dead Sea Scrolls*, 107.
114. Both the verbal and noun forms of תקף are used throughout 1QapGen.

the eschatological judgment (XIII), and columns XX–XXII of the Abram narrative. Column 0, line 5, reads "You will strengthen (תתקף) Your anger," in reference to God's anger prior to the Flood judgment. Column I, line 22,[115] preserves the phrase "a strong (תקיף)[116] bond/prisoner," apparently relating תקף to the wicked. The term then appears again in relation to both of Noah's visions. In Noah's declaration of his righteousness, leading into his first vision, column VI, line 6, states "I (Noah) held fast to righteousness and strengthened (ואתקפת) myself in wisdom." Here, תקף is associated with righteous Noah who would be delivered, as opposed to the wicked ones of his first vision who would be judged. תקף appears again in Noah's eschatological vision in which he sees "the four winds of heaven blowing powerfully (בתקוף) and violently against this olive tree" (XIII:16). Here, the term is likely associated with the judgment of Adam's descendants in the Flood. Thus, the author of 1QapGen appears to use תקף as a literary tool to weave together the Flood with the eschatological judgment.

תקף is not only woven through the Noah story, but also through the Abram story, forming a thematic unity across 1QapGen. In column XX, line 14, Sarai has been taken from Abram "by strength/force" (בתוקף) and the Lord responded by sending afflictions that grew more powerful (תקפו) (XX:18). God then promises Abram that "I am with you and will be for you a support and strength (ותקף). I am a shield over you and a buckler against those stronger (לתקיף) than you" (XXII:30–31).

Throughout 1QapGen the use of תקף contrasts the Watchers and the wicked ones, who are judged, against the righteous ones and God, who judges the wicked. Of particular importance is the recurring use of תקף in the Noah story which serves as a literary device connecting the Flood and eschatological judgments against the wicked.

Column I, line 25,[117] preserves the phrase ולקלל לכול בשרא (and as a curse on all flesh) in the context of God's anger and imminent judgment against the wickedness of the antediluvian world. The phrase כל־בשר (all flesh) is notably found throughout the Genesis Flood narrative[118] in which corrupt כל־בשר (all flesh) is destroyed in the Flood while righteous Noah

---

115. Column I, line 22, is rendered as line 21 according to Machiela's edition of 1QapGen.

116. Fitzmyer and Machiela render this as תקיף while it has also been read as תקוף. See Abegg Jr., with Bowley and Cook, in consultation with Tov, *The Dead Sea Scrolls Concordance*, 944.

117. Machiela's edition of 1QapGen renders this as column I, line 24.

118. See Genesis 6:12, 13, 17, 19; 7:15, 16, 21; 8:17; 9:11, 15, 16, 17.

and his family are preserved. Dorothy Peters observed how the prophetic literature "envisioned judgment on כל־בשר by fire or sword."[119] For example, Isaiah 66:16 states, "For by fire and by His sword the LORD will judge all flesh (כל־בשר)." Thus, the Hebrew Bible employed the phrase כל־בשר in the context of both, the Flood judgment and the eschatological judgment by fire. 1QapGen (columns 0–I) refers to God's anger against the wicked antediluvian world and its imminent destruction. These columns also employ the language of "heat" and "fire," along with "curse on all flesh." The overall themes of Flood judgment (columns 0–XII) and eschatological judgment (columns XIII–XV) provide further literary context that these early columns not only anticipated the Flood judgment, but also the eschatological judgment. Peters concluded, "The simplest explanation, in keeping with the imminent and eschatological themes in the *Genesis Apocryphon*, is that the 'curse on all flesh' is a phrase meant to refer to both types of judgments, primordial and eschatological."[120]

Columns II–V

The lengthy narrative of columns II–V deal with Noah's birth, Lamech's concern about the legitimate conception of the child Noah, and his connection to the story of the Watchers. Column II opens with Lamech's concern that the child's conception was not from him, but from "the Watchers (עירין), and the seed from the Holy Ones (קדישין), and to Nephil[im] (ולנפיל[ין])" (II:1). In column II, lines 8–18, Bitenosh responds to Lamech that the child is, in truth (בקושט) (lines 10, 18), his seed (זרעא) (line 15) and not the seed of the Watchers (or sons of heaven). Bitenosh appeals to the "heat" (בחום) of lovemaking in regard to this child's conception (II:10), recalling the language in column 0, line 6, of the "heat" of God's anger toward the wicked. Thus, the righteous seed, which would be delivered from judgment, is conceived "in heat" (בחום) (II:10), while the wicked would face "the heat" (חמת) of God's anger (0:6). Bitenosh tells Lamech that "this seed (זרעא) is from you, and from you this conception, and from you the planting of this fruit (נצבת פריא)" (II:15). This reference to the "planting of this fruit" (נצבת פריא) in column II anticipates Noah's claim in column VI, line 1, (introducing his first vision) that he was "planted for righteousness" (לקושט נציבת) from birth. This reference also anticipates Noah's eschatological vision in

---

119. Peters, *Noah Traditions in the Dead Sea Scrolls*, 108.
120. Ibid.

which his "seed" (זרעא) would be established as a "righteous planting" (לנצבת קושט) forever (XIV:9–15).[121] Thus, a connection is made between the righteous seed, Noah, who would be delivered in the Flood and his righteous seed who would be delivered from the eschatological judgment.

In columns III–V Enoch addresses the child Noah as truly (בקושט) (V:9) being Lamech's seed, not the seed of the Watchers. Enoch tells Methuselah to tell his son, Lamech, that "the child is truly (בקושט) from you and not from the sons of heaven" (V:10). Further, the language of wickedness, violence, and pending judgment throughout these columns also anticipate the coming Flood. Thus, the birth narrative presents Noah as the righteous "seed," not the "seed" of the Watchers.

In summary, columns II–V present Noah as the righteous seed who would be delivered, and not as the lineage of the wicked who would be judged in the Flood. The author recalls themes (e.g. "heat") from earlier columns (0–I) and introduces themes (e.g. "righteous planting") later found in relation to Noah's vision concerning imminent judgment (VI–VII) and his vision of eschatological judgment (XIII–XV). Noah's birth narrative then serves an important function in the author's connection of the Flood and eschatological judgments.

Columns VI–VII and XIII–XV: Noah's Visions

Within the Noah narrative of 1QapGen the author inserts Noah's visions, which appear to serve as a literary device, further connecting the imminent Flood judgment with the eschatological fiery judgment. The visions Noah receives in 1QapGen are unique and do not occur in any other Second Temple period literature.[122] Crawford notes that Noah's visionary capacity "places Noah on the same level as Enoch," adding an apocalyptic tone to these columns.[123]

Columns VI:11 to VII:5 contain a narrative of a vision Noah receives concerning the deeds of the "sons of heaven" (בני שמין) (VI:11–22) and the subsequent Flood judgment (VI:25–26) due to their conduct. These columns also further develop themes found in the birth narrative (II–V). In the opening lines of column VI, preceding the vision, the text reaffirms Noah as the true seed and "righteous planting" through Noah's first person

---

121. Ibid., 109.
122. Crawford, *Rewriting Scripture in Second Temple Times*, 114.
123. Ibid., 111.

speech: "from iniquity; and in the womb of her who bore me I came forth for truth/uprightness (קושט); and when I came forth from my mother's womb, I was planted for truth/uprightness (לקושט נציבת)" (VI:1). This recalls Bitenosh, telling Lamech that "this seed (זרעא) is from you, and from you this conception, and from you the planting of this fruit (נצבת פריא)" (II:15). Thus, Noah is not of the lineage of the "sons of heaven" (Watchers), whose wicked deeds are revealed in the vision, resulting in judgment. In contrast, Noah is the true seed and righteous planting who "found grace, prominence, and justification in the eyes of the Lord" (VI: 23) while the deeds of the "sons of heaven" were provoking God's judgment.[124] This vision also anticipates the eschatological vision (XIII–XV) in which Noah's "seed" (זרעא) would be "established" (קום) as a "righteous planting" (לנצבת קושט) forever (XIV:9–15).

After the Flood and the landing of the ark, Columns XIII–XV record Noah's eschatological vision(s) which he received while in his sleep (cf. XV:21). The vision of columns XIII–XIV deals with the past destruction and the immediate future. The beginning of the vision in column XIII, lines 8–12 read:

> 8. [ ] ... the wood [the bir]ds of the heavens, the wild beasts of the field, the [livesto]ck of the soil, and the creeping things of the dry ground going ... [ ] ... 9. [ ] ... the stones and the clay objects, they were chopping and taking it for themselves. As I continued watching, the gold, the sil[ver], 10. The ..., iron, and all of the trees, they were chopping and taking of it for themselves. As I continued watching, the sun, the moon, 11. and the stars, they were chopping and taking of it for themselves. I kept watching until they brought to an end the swarming creatures of the earth and the swarming creatures of the water. 12. So the water ceased, and it ended. (XIII:8–12)

Immediately noticeable is the echoing of earlier universal language employed in Noah's first vision (columns VI–VII), dealing with the wickedness of the antediluvian world and the imminent Flood judgment. Column XIII, line 8, echoes "... to humans, and cattle, and wild animals, and birds" in VI:26, while lines 10–11 echo "... every heavenly body: the sun, the moon and the stars, and the Watchers" in VII:2. This destruction and pillaging of the earth in lines 8–11 likely refers to the deeds of the Watchers

---

124. Peters, *Noah Traditions in the Dead Sea Scrolls*, 111.

and their wicked offspring (cf. *1 En* 7).[125] Line 12 then states: "so the water ceased, and it ended." This, perhaps, is referencing the floodwaters. Lines 13–14 then introduce an olive tree:

> 13. I turned to see the olive tree, and how the olive tree had grown in height! [This continued] for many hours, with a bursting forth of many branches . . . [ ] . . . 14. Good and beautiful fr[uit] . . . and appearing in them. I was pondering this olive tree, and the great abundance of its leaves [ ] . . . (XIII:13–14)

This olive tree is likely Adam and his descendants. This seems more apparent as lines 16–17 inform: "the [four] winds of heaven blowing powerfully (בתקוף) and violently against this olive tree, knocking off its branches and breaking it to pieces . . . . It struck it, caused some of its leaves and fruit to fall from it, and scattered it to the winds." The use of תקף recalls earlier usage in relation to the Flood judgment.

In column XIV, an angelic emissary introduces a cedar, which is identified as Noah: "[Now] listen and hear! You are the great cedar tree that was standing before you on top of mountains in your dream, [and] the shoot which emerged from it, gre[w h]igh, and was rising up from its height (as) three sons." In lines 11–17, the cedar has three shoots attached at its root, which are Noah's sons. Within this section the narrative states: "Now the first son will not separate from you for all of his days, and among his seed (ובזרעה) shall your name be recalled . . . the first son shall come forth as a righteous planting (לנצבת קושט) for all . . . established forever" (XIV:12–14). Thus, the first shoot (Shem) will never depart from Noah and will bring forth a "righteous planting." This appears to be an intentional link to column II, line 15, where Bitenosh tells Lamech that ". . . this seed (זרעא) is from you, and from you this conception, and from you the planting of this fruit (נצבת פריא)." This also echoes Noah's claim in column VI, line 1, that he was "planted for righteousness" (לקושט נציבת) from birth. The recurrence of this "righteous planting" (לנצבת קושט) in column XIV links to Noah, who was delivered in the Flood judgment, and now extends to Noah's seed (זרעא) who would be established as a "righteous planting" (לנצבת קושט) forever (XIV:9–15). At this point, the vision(s) of columns XIII–XIV have addressed the past destruction of the olive tree (the Flood judgment) and established Noah as the cedar, whose first shoot would be established forever as a righteous planting in light of the eschatological judgment.

---

125. Crawford, *Rewriting Scripture in Second Temple Times*, 114.

In column XV, Noah's vision is apocalyptic and eschatological, providing further links to the Flood judgment:

> 9. the ends of the earth. As for the fact that you saw all of them crying out and turning away, the majority of them will be evil (רשיעין). As for the fact that you saw [ ] 10. the Great Warrior coming from the south of the earth, sickle in hand and fire (ונורא) with Him, He has crushed all ... [ ] 11. ... [ ] ... and the Mighty Lord, He is the One who will come from the south of the earth [ ] ... 12. [ ] the torches and the evil one (ורשעא). And He threw all the rebellious ones (פשעיא) onto the fire (נורא) [ ] 13. and they will seal ... As for the fact that you saw that they plucked up ... [ ] south 14. ... [ ] ... a chain on them, four mighty angels [ ] 15. [ ] ... for them a chain, from all peoples of the earth who will not have power over (XV:9–15)

This vision portrays the destruction of the wicked and rebellious by the "Great Warrior," the "Mighty Lord," who "will come from the south of the earth" (XV:10–11). The "Great Warrior" (לגברא רבא) is literally a great "man/warrior" (root גבר), which is identified as a Divine being (the Mighty Lord) in line 11 (cf. Dan 7:9–14). In the phrase, "He is the one who will come from the south of the land," the pronoun הוא refers to the גברא, the "man" in line 10.[126] This Divine "man" will "come from the south of the earth/land." The text literally reads מן ימין ארעא "from the right hand of the land." This language recalls Deborah's Song in Judges 5:4–5, where the Lord marches to battle from Edom, and Isaiah 63:1, where the Lord comes from Edom to save Israel.[127]

This "Great Warrior" (Divine "man") will come with "the sickle (מגלא) in His hand, and the fire (נורא) with Him" (XV:10). These are symbols of coming judgment.[128] For example, in the New Testament, the Son of Man has in His hand a "sharp sickle" in which He reaps the earth, and an angel then thrusts a "sharp sickle" into the earth, throwing it into the "wrath of God" (Rev 14:14–20). Reference to "fire" is also found in relation to this eschatological wrath (14:18).

Column XV, line 12, reads: [פש]עיא כול נורא על ורמי (and He threw all the wicked/rebellious ones onto the fire). This recalls the earlier use of

---

126. Fitzmyer, *The Genesis Apocryphon of Qumran Cave 1 (1Q20)*, 169.

127. Crawford, *Rewriting Scripture in Second Temple Times*, 115. Crawford also identifies the reference in *1 Enoch* 1:4, where the Lord comes from the south (Sinai).

128. Fitzmyer, *The Genesis Apocryphon of Qumran Cave 1 (1Q20)*, 169.

"heat" (חמת) (0:6) and "fire" (נור) (0:13) in relation to God's anger toward the wickedness of the antediluvian world prior to the Flood judgment. Also, in the birth narrative (II–V), the child, Noah, is referred to as a נור (fire/light). Noah is presented in the birth narrative as the true seed who will be delivered from the imminent judgment. This reference to the child, who would be delivered from the Flood judgment, as a נור provides a further subtle anticipation of the eschatological fiery judgment. Thus, the use of נור in column 0, the birth narrative (V), and Noah's eschatological vision (XV), shows another lexical layer of unity in the Noah narrative of 1QapGen. This idea of judgment by fire is also common in apocalyptic literature (Dan 7:11; Rev 14:17–19; 20:11–15; *1 En* 90:24–27).[129]

The Flood as an Archetype of Eschatological Judgment: Conclusions

Throughout the Noah narrative, the author introduces, recalls, and weaves together themes from distinct literary sections, connecting the imminent Flood judgment with the eschatological fiery judgment. The literary development of the Flood as an archetype of eschatological judgment is apparent.

---

129. Crawford, *Rewriting Scripture in Second Temple Times*, 115.

Qumran Interpretation of the Genesis Flood

Introduction	Noah's Birth Narrative	Noah's Visions	
Columns 0–I	**Columns II–V**	**Columns VI–VII**	**Columns XIII–XV**
God's anger against the wickedness of the antediluvian world	Noah is the true "seed" and "righteous planting" who would be delivered, not the seed of the wicked, who would be judged in the Flood	Noah's declaration that he was "planted for righteousness" and vision of wicked deeds of the "sons of heaven" (Watchers) and ensuing Flood judgment due to their conduct	Noah's vision of the previous destruction of the wicked (olive tree); his "seed" established forever as a "righteous planting," while the wicked are cast into the "fire" in eschatological judgment
You will intensify (תקף) Your anger (רגזך) (0:5) The wicked face the heat (חמת) of Your anger (רגזך) (0:6) Your hand is near to strike (לממחה) (0:12) a fire (נור) which is seen (0:13) as a curse on all flesh (ולקלל לכול בשרע) (I:25)	Noah, in truth (בקושט) is the seed (זרעא) of Lamech, not Watchers (II:10, 15, 18) Noah, who would be delivered, is conceived in the heat (בחום) of lovemaking (II:10) This seed (זרעא) and planting of this fruit (נצבת פריא) belongs to Lamech (II:15) Noah, in truth (בקושט) is the seed (זרעא) of Lamech, not Watchers (V:10) The child, Noah, is a fire (נור) (V:13)	Noah is conceived in truth (בקושט) and planted for righteousness (לקושט) (נציבת) (VI:1) Noah held fast to righteousness (קושט) and strengthened (תקף) himself in wisdom (VI:6)	The winds of heaven blow powerfully (תקף) and violently against the olive tree (XIII:16–17) Noah's seed (זרעא) established forever as a righteous planting (לנצבת קושט) (XIV:12–14) The Mighty Lord throws all the wicked/rebellious ones onto the fire (נור) (XV:12)
Language recurs in later columns	Language echoes previous columns and recurs in later columns	Language echoes previous columns and recurs in later columns	Language echoes previous columns
Anticipates imminent Flood judgment and eschatological judgment	Anticipates imminent Flood judgment and eschatological judgment	Anticipates eschatological judgment	Recalls Flood judgment

The early columns of 1QapGen introduce themes ("heat," "fire," "strength") which are developed in the author's presentation of the Flood as an archetype of eschatological judgment. Columns II–V present Noah as the righteous "seed" who would be delivered, and not as the lineage of the wicked who would be judged in the Flood. The author recalls themes (e.g. "heat") from earlier columns (0–I) and introduces themes (e.g. "righteous planting") later found in relation to Noah's vision concerning imminent judgment (VI–VII) and his vision of eschatological judgment (XIII–XV). The language of Noah's first vision (col. VI–VII) echoes previous columns, while anticipating the eschatological vision (col. XIII–XV). Noah's eschatological vision(s), concerning the destiny of his seed as an eternal righteous planting and the wicked being thrown onto the fire (col. XIII–XV), recalls language from previous columns (including Noah's first vision), drawing a further connection between the two judgments.

Just as Noah, the true seed and righteous planting, was delivered while the wicked were judged in the Flood, so too Noah's seed, the righteous planting, would be delivered while the wicked are thrown onto the fire in the eschatological judgment. This idea apparently resonated with the Qumran community's understanding that they were the true seed who were living in the last days and would be delivered from the eschatological judgment, while the wicked would be judged.[130] In 1QapGen, Noah is presented as the righteous archetype of deliverance for the righteous seed in the eschatological judgment. Thus, by correlation, the Flood (from which Noah was delivered) is presented as the archetype of the fiery eschatological judgment.

The Landing of the Ark: Lubar and the Promised Land

Where was the landing place of the ark during the global Flood event? The Bible only mentions that "the ark rested ... on the mountains of Ararat (הרי אררט)" (Gen 8:4). The mountainous region of Ararat is located in eastern Asia Minor (modern Turkey). The Genesis account does not explicitly provide any more detail as to the specific location or mountain the ark rested upon. Thus, Jewish exegetes during the Second Temple period sought to

---

130. Cf. CD IV:10–18; 1QpHab VII:10–14; 1QH VIII:4–14. See Dimant, "Noah in Early Jewish Literature," 136. Dimant, among others, also confirms, "Such an analogy appealed to the Qumran community in particular, as it corresponds to the community's self-image as a small group living on the verge of the final age."

Qumran Interpretation of the Genesis Flood

provide more specific locations. The Second Temple period literature sets forth several views. For example, *Jubilees* (5:28) specifies Mount Lubar as the mountain the ark landed on, while the *Sibylline Oracles* (1.261–274) places the landing of the ark in Phrygia and Josephus (*Antiquities* 1.92) mentions Armenia.[131] The Qumran literature, including 1QapGen, also contributes to this discussion.

Concerning 1QapGen, two questions are raised: *where* did Noah's ark come to rest and *how* does the author of 1QapGen employ this geographical information? Does the author of 1QapGen merely provide the geographical information out of passing interest or filling-in information for the reader? Or does the author employ the geographical information as a literary device with certain theological goals in mind?

The Landing of the Ark on Mount Lubar

Column X, line 12, reads: "the ark rested on one of the mountains of Hurarat (Ararat)" (תבותא נחת חד מן טורי הוררט). This reflects closely the biblical reading: "the ark rested ... on the mountains of Ararat (הרי אררת)" (Gen 8:4).[132] However, 1QapGen differs slightly in that the ark came to rest on *one* of the mountains of Ararat. In Column XII, line 13, the author appears to identify the specific mountain the ark rested upon, noting Noah's planting of a vineyard "on Mount Lubar" (בלובר טורא). *Jubilees* 5:28 mentions the landing of the ark on "the top of Lubar, one of the mountains of Ararat." The 1QapGen identification of Noah's planting a vineyard on Mount Lubar (XII:13) is found also in *Jubilees* 7:1: "Noah planted a vineyard on the mountain on which the ark rested, whose name is Lubar, one of the mountains of Ararat." Thus, *Jubilees* identifies this mountain upon which Noah planted a vineyard as the same mountain the ark landed upon. A clear link is made in 1QapGen between "Mount Lubar" in XII:13 and the landing of the ark in X:12. The identification of לובר (Lubar) is also found in other Qumran fragments. 4Q244, fragment 8, preserves "2. [ ] after the flood [ ] 3. [ ] Noah from [Mount] Lubar [ ] (נוח) [ ] מן בתר מבולא [מן לובר]טורא[" while 6Q8 also mentions לובר (Lubar). Thus, 1QapGen, 4Q244, 6Q8, and *Jubilees*, all give the name of the specific mountain as לובר

---

131. Machiela, "Flood," 646.

132. 1QapGen reads הוררט, an alternate spelling for אררת (Ararat). Fitzmyer notes the peculiarity of the form in 1QapGen. Falk points out that the spelling is preserved in SP, tying it to the pre-Samaritan tradition. הוררט is also the spelling found in 4Q252.

(Lubar).¹³³ Fitzmyer sees the identification of Mount Lubar as noteworthy, because "Ararat" is the Old Testament name of a *locality* (or region), not a specific *mountain*.¹³⁴ While Lubar is identified as the ark's specific landing place in the mountains of Ararat, it appears the author of 1QapGen was chiefly interested in employing the geographical information as a literary device, linking the Noah and Abram narratives for a theological purpose.

Mount Lubar and the Promised Land

1QapGen records the landing of the ark on one of the mountains of Ararat (X:12), which is later identified as Mount Lubar (XII:13). Immediately after the landing of the ark in X:12 the text provides Noah's first person account of the sacrifice offered up:

> 12. the ark rested on one of the mountains of Ararat, and the eternal fire. . . 13. . . . [ ] . . . and I atoned for all the earth in its entirety. To begin, the [he-goat] was 14. placed u[pon] first, and after it came upon . . . [ ] and I burned the fat upon the fire. Second, . . . [ ] 15. [Th]en . . . all of their blood to the base of the altar and [I] poured it out, and all of their flesh I burned upon the altar. Third, I offered the young turtledoves 16. wi[th] them upon the altar; their blood and all of them upon it. I gave fine wheat flour, mixed together with oil containing incense, as their meal offerings. 17. . . . portion of . . . I said a blessing, and was putting salt on all of them, and the scent of my offering rose up to the [he]avens. 18. Then the Most High b[lessed] . . . (column X, lines 12–18)

In lines 13–18, Noah makes a sacrifice, as also recorded in Genesis 8:20–21 (which records that Noah built an altar and offered clean animals and birds). However, line 13 reads: ". . . and I atoned for all the earth in its entirety" (ועל כול ארעא כולה כפרת). The text literally reads ". . . and for the whole earth, all of it, I atoned." 1QapGen refers to the sacrifice as an "atoning"

---

133. See Steiner, "The Mountains of Ararat, Mount Lubar, and הר הקדם," 247–49. Since a number of works which mention לובר were written in Aramaic, Steiner has proposed looking for an Aramaic etymology. Indeed, he notes an Aramaic word לובר used to describe wood in a 5th century B.C. Elephantine document authorizing the repair of a boat (p. 247). Further, there is a connection between the Aramaic לובר and the Akkadian *labiru* used to describe wood. Steiner suggests that לובר is an Aramaic word of Akkadian origin, meaning "ancient" (p. 249).

134. Fitzmyer, *The Genesis Apocryphon of Qumran Cave 1 (1Q20)*, 163.

Qumran Interpretation of the Genesis Flood

sacrifice (כפרת "I atoned"), which differs from the Genesis account. This phrase is the same as in *Jubilees* 6:2, except 1QapGen is in first person.

Several observations are noteworthy concerning this atoning sacrifice on Mount Lubar. First, the context of 1QapGen is that the earth had been morally defiled by the wicked deeds of the "Watchers" or "sons of heaven" (VI:11), the "sons of the earth" (VI:16), and the blood shed by the "Nephilim" (VI:19). The wickedness of the sons of heaven and humanity, which defiled the earth, is also mentioned in Genesis 6:2-4, 11-13; 8:21; 9:14.[135] As a result, the Flood then destroyed the earth and its inhabitants. Fitzmyer observed an important connection with this "atoning" sacrifice: "Most likely the liturgical use of כפר is found here . . . In many OT passages *kippēr* is used to denote the removal of stains of sin from Temple servants or cultic objects."[136] Thus, a link is made between Noah's sacrifice and the later Temple sacrifices.

Second, lines 13-18 record Noah following the provisions for sacrifice laid out in Leviticus.[137] Crawford views Noah's sacrifice as presenting Noah as a righteous patriarch who followed the Torah well before Moses.[138]

Third, the ark comes to rest on one of the mountains of Ararat (X:12) and Noah makes an atoning sacrifice (X:13-18), apparently while still in the ark.[139] Column XI, line 1, mentions Noah "at the door of the ark" as the waters receded. Then column XI, line 11, reads: "[Then] I, Noah, went out and walked throughout the land." Thus, when reading the 1QapGen text chronologically, Noah atones for the land before disembarking from the ark. Daniel Falk has suggested ". . . the possibility that the author of *Genesis Apocryphon* regards it as essential that Noah built his altar on the ark specifically because of its *location*. Only one such location could be so compelling; that is, if the ark were seen to have come to rest directly on the rock

---

135. Peters, *Noah Traditions in the Dead Sea Scrolls*, 112; Fitzmyer, *The Genesis Apocryphon of Qumran Cave 1 (1Q20)*, 153.

136. Fitzmyer, *The Genesis Apocryphon of Qumran Cave 1 (1Q20)*, 153.

137. Crawford, *Rewriting Scripture in Second Temple Times*, 112. Crawford identifies Noah "first evidently (although the text is not preserved) offering a calf, then a sheep or a goat (Lev 4:27-5:26), burning the fat and sprinkling the blood (Lev 4:17, 18, 25, 30), then offering turtledoves (Lev 5:7-10). Finally, Noah offers a grain offering as called for in Lev 6:15."

138. Ibid.

139. Falk, *The Parabiblical Texts: Strategies for Extending the Scriptures among the Dead Sea Scrolls*, 38.

where the later Temple altar would stand in Jerusalem."[140] This suggestion is intriguing since the text already mentions the atoning sacrifice of Noah which anticipates temple sacrifice and follows the prescriptions for sacrifice in Leviticus (X:12–18). But was the sacrifice on the mountain, while still in the ark, intended to convey that the author of 1QapGen believed Mt. Moriah was the actual location Noah's ark landed on? It is proposed here that the 1QapGen narrative of Noah's sacrifice is better understood as a literary device connecting priestly Noah and the mountain the ark rested upon to the holy mountain in Jerusalem.

The linking of the Noah story to the Promised Land is evident in the description of Noah's survey of the land. Column XI, line 1, records Noah "at the door of the ark." Line 9 then reads, ". . . the mountains and the wilderness, the hinterlands and [the] co[astlands,]a[l]l . . . ," which appears to describe in more expanded detail what Noah observed from the ark (cf. Gen 8:13–14). Machiela views this innovation as emphasizing the extensive scope of what Noah saw from the top of Mount Lubar.[141] In column XI, line 11, Noah disembarks from the ark and surveys the land: "[Then] I, Noah, went out and walked throughout the land, through its length (לאורכהא - root אורך) and through its width (ולפותיהא - root פותי), [ ] . . . ." Crawford suggests that the purpose of Noah's traversal of the land "seems to be to take possession symbolically of the land."[142] The description of Noah viewing the land from a height and then walking through its length and width anticipates Abram's survey from a height and walking through the land in column XXI (cf. Gen 13:14–18).[143] Abram views the land the Lord will give him and his descendants, from a height (XXI:9–12). Then in column XXI, lines 13–14, the Lord commands Abram to survey the land: "Get up, walk around, go and see how great is its length (ארכהא - root אורך) and its width (פתיהא - root פותי). For I shall give it to you and to your descendants . . . ." Thus, a direct literary link is made between Noah and Abram, tying the land Noah surveyed to the land promised to Abram and his descendants. The link between Noah and Abram is further made explicit in XI:15, where God spoke to Noah saying, "Do not fear, O Noah. I am with you"–clearly drawn from God's words to Abram in Genesis 15:1.

---

140. Falk, "In the Door of the Ark: Noah's Prayer and Sacrifice in Genesis Apocryphon," as cited in Peters, *Noah Traditions in the Dead Sea Scrolls*, 112.

141. Machiela, "Each to His Own Inheritance," 55.

142. Crawford, *Rewriting Scripture in Second Temple Times*, 113.

143. Machiela, "Each to His Own Inheritance," 55.

For what purpose does the author make this connection? Machiela concludes that the author is concerned with a particular goal: the right of Israel to the Promised Land.[144] The immediate literary context appears to support this idea. Noah's first person speech in Column XI, lines 13–15, reads:

> 13. Again, I blessed the One who had compassion on the land, and who removed and obliterated from it 14. all those doing violence and wickedness and deceit, but rescued the righteous man . . . 15. And . . . appeared to me from heaven, speaking with me and saying to me, "Do not fear, O Noah. I am with you and with those of your sons who will be like you forever." (column XI, lines 13–15)

Peters views these lines as the theme of the entire Noah narrative in 1QapGen.[145] This is for good reason. The land motif is fundamentally connected to the author's presentation of Noah, who was delivered from the Flood judgment, as the righteous archetype for the righteous who would be delivered from the eschatological judgment. Just as Noah inherited the renewed land (cleansed from the wicked), his righteous seed would also inherit the land. Lines 13–14 mention specifically that the Lord had compassion on *the land* in Noah's day and ". . . removed and obliterated from it all those doing violence and wickedness and deceit" from the land, while rescuing righteous Noah to inhabit the renewed land. So too, the wicked had no right to the Promised Land and would be removed from the land in the eschatological judgment. The narrative of the landing of the ark and Noah's subsequent survey of that land in 1QapGen links the land of righteous Noah to the Promised Land of Abram, legitimizing the right of the righteous seed to the land. This would have appealed to the Qumran community, who viewed themselves as the righteous seed who would be delivered from the eschatological judgment, while the wicked would be removed from the land. Thus, the mountain which the ark landed upon and that land surveyed by Noah is an important archetype for the Promised Land.

The Flood: Restoration of Eden and Anticipation of the Promised Land

The author of 1QapGen viewed the Flood not only as an agent of judgment upon the earth and its inhabitants, but also as ushering in a new creation,

---

144. Ibid., 50.
145. Peters, *Noah Traditions in the Dead Sea Scrolls*, 113.

with Noah as a new Adam. While Noah's sacrifice on the ark and traversal through the "length" and "width" of the land are linked to Abram and the Promised Land, the author also invokes Eden to the reader's mind in columns XI–XII.

First, after offering the sacrifice, Noah leaves the ark and walks around on a mountain top, Eden-like paradise: "[Then] I, Noah, went out and walked throughout the land, through its length and through its width, [ ] ... upon it, pleasure (עדן) in their leaves and in their fruit. The entire land was full of grass, herbs, and grain" (XI:11–12). Note the description in line 12 of the "pleasure in their leaves and in their fruit." The noun translated "pleasure" is עדן, which recalls directly גן עדן, "the Garden of Eden" (cf. Gen 2:8).[146] Thus, a lexical link between the mountain which the ark landed on and Eden is made. The connection of the Garden of Eden as a holy mountain is made by the prophet Ezekiel.[147]

Second, the dominion mandate in column XI, lines 16–17, reflects Genesis 9:1–3, which recalls directly the creation mandate in Genesis 1:28–30. However, a comparison between the Genesis passages (1:28–30; 9:1–3) and 1QapGen reveals some differences which seem to reflect intentional exegesis on the part of the 1QapGen author.

---

146. Fitzmyer, *The Genesis Apocryphon of Qumran Cave 1 (1Q20)*, 155.

147. The idea of the Garden of Eden as the holy mountain of God is found in Ezekiel 28:13–16. The "king of Tyre" is said to have been "in Eden, the Garden of God" (v. 13). He is then described as "the anointed cherub" who was "on the holy mountain of God" (v. 14) and was subsequently cast out of "the mountain of God" (v. 16), due to his iniquity (v. 15).

Qumran Interpretation of the Genesis Flood

Genesis 1:28–29	Genesis 9:1–3	1QapGen XI:16–17
'Be fruitful and **multiply; fill the earth** and subdue it; **have dominion** (rule) over the fish of the sea, over the birds of the air, and over every living thing that moves on the earth. And God said, 'See, **I have given you every herb that yields seed which is on the face of the earth, and every tree whose fruit yields seed; to you it shall be for food**.'	'**Be fruitful and multiply**, and **fill the earth**. And the **fear of you** and the **dread of you** shall be on every beast of the earth, on every bird of the air, on all that move on the earth, and on all the fish of the sea. They are given into your hand. **Every moving thing that lives shall be food for you. I have given you all things, even as the green herbs**.'	'**Be fruitful and multiply**, and **fill the earth**; **have dominion** (rule) over all of them; over its seas and over its wildernesses, over its mountains and over everything that is in them. **I am now [gi]ving to you and to your sons everything for food; that of the vegetation and herbs of the land**. But you shall not eat any blood. The awe and fear of you'

The text of Genesis 9:1–3 directly recalls Genesis 1:28–29, repeating the creation mandate to "be fruitful and multiply; fill the earth." However, there are two pointed differences. First, Genesis 1:28 commands man to "subdue" the earth and to "have dominion/rule over)" all the animals, while Genesis 9:2 states that "the fear of you and the dread of you" shall be upon the animals. Second, Genesis 1:29–30 records the provision of vegetation alone as food for man and animals, whereas Genesis 9:3 allows for the eating of meat, even as the vegetation.

While 1QapGen reflects Genesis 9:1–3, several noteworthy differences further reveal the author's exegesis. First, column XI, line 16, adds the phrase: "and have dominion (rule) over them all" (ושלט בכולהון).[148] This reflects the creation mandate in Genesis 1:28, not Genesis 9:1–2. Daniel Falk sees this addition by the 1QapGen author as claiming that "the dominion was regained or renewed with Noah."[149] Second, 1QapGen modifies Genesis 9:3, with the reading, "I am now [gi]ving to you and to your sons everything for food; that of the vegetation and herbs of the land," omitting the provision to eat meat. Falk concludes that 1QapGen ". . . asserts that with Noah there is a return to paradise conditions of Gen 1:28–30: harmonious relations between humans and animals, and vegetation only for

---

148. The addition of שלט (have dominion; rule over) in XI:16 is the same root the Targumim use at Genesis 1:28.

149. Falk, "Anatomy of a Scene," 28.

food."[150] Thus, Genesis 9:1–3 is modified by the author of 1QapGen to be understood as a restatement of the mandate to Adam in Genesis 1:28–30 in which dominion was restored to Noah.

Last, column XII, line 13, records Noah's first person words: "[Then] I, along with all of my sons, began to cultivate the earth. I planted a great vineyard on Mount Lubar . . . ." This description of Noah planting a vineyard recalls the Garden of Eden. Further, the planting of this vineyard is said to be on Mount Lubar, which recalls Noah's traversal of the mountain top, Eden-like land in XI:11–12.

1QapGen presents the Flood narrative as ushering in a new creation with a renewed land (recalling Eden) and Noah as a new Adam through: 1) Noah's survey of the Eden-like land (XI:11–12), 2) the dominion mandate of Genesis 1:28–30 restored to Noah (XI:16–17), and 3) Noah's planting of a vineyard on Mount Lubar (XII:13). Coupled with the link between Noah and Abram, tying the land Noah surveyed (column XI) to the land promised to Abram and his descendants (column XXI), the author of 1QapGen presents the Flood narrative as a vital link between Eden and the Promised Land. Noah is presented as a new Adam and proto-Abraham.

Flood Interpretation in 1QapGen: Conclusions

The Noah narrative (columns 0–XVII) of 1QapGen appears to deal primarily with the figure of Noah as a righteous archetype. Concerning the author's interpretation of the Flood, the narrative of the Flood event itself is extremely fragmentary. Nonetheless, this ancient text is still a treasure trove for gleaning Second Temple period interpretation(s) of the Genesis Flood and how it was used. First, the cause(s) of the Flood in 1QapGen is attributed to both, wicked humanity and the Watchers, in which the story of the Watchers is primary. Second, Noah is presented as the righteous archetype of deliverance for the righteous seed in the eschatological judgment. Thus, the Flood (from which Noah was delivered) is presented as the archetype of the fiery eschatological judgment. Third, the narrative of the landing of the ark and Noah's subsequent survey of that land in 1QapGen links the land of righteous Noah to the Promised Land of Abram, with the intended purpose of legitimizing the right of the righteous seed to the land. Fourth, 1QapGen presents the Flood narrative as ushering in a new creation with a renewed

150. Ibid.

land and Noah as a new Adam. Thus, the Flood narrative also serves as a vital link between Eden and the Promised Land.

The author, using multiple sources, skillfully links the Noah narrative with the Abram narrative through literary devices, such as lexical and thematic links, for an intended purpose. At the forefront of the author's presentation of Noah and Abram as righteous archetypes of deliverance is the *land* they inherited. Thus, the author's interpretations of certain aspects of the Genesis Flood are employed for certain intended purposes and should be understood in this context.

CHAPTER THREE

COMMENTARY ON GENESIS (4Q252)

Discovery of 4Q252

4Q252 (*COMMENTARY ON GENESIS*) was discovered by Bedouin in 1952 among some 600 manuscripts, represented by thousands of fragments, in Cave 4. This manmade cave was carved into the soft sandstone marl terrace upon which Khirbet Qumran sits and also lies within the Sabbath limit of 1,000 cubits from the site itself. Cave 4 produced, by far, the largest stash of these timeless treasures. However, due to the large volume of these fragmentary manuscripts and a number of other reasons, the publication of many of these manuscripts was significantly delayed. It was not until the early and mid-1990s that preliminary publications of the text of 4Q252 became available to scholars.[1] The official edition of 4Q252 was then published in 1996 by George Brooke in volume 22 of the *Discoveries in the Judaean Desert* series.

---

1. The Hebrew text of 4Q252 was published in the early to mid-1990s in several works: Wacholder and Abegg, *A Preliminary Edition of the Unpublished Dead Sea Scrolls: The Hebrew and Aramaic Texts from Cave Four II* (1992); Eisenman and Wise, *The Dead Sea Scrolls Uncovered* (1992); Fragment 1 was published in preliminary form by Lim, "The Chronology of the Flood Story in a Qumran Text (4Q252)," 288–98; A complete transcription of the Hebrew text was provided by Brooke, "The Thematic Content of 4Q252," 33–59.

Qumran Interpretation of the Genesis Flood

Qumran Cave 4 (Photograph by Jeremy D. Lyon)

Physical Description of 4Q252

4Q252 consists of six fragments of a Hebrew text written in Jewish script. Paleographic investigation shows that 4Q252 was penned in an early Herodian hand, dating the manuscript to the last half of the first century B.C. (50–1 B.C.).[2] Several physical features indicate that the manuscript was likely written on a single sheet of leather containing six columns.[3] The scroll's original length likely would have been around 60 centimeters.[4] By and large, the top part of the manuscript has been preserved, with column I extending to the bottom margin, containing 22 lines of text. Fragment 1, the best preserved and largest fragment, preserves most of column I and a significant amount of column II, which contain material covering the

---

2. Brooke, "Commentary on Genesis," 300; Crawford, *Rewriting Scripture in Second Temple Times*, 130.

3. Ibid.

4. Brooke, "Commentary on Genesis," 300.

Genesis Flood. The extant portions of 4Q252 contain interpretations of selected texts from Genesis 6–49.

This large fragment of 4Q252 preserves most of column I and a good portion of column II (Courtesy of the Leon Levy Dead Sea Scrolls Digital Library; IAA, photo: Shai Halevi)

Is the beginning of the manuscript preserved in fragment 1, with what has been dubbed "column I," or were there originally more columns of text? Ida Fröhlich concluded that the beginning of the manuscript is missing based on the traces of stitching on the right edge of fragment 1.[5] However, George Brooke is confident that column I is the beginning of the manuscript based on two physical features: 1) the likely traces of the scroll's fastening to the right of the column and 2) the discoloration of the first 5 to 6 centimeters of the reverse side of the leather, indicating that these first centimeters formed the outside of the scroll when rolled up.[6] Though there cannot be

5. Fröhlich, "Themes, Structure and Genre of Pesher Genesis," 81.
6. Brooke, "The Thematic Content of 4Q252," 36. See Crawford, *Rewriting Scripture in Second Temple Times*, 130. Crawford agrees with Brooke's assessment of 4Q252 being written on a single sheet of leather consisting of six columns. Moshe Bernstein has also revised his previously held view, coming into agreement with Brooke. See Bernstein, "4Q252: Method and Context, Genre and Sources," 63–64. Brooke also recognizes a few textual difficulties to this view (pages 36–37). First, if there was no text preceding

absolute certainty, it seems likely that fragment 1 contains the beginning of the text and that the whole manuscript consisted of six columns on a single sheet of leather. Thus, the extant fragments, which contain lines from all six columns, provide an outline of the complete text, in fragmentary form.⁷

History of Research on 4Q252

While there was significant delay in publishing the numerous Cave 4 fragments, scholarly research on 4Q252 finally commenced in full force in the early to mid-1990s. Much of the research focuses on the manuscript as a whole or specifically deals with the first two columns dealing with the Genesis Flood. Though numerous scholars have made significant contributions, George Brooke and Moshe Bernstein remain the two major figures in 4Q252 research. The following is a brief history of research on 4Q252.

Timothy H. Lim

A preliminary publication of columns I and II, from fragment 1, was produced by Timothy H. Lim in the *Journal of Jewish Studies* in 1992.⁸ The article, titled "The Chronology of the Flood Story in a Qumran Text (4Q252)," provided "a preliminary transcription, translation and study of two of the three columns of 4Q252 fr. 1 (PAM 43.253)."⁹ After the transcription and translation of the first two columns, Lim provides line-by-line textual notes. A discussion of the sectarian exegetical nature of 4Q252 and the chronology of the Flood concludes the article. Lim's preliminary edition of columns I–II finally opened up scholarly discussion on the Flood material in 4Q252, decades after being discovered. Ronald Hendel, for example, noted that Lim's preliminary publication "has occasioned some renewed

---

column I, then the use of קצם (their end) in column I, line 1, would appear to have no clear antecedent. This could easily be resolved if there were text preceding this. However, Brooke contends the author may have not been compelled to provide a clear antecedent, assuming the readers were familiar with the content. Second, the author of 4Q252 sometimes indicates new sections in the work with spaces and there is no room for a space at the beginning of column I which would introduce the Flood material as a new section. However, Brooke notes that "it is customary scribal practice to begin the first column of a text at the margin."

7. Crawford, *Rewriting Scripture in Second Temple Times*, 131.
8. Lim, "The Chronology of the Flood Story in a Qumran Text (4Q252)," 288–98.
9. Ibid., 288.

interest in the problem of the flood chronology in Genesis 7–8."[10] Lim's textual notes and discussion of the Flood chronology in 4Q252 are directly relevant to this current research on Flood interpretation at Qumran.

George Brooke

In 1994, George Brooke provided a transcription of the complete extant text of 4Q252 (six columns) in an article titled, "The Thematic Content of 4Q252." Brooke sought to determine the purpose behind the collection of selected biblical passages by the author/compiler of 4Q252 by examining the content and organization of the scroll. He provides a nice physical description of the manuscript and then discusses the scroll's content section-by-section. Brooke concluded that it was "not possible to present a systematically argued structural analysis of 4Q252."[11] However, he views the author/compiler of 4Q252 as understanding himself and his readers as those who had the right to the land.[12] Thus, Brooke saw a thematic purpose starting to emerge. In another 1994 article, titled "The Genre of 4Q252: From Poetry to Pesher," Brooke provided more detailed physical descriptions of the manuscript and summarized each pericope of interpretation. This he does, in an attempt to reconstruct the structure and purpose of the text as a whole.[13] He understands the text of 4Q252 as exegesis through the author's use of a variety of genres and a range of interpretive techniques.[14]

In 1996, George Brooke published "4Q252 as Early Jewish Commentary," in which he addressed the varied responses to the different genres employed and concludes that 4Q252 is a "highly distinctive commentary."[15] Also, in 1996, Brooke's official edition of 4Q252 was published in volume 22 of the *Discoveries in the Judaean Desert* series.[16] This edition of the complete extant text of 4Q252 included orthographic details, transcription and translation of the text, notes on the readings, further editorial comments, and notes on the biblical text. Thus, through the official edition of 4Q252 and his numerous articles, Brooke's research has become foundational to

10. Hendel, "4Q252 and the Flood Chronology of Genesis 7–8," 72.
11. Brooke, "The Thematic Content of 4Q252," 54.
12. Ibid., 55.
13. Brooke, "The Genre of 4Q252: From Poetry to Pesher," 160–79.
14. Ibid., 179.
15. Brooke, "4Q252 as Early Jewish Commentary," 385–401.
16. Brooke et al., *Qumran Cave 4, XVII: Parabiblical Texts, Part 3*.

Moshe Bernstein

In 1994, Bernstein published an article in *The Jewish Quarterly Review* titled, "4Q252: Method and Context, Genre and Sources," in response to Brooke's article, "The Thematic Content of 4Q252."[17] Bernstein discusses differences with Brooke's approaches concerning their conceptions of the different genres, presuppositions, and methodology in analyzing the text.[18] Bernstein sees a connection in the disparate texts of 4Q252 only in the light they shed on exegetical difficulties for the author. Thus, the individual sections of 4Q252 are responses to different exegetical difficulties with the biblical text.[19] Bernstein's scholarly and critical interaction with Brooke's research is invaluable in seeking to evaluate critically the text of 4Q252. Bernstein published another article in 1994, titled "4Q252: From Re-Written Bible to Biblical Commentary," in which he views 4Q252 as different from any Qumran text, representing the first steps toward non-esoteric, expository biblical commentary.[20] Bernstein provides a section-by-section commentary on the text of 4Q252 and an assessment of approaches taken by Lim and Eisenman–Wise to the 4Q252 text, making this study a valuable resource. Bernstein also contributed a book chapter, titled "Noah and the Flood at Qumran," in *The Provo International Conference on the Dead Sea Scrolls: New Texts, Reformulated Issues, and Technological Innovations*, where he included discussion of 4Q252 among other texts.[21] Bernstein's overall work on 4Q252 has, alongside Brooke's research, become standards for 4Q252 research.

Ida Fröhlich

1994 proved to be a very prolific year for published works on 4Q252 as Ida Fröhlich also produced an article, "Themes, Structure and Genre of Pesher

17. Bernstein, "4Q252: Method and Context, Genre and Sources," 61–79.
18. Ibid., 62.
19. Ibid., 78–79.
20. Bernstein, "4Q252: From Re-Written Bible to Biblical Commentary," 1–27.
21. Bernstein, "Noah and the Flood at Qumran." This 1999 publication is on the 1996 Provo International Conference on the Dead Sea Scrolls.

Genesis," in response to George Brooke's article, "The Thematic Content of 4Q252."[22] Fröhlich sought whether an analysis of the structure of 4Q252 was possible, and the basis upon which an analysis could be made.[23] Fröhlich provided discussion of the six columns of text, concluding that 4Q252 is a collection of interpretations in various forms of the Genesis text, which deals with the wicked and the righteous from different generations of human history that lose or inherit the land.[24] Fröhlich's study of 4Q252 adds to the discussion of genre, literary structure, and purpose of 4Q252.

Literary Genre and Content of 4Q252

4Q252 is a complex commentary, containing interpretations on selected portions of Genesis 6–49 and following the order of the Genesis text itself.[25] The content of the extant manuscript begins with the Flood narrative and continues with Noah's curse of Canaan, Abram's entry into the land, the covenant of the pieces, the destruction of Sodom and Gomorrah, the binding and blessing of Isaac, the defeat of the Amalekites, and Jacob's blessings. Thus, 4Q252 covers a substantial amount of biblical text, unlike 1QapGen, for example, which covers only the Noah and Abram narratives (Gen 6–15). 4Q252 also assumes and works under the Genesis base text as its authority. Thus, 4Q252 is a commentary on selected passages from Genesis 6–49.

4Q252 is unique among the Qumran literature as the contents are represented by a variety of different types of biblical interpretation, including rewritten Bible, halakhic exegesis, and *pesher*-type commentary. Each section of commentary has its own distinctive character. For example, the best preserved portion of 4Q252 (cols. I–II) contains a rewritten form of the Flood narrative (I:1–II:5). Column II, lines 5–8, provide poetic commentary on the curse of Canaan. In column III, halakhic exegesis is employed in the retelling of the destruction of Sodom and Gomorrah. However, in columns IV and V the genre changes with the citation of the Genesis base text given first, followed by exegetical comment. The blessings of Jacob (IV:3–VI:2) are interpreted in the same manner as the sectarian *pesharim*.

22. Fröhlich, "Themes, Structure and Genre of Pesher Genesis," 81–90.

23. Ibid., 81.

24. Ibid., 89–90.

25. The extant text, consisting of six columns, contains exegetical remarks beginning with Genesis 6:3 and following with 7:10–12; 7:24; 8:3–6; 8:8–14; 8:18; 9:24–27; 11:31; 15:9; 15:17; 18:31–32; 22:10–12; 28:3–4; 36:12; 49:3–4; and 49:10.

Thus, a shift in the style of commentary occurs in the text of 4Q252.[26] The abrupt changes between the various sections of 4Q252 and the great variety of genres of interpretation can be explained by the author/compiler working from different sources, written in different styles.[27] George Brooke concludes that the text of 4Q252 is "... exegesis displayed through the use of a great variety of forms and using a range of interpretive techniques."[28] Ida Fröhlich understands 4Q252 as consisting of two genres: 1) *narrative* on different themes characterized by chronological matters (Noah and the Flood, Abraham traditions) and 2) *exegesis* of biblical verses (Amalek, Jacob's blessings).[29] Bernstein views 4Q252 as representing a new genre, perhaps "proto-biblical commentary," somewhere between rewritten Bible and biblical commentary.[30] Further, he views the presence of rewritten Bible and formal commentary side-by-side as likely indicating the transitional nature of this genre. Brooke agrees that the use of varied genres in 4Q252 "permits us to see early Jewish interpretation in transition."[31] In summary, 4Q252 is a unique form of biblical commentary covering only selected passages from Genesis 6–49 (following the order of the text itself) and containing various styles of commentary, from rewritten form to formal commentary.

Literary Structure of 4Q252

The diversity of genres and interpretive methods between the various sections of 4Q252 raises an important issue: should the various sections be read as an integrated whole? Is there an overall compositional unity and purpose behind the various sections included in the text? In particular, this

---

26. This shift in exegetical method is generally recognized. For example, see Crawford, *Rewriting Scripture in Second Temple Times*, 131.

27. Several scholars have set forth this explanation. See Brooke, "Commentary on Genesis," 300; Bernstein, "Method and Context, Genre and Sources," 77; Crawford, *Rewriting Scripture in Second Temple Times*, 131.

28. Brooke, "The Genre of 4Q252: From Poetry to Pesher," 178–79.

29. Fröhlich, "Themes, Structure and Genre of Pesher Genesis," 81–90.

30. Bernstein, "Method and Context, Genre and Sources," 76.

31. Brooke, "4Q252 as Early Jewish Commentary," 401. Brooke also notes that "... 4Q252 represents 'a middle course' ... between rewritten biblical texts and explicit exegesis ... not only because there is a mixture of explicit exegesis and implicit interpretation, but also because in the pericopae which look most like rewritten Bible there is some explicit exegesis and conversely in the pericopae where it looks most obviously as if there is explicit exegesis, that is done through the implicit use of other biblical materials" (392).

can affect how one reads and analyzes the Flood section (I:1–II:5). Is the Flood section to be read and understood on its own or as an integrated part of an overall unified message and purpose behind these various sections?

Bernstein suggests that due to the kinds of exegetical issues dealt with being so different from one another, one should not view the various sections of 4Q252 as an integrated whole.[32] In his estimation, "What connects these disparate texts is the light that they shed, in the view of the compiler, on exegetical difficulties in the Hebrew Bible."[33] Thus, 4Q252 is seen as a collection of exegetical remarks on various passages from Genesis 6–49 with no intended unifying message/theme for the work as a whole. One can analyze the individual pericopae, but there is no underlying reason to read these individual sections as an integrated whole since the only unifying factor between these texts is their connection to the biblical text.[34] Thus, for example, one can focus solely on the interpretive details of the Flood section (I:1–II:5) and not how it may possibly relate to other sections as a unified whole. While Bernstein does not see an overall unity of purpose behind the various exegetical sections of 4Q252, can an overall literary unity be discerned?

George Brooke sees an overall unified literary structure in 4Q252 based on a combination of themes in a temporal scheme. Thus, there is an ordered historical reading of the selected passages from Genesis for an intended purpose. Provided below is an adaptation of Brooke's literary outline of 4Q252:[35]

---

32. Bernstein, "4Q252: From Re-Written Bible to Biblical Commentary," 26.
33. Bernstein, "4Q252: Method and Context, Genre and Sources," 77.
34. Ibid., 78.
35. Brooke, "The Genre of 4Q252: From Poetry to Pesher," 175. Brooke also notes that much of this overall structure is found in the admonition of the *Damascus Document* (CD), providing parallels between 4Q252 and CD (176). See Brooke, "4Q252 as Early Jewish Commentary," 398.

Qumran Interpretation of the Genesis Flood

I. *The Past, Determinative of the Present*

    A. Exegetical Chronicle: The Flood (Period Before Flood Judgment, Flood Chronology, Noah in the Land)

    B. Poetic Commentary: Noah's Curse on Canaan

    C. Exegetical Chronicle: Abram's Entry into the Land and Covenant of the Pieces

II. *The Present*

    A. Haggadah: Isaac Rather than Ishmael

    B. Halakhic Exegesis: Destruction of Sodom and Gomorrah

    C. Abbreviated Narrative: Abraham's Faithful Binding of Isaac

    D. Exegesis: Isaac's Blessing on Jacob

III. *The Future, Anticipated in the Present* (Realization of the Community's Hopes)

    A. Exegesis: Complete Defeat of Amalek

    B. Pesher: Jacob's Blessings

The exegetical presentation of certain selected themes appears to indicate that the author of 4Q252 viewed himself and his community as living in the land promised to Abraham, but still awaiting the future messianic age.[36] Thus, Brooke suggests that this commentary may also have served as a "quasi-legal document," which validates the possession of the land for the author and his community.[37]

Bernstein responded that Brooke's thematic and structural discussion was "premature," arguing that Brooke 1) appeared too eager to have 4Q252 conform to Qumran literature and thus 2) presupposed theological patterns which prevented objective analysis of each section.[38] Bernstein rightly seeks to understand the text of 4Q252 on its own terms as it relates strictly to its underlying biblical text, without prematurely invoking Qumran ideologies. However, based on examination of the text itself, 4Q252 should likely be understood as *Qumran* exegesis of the biblical base text for a number of reasons: 1) the text is dated to the Qumran period, 2) the text was found at Qumran, 3) a number of theological themes in the text conform

---

36. Brooke, "4Q252 as Early Jewish Commentary," 397.
37. Brooke, "The Genre of 4Q252: From Poetry to Pesher," 174–78.
38. Bernstein, "4Q252: Method and Context, Genre and Sources," 75.

to Qumran concerns (e.g. chronology, calendar, messianism), and 4) the text explicitly mentions the Qumran sectarian term היחד (the Community) (V:5). Thus, Bernstein's criticisms of Brooke appear to be unwarranted. The nature of this exegetical work as being Qumran exegesis can be derived through analysis of the text itself and theological patterns can likely be discerned through analysis of the text as well. Thus, Brooke's understanding of an overall unity in the composition of these various exegetical sections may be justified.

Ida Fröhlich also discerned a unified literary structure behind the collection of texts in 4Q252. Columns I–III (a narrative retelling) form a historical sequence beginning with the Flood, while columns IV–V (exegesis) deal with the future eschatological age when Israel's enemies will be destroyed and the righteous will inherit the land. Structurally, Fröhlich observed a literary arrangement in 4Q252 of four consecutive series of counterparts (summarized below) which develops a unified purpose:[39]

Text	Consecutive Series of Counterparts
I:1–II:5	Something from the history of man before the Flood
	Rescue of Noah from the Flood and his "landing"
II:5–8	Curse of Canaan; subjugation to brothers (violation of sexual taboo)
II:8–13	Abram's entry into the land; God's covenant with him
III:1–6	Sin/destruction of Sodom and Gomorrah (violation of sexual taboo)
III:6–14	The *aqedah* (Abraham merits the covenant); blessing of Isaac
IV:1–7	Destruction of Amalek; curse of Reuben (violation of sexual taboo)
V:1–VI:3	Eternal reign of Judah; blessing of other sons of Jacob

This series of texts contrasts the wicked and the righteous. In each case, the sin involves some sort of sexual violation. This appears tenuous for the first section of 4Q252 (I:1–II:5) as the story of the Watchers (sons of God) and daughters of men (Gen 6:1–4) is not explicitly presented.[40] However, Fröhlich (unlike Brooke and Bernstein) holds that the beginning of 4Q252 is missing. Thus, one could surmise that this missing part of the

39. Fröhlich, "Themes, Structure and Genre of Pesher Genesis," 89.

40. In the Flood section, discussion begins with interpretation of Genesis 6:3, which is part of the narrative concerning the Watchers (sons of God) and the daughters of men. Thus, this idea of a sexual violation can be understood for the Flood section as well, though it is recognized that there is no explicit statement extant in the text.

text likely included the story of the Watchers and the wickedness before the Flood. This is possible, but unlikely as Brooke has demonstrated that column I is most likely the beginning of the document. Nonetheless, in each case punishment of the wicked is destruction or subjugation, while the righteous are rescued and/or inhabit the land. Fröhlich, like Brooke, recognizes the various interpretations deal with the wicked and the righteous represented in consecutive *periods of history*. While Fröhlich's breakdown of the literary structure differs from Brooke's somewhat, the end result appears basically the same as the purpose of 4Q252 is viewed as validation of the possession of the land for the righteous (past, present, and future).

In conclusion, an overall compositional unity and purpose behind the selection of various forms of interpretations in 4Q252 appears evident. A temporal scheme and some sort of a series of counterparts are observed in the text. However, due to the fragmentary nature of the manuscript any conclusions must maintain a degree of tentativeness. In that vein the structure of this complex commentary is understood here in an adapted form:

Literary Genre(s)		Topical/Thematic Outline	
C O M M E N T A R Y	Rewritten Bible	\multicolumn{2}{l	}{The Past, Determinative of the Present}
		I:1–3	*Exegetical Chronicle*: The 120 years of Gen 6:3 (period until Flood judgment)
		I:3–II:5	*Exegetical Chronicle*: Chronology of the Flood (Noah delivered)
		II:5–8	*Poetic Commentary*: Noah's Curse of Canaan
		II:8–13	*Exegetical Chronicle*: Abram's entry into the land and the covenant of the pieces
		III:1–6	*Halakhic Exegesis*: Destruction of Sodom & Gomorrah
		III:6–14	*Exegesis*: The *aqedah* (Abraham merits the covenant) and Isaac's blessing
		\multicolumn{2}{l	}{The Future, Anticipated in the Present}
		IV:1–3	*Exegesis*: The destruction of Amalek (traditional enemy of Israel) "in the last days" (באחרית הימים)
	Pesher Commentary (Citation-plus-comment)	IV:3–VI:2	Section Heading: "The Blessings of Jacob" The eternal, messianic rule of Judah

Certain exegetical themes emerge in 4Q252 which likely guided the author's selection of Genesis passages. The various genres employed by the author indicate the use of sources for 4Q252. The author/compiler of 4Q252 employed earlier, non-sectarian sources in the rewritten Bible section (I:1–IV:3) along with the sectarian *pesher* commentary in IV:3–VI:2. However, the author/compiler used these non-sectarian sources for the sectarian interpretive goal of the work: validating the possession of the land for the righteous (past, present, and future).[41] Thus, while the overall composition of 4Q252 is understood as serving a Qumran sectarian purpose, the various exegetical sections may or may not have theological agendas. Hence, the various individual sections can still be examined individually. Indeed, the Flood section in particular, has garnered much attention from scholars. This section (I:1–II:5) consists of two distinct parts. The first section (I:1–3) deals with the interpretation of the 120 years of Genesis 6:3 while the rest

---

41. See Crawford, *Rewriting Scripture in Second Temple Times*, 141–42.

of the Flood material (I:3–II:5) concerns the chronology of the Flood itself. The substantial amount of extant Flood material in 4Q252 reveals various aspects of Qumran Flood interpretation.

The 120 Years in Genesis 6:3 as the Period before the Flood

There was a dispute in antiquity regarding Genesis 6:3 which reads: "And the LORD said, 'My Spirit shall not strive with man forever, for he is indeed flesh; yet his days shall be one hundred and twenty years.'" Do the "120 years" of Genesis 6:3 refer to the shortened lifespan of man or the period of time remaining for man until the Flood? The opening lines of column I begin with a rewritten form of Genesis 6:3 which seeks to resolve this chronological ambiguity in the biblical text.

1 בשנת ארבע מאות ושמונים לחיי נוח בא קצם לנוח ואלוהים
2 אמר לא ידור רוחי באדם לעולם ויחתכו ימיהם מאה ועשרים
3 שנה עד קץ מי מבול ומי מבול היו על הארץ

> 1. In the four hundred and eightieth year of Noah's life their end came to Noah. And God said 2. "My Spirit will not dwell among man forever," and their days were determined at one hundred and twenty 3. years until the end of the waters of the Flood. And the waters of the Flood were upon the earth. (column I, lines 1–3a)

Line 1 provides additional information to the biblical material: "In the four hundred and eightieth year of Noah's life their end came to Noah." While there is no mention of "the four hundred and eightieth year" in the biblical text, this can easily be derived by subtracting 120 years from the 600th year of Noah's life. Line 1 places God's statement in lines 2–3 in the 480th year of Noah's life. Thus, the mention of the 480th year of Noah's life indicates God's statement came precisely 120 years before the 600th year of Noah's life when the Flood came (lines 3–4).

In the phrase, "their end came to Noah" (בא קצם לנוח), the pronominal suffix of קצם (their end) requires an antecedent which is not provided in the extant text.[42] This raises the question: *whose* end came to Noah? קצם could refer to the offspring of the "sons of God" (Watchers) and the "daughters of

---

42. This has been explained by the use of sources by the author/compiler of 4Q252 who likely assumed the readers would be familiar with the Genesis base text. See Brooke, "The Genre of 4Q252: From Poetry to Pesher."

men" (Gen 6:1–4) and/or wicked humanity in general.⁴³ Timothy Lim identifies the antecedent as "all flesh," which is directly linked to God's statement to Noah in Genesis 6:13: קץ כל בשר בא לפני (The end of all flesh has come before Me).⁴⁴ Lim also notes the use of plural pronominal suffixes in 6:13 which further supports this link with the plural pronominal suffix (קצם) in line 1 of 4Q252.⁴⁵ This "all flesh" identification would appear to encompass both, the offspring of the Watchers with human women and humanity in general. This link with Genesis 6:13, where God speaks to Noah concerning the end of all flesh, further indicates that בא קצם לנוח portrays the idea of the end of all flesh "having come to Noah's knowledge."⁴⁶ What is important to note here is that "their end" came to Noah in the 480th year of his life (line 1) and a 120 year period was "determined" before they would be destroyed by the Flood (lines 2–3) in the 600th year of Noah's life (lines 3–4).

Lines 2–3 interpret Genesis 6:3 in a rewritten form, recording God's statement to Noah in his 480th year: "My Spirit will not dwell among man forever, and their days were determined at one hundred and twenty years, until the end of the waters of the Flood." Genesis 6:3 reads והיו ימיו מאה ועשרים שנה (yet his days shall be one hundred and twenty years), while 4Q252 reads ויחתכו ימיהם מאה ועשרים שנה (and their days were determined at one hundred and twenty years). Bernstein notes how 4Q252 emphasizes the "decretal force" of והיו ימיו by the use of ויחתכו ימיהם (and their days were determined) (cf. Dan 9:24).⁴⁷ Further, the use of ויחתכו, which in later Hebrew means 'to decide, render judgment,' may emphasize the nature of God's decree as immutable.⁴⁸ The fact that there is no mention in the text of this being a period for repentance also appears to support the idea that this judgment was inevitable. Such a deterministic restating (ויחתכו ימיהם) of Genesis 6:3 (והיו ימיו) would not be unexpected from a Qumran text. The phrase "and their days were determined at one hundred and twenty years" is then modified by the additional phrase עד קץ מי מבול (until the end of the

---

43. Crawford, *Rewriting Scripture in Second Temple Times*, 133.

44. Lim, "The Chronology of the Flood Story in a Qumran Text (4Q252)," 291.

45. Ibid., 291. Genesis 6:13: "And God said to Noah, 'The end of *all flesh* has come before Me, for the earth is filled with violence *through them*; and behold, *I will destroy them* with the earth'" (italics added).

46. Ibid., 291.

47. Bernstein, "4Q252 i 2 לא ידור רוחי באדם לעולם: Biblical Text or Biblical Interpretation?" 426. The only other occurrence of the root of ויחתכו is found in Daniel 9:24: "Seventy weeks are determined (נחתך) against your people and against your holy city."

48. Bernstein, "4Q252: From Re-Written Bible to Biblical Commentary," 6.

waters of the Flood), which explicitly identifies the 120 years as the period of time determined for man until the Flood. Bernstein notes that 4Q252 agrees with a number of ancient sources by understanding the 120 years as the period of time until the Flood, but differs from them by not ascribing to this period the opportunity for repentance.[49]

In summary, the opening lines of 4Q252 teach that the "120 years" of Genesis 6:3 do not refer to the shortened life-span of man, but to the period of time given to man until the Flood. First, the mention of the 480th year of Noah's life in line 1 places God's statement in that same year, 120 years before the 600th year of Noah's life when the Flood came (lines 3–4). Second, קצם (their end) likely refers to "all flesh" (cf. Gen 6:13), who would be destroyed when the Flood came. Last, the phrase עד קץ מי מבול (until the end of the waters of the Flood) explicitly identifies the 120 years as the period of time determined for man until the Flood (lines 2–3).

The Chronology of the Flood and the Solar Calendar

The Flood narrative of 4Q252 (I:3–II:5) is a highly selective exegetical retelling of the Genesis Flood account, with a particular interest in chronology. In this retelling of the year-long Flood the author gives attention only to the biblical passages which pertain to Flood chronology (Gen 7:11–12, 17, 24; 8:3–6, 8–14).[50] There is no discussion in the text of other elements from the biblical narrative (building of the ark, entrance into the ark, the destructive effects of the Flood, judgment upon all flesh, God's covenant) which would detract from the goal of the author's retelling.[51]

In the biblical narrative the events of the Flood are dated according to days of *months*. However, in 4Q252 the events are dated not only according to days of *months*, but also days of *weeks*. In addition, other events that are more vaguely dated in the biblical material are explicitly dated in 4Q252, which supplies the date of the month and day of the week.

---

49. Ibid.

50. According to Daniel Falk, 4Q252 deals with approximately 20% of the biblical text (Gen 6:3—8:18). See Falk, *The Parabiblical Texts*, 130.

51. Brooke, "The Genre of 4Q252: From Poetry to Pesher," 166. George Brooke understands this narrative as a "deliberately abbreviated" retelling by the author in which "nothing superfluous to this concern [chronology] is allowed to clutter this retelling."

COMMENTARY ON GENESIS

Genesis (MT)	4Q252
7:11	I:3–5
בשנת שש־מאות שנה לחיי־נח בחדש השני בשבעה־עשר יום לחדש ביום הזה נבקעו כל־מעינת תהום רבה וארבת השמים נפתחו	ומי מבול היו על הארץ בשנת שש מאות שנא לחיי נוח בחודש השני באחד בשבת בשבעה עשר בו ביום ההוא נבקעו כול מעינות תהום רבה וארבות השמים נפתחו
7:12	I:5–7
ויהי הגשם על־הארץ ארבעים יום וארבעים לילה	ויהי הגשם על הארץ ארבעים יום וארבעים לילה עד יום עשרים וששה בחודש השלישי יום חמשה בשבת
7:17	
ויהי המבול ארבעים יום על־הארץ וירבו המים וישאו את־התבה ותרם מעל הארץ	
7:24	I:7–9
ויגברו המים על־הארץ חמשים ומאת יום	ויגברו המים על הארץ חמשים מאות יום עד יום ארבעה עשר בחודש השביעי בשלושה בשבת ובסוף חמשים ומאת יום חסרו המים שני ימים יום הרביעי ויום החמישי
8:3	
וישבו המים מעל הארץ הלוך ושוב ויחסרו המים מקצה חמשים ומאת יום	
8:4	I:9–10
ותנח התבה בחדש השביעי בשבעה־עשר יום לחדש על הרי אררט	ויום הששי נחה התבה על הרי הוררט ה[וא יו]ם שבעה עשר בחודש השביעי
8:5	I:11–12
והמים היו הלוך וחסור עד החדש העשירי בעשירי באחד לחדש נראו ראשי ההרים	והמים הי[ו] הלוך וחסור עד החודש [הע]שירי באחד בו יום רביעי לשבת נראו ראשי ההרים
8:6	I:12–14
ויהי מקץ ארבעים יום ויפתח נח את־חלון התבה אשר עשה	ויהי מקץ ארבעים יום להראות ראשי ההר[ים ויפ]תח נוח את חלון התבה יום אחד בשבת יום עשרה בעש[תי עשר] החודש

85

Qumran Interpretation of the Genesis Flood

Genesis (MT)	4Q252
8:10	I:15–17
ויחל עוד שבעת ימים אחרים ויסף שלח את־היונה מן־התבה	ויחל עוד שבעת ימים א[חרים] ויוסף לשלחה ותבוה אליו ועלי זית טרף בפיה [הוא יום עשרים] וארבעה לעשתי עשר החודש באחד בשב[ת
8:12	I:18–20
וייחל עוד שבעת ימים אחרים וישלח את־היונה ולא־יספה שוב־אליו עוד	ומקץ שבעת ימים אחר[י]ם שלח א[ת ה]יונה ולוא יספה לשוב עוד הוא יום א[ח]ד לשנים עשר החודש [באחד] בשבת
8:13	I:20–22
ויהי באחת ושש־מאות שנה בראשון באחד לחדש חרבו המים מעל הארץ ויסר נח את־מכסה התבה וירא והנה חרבו פני האדמה	ומקץ שלוש[ים יום לשלח את היונ]ה אשר לוא יספ[ה] שוב עוד חרבו המ[י]ם מעל הארץ ו[י]סר נוח מכסה התבה וירא והנה [חרבו יום רביעי לשבת] באחד בחודש הריאשון
8:14	II:1–3
ובחדש השני בשבעה ועשרים יום לחדש יבשה הארץ	באחת ושש מאות שנה לחיי נוח ובשבעה עשר יום לחודש השני יבשה הארץ באחד בשבת ביום ההוא יצא נוח מן התבה לקץ שנה תמימה לימים שלוש מאות ששים וארבעה באחד בשבת

The author's exact expression of the days of the week varied slightly, while שבת is uniformly employed for "week."[52] This additional use of days and weeks for dating the events of the Flood in 4Q252 is noteworthy. The dates of the Flood in 4Q252 correspond to the solar calendar, in which the 364-day year is divided into 52 weeks. Thus, the week is primary and the month is secondary for dating these events within the author's purposes in 4Q252. The events marked by days and weeks in 4Q252 include the beginning of the Flood (I:3–5), the period of rainfall before the ark was lifted off the ground (I:5–7), the ending of the waters prevailing (I:7–9), the initial subsiding of

---

52. I:3–5 באחד בשבת; I:5–7 חמשה בשבת; I:7–9 בשלושה בשבת; I:12יום רביעי לשבת; I:13–14 יום רביעי לשבת; I:17 באחד בשב[ת; I:19–20 באחד בשבת; I:21–22 יום אחד בשבת; II:2–3 באחד בשבת (2).

waters (I:9), the ark resting on the mountains (I:9–10), the waters subsiding and mountain tops appearing (I:11–13), the opening of the ark window (I:13–14), the dove's second flight (I:15–17), the dove's third flight (I:18–20), the waters drying up from the earth (I:20–22), and the land drying up with Noah's exit from the ark (II:1–5). Importantly, through this additional information of days and weeks, the author/compiler of 4Q252 highlights the fact that none of the dated events during the Flood occurred on a seventh day of the week (Sabbath) or any of the principal days of a festival.

In column I, lines 6–7, the author provides an explicit date, whereas the biblical text does not. The biblical text mentions only the period of "forty days and forty nights" of rain until the ark was lifted up from the ground (Gen 7:12, 17). However, column I, lines 6–7, explicitly dates the end of the "forty days and forty nights" to 3/26/600 by counting the forty days from 2/17/600. In this case, the author also points out that this occurred on "the fifth day of the week."

In column I, lines 7–10, the author of 4Q252 addresses an exegetical problem concerning the waters prevailing 150 days and the ark landing on 7/17/600. The biblical text records that "the waters prevailed on the earth one hundred and fifty days" (Gen 7:24) and that "at the end of the hundred and fifty days the waters decreased" (Gen 8:3), with the ark *then* resting "in the seventh month, the seventeenth day of the month, on the mountains of Ararat" (Gen 8:4). With the use of the 364-day solar calendar in 4Q252 the 150-day period of prevailing waters ended on the fourteenth day of the seventh month, a few days short of the biblical date of the ark coming to rest on the seventeenth day of the seventh month. The author of 4Q252 attempts to resolve this chronological conundrum:

> 7. And the waters prevailed upon the earth one hundred and fifty days, 8. until the fourteenth day in the seventh month, the third (day) of the week. At the end of 9. one hundred and fifty days, the waters came down two days, the fourth day and the fifth day, and the 10. sixth day, the ark rested in the mountains of Hurarat (Ararat); it was the seventeenth day of the seventh month. (column I, lines 7–10)

The author interprets the subsiding of the waters at the end of 150 days (Gen 8:3) as occurring *prior* to the ark landing on 7/17/600 (Gen 8:4). Based on this understanding, the author supplied an additional two days of the waters subsiding between the end of the prevailing waters and the landing of the ark: "At the end of one hundred and fifty days, the waters came down two days, the fourth day and the fifth day, and the sixth day (of the week) the ark rested" (lines 8–10).[53] Lim observed that ". . . the addition of two extra days means that the ending of the mighty waters (8:3) and the resting of the ark (8:4) were understood to be sequential rather than simultaneous."[54] Thus, the author has resolved this chronological conundrum by understanding the 150-day period of prevailing waters ending on 7/14/600 and the ark landing on 7/17/600 as two separate events. Further, Brooke pointed out that the author's addition of two days placed the end of the prevailing waters on the eve of Sukkot[55] and the landing of the ark on the eve of the Sabbath.[56] The end result is that the author has also simultaneously avoided dating either event on a principal feast day or a seventh day (Sabbath).

Column II, lines 1–5, concludes this chronological commentary on the Flood with explicit statements concerning the ending of the Flood, Noah's departure from the ark, and the duration of the Flood:

> 1. in the year six-hundred and one of Noah's life, on the seventeenth day of the second month 2. the land dried up, on the first (day) of the week. On that day, Noah went out of the ark, at the end of a complete 3. year of three-hundred and sixty-four days, on the first (day) of the week. On the seventh 4. . . . one and six . . . Noah from the ark, at the appointed time of a complete 5. year. *vacat* (column II, lines 1–5)

Lines 1–2 place the end of the Flood on 2/17/601 (the first day of the week), precisely one year after the fountains of the great deep were broken up and the windows of heaven were opened on 2/17/600 (the first day of the week) (I:3–5). This understanding that the Flood lasted exactly

---

53. Bernstein, "4Q252: From Re-Written Bible to Biblical Commentary," 8.

54. Lim, "The Chronology of the Flood Story in a Qumran Text (4Q252)," 292.

55. Leviticus 23:33–35, 39: "Then the LORD spoke to Moses, saying, 'Speak to the children of Israel: 'The fifteenth day of this seventh month shall be the Feast of Tabernacles for seven days to the LORD. On the first day there shall be a holy convocation. You shall do no customary work on it . . . on the fifteenth day of the seventh month, when you have gathered in the fruit of the land, you shall keep the feast of the LORD for seven days; on the first day there shall be a Sabbath-rest, and on the eighth day a Sabbath-rest.'"

56. Brooke, "The Thematic Content of 4Q252," 39. The one hundred and fifty days of waters prevailing ended on the fourteenth day of the seventh month. Sukkot began on the fifteenth day of the seventh month. The fifteenth was a "Sabbath-rest" in which no work was done (cf. Lev 23:33–44; see previous footnote). The ark then landed on the seventeenth day of the seventh month, the sixth day of the week. Thus, the ark landed prior to the Sabbath, which occurred on the eighteenth day of the seventh month.

one year is attested elsewhere in Second Temple period literature. The Septuagint (LXX) presents the Flood as lasting for an exact year, but with the Flood beginning on 2/27/600 (MT 2/17/600) and ending on 2/27/601 (MT 2/27/601).[57] *Jubilees* 5:21–32 also corresponds to 4Q252, dating the Flood from 2/17/600 to 2/17/601. However, *Jubilees* 5:32 makes a distinction between the end of the year-long Flood on 2/17/601 and the departure of the animals from the ark on 2/27/601. Further, it is not until 3/1/601 that Noah leaves the ark (*Jubilees* 6:1), while 4Q252, line 3, understood Noah to have exited the ark "on that day" the Flood ended (2/17/601). Also, *1 Enoch* 106:15 refers to "a deluge and a great destruction for one year." Consequently, Second Temple period literature indicates that 4Q252 was not unique in its understanding of the Flood lasting exactly one year. Bernstein noted that the year-long Flood chronology presented in 4Q252 ". . . is not at all surprising in the context of the other ancient sources."[58] Nonetheless, the addition of the days and weeks provided by 4Q252 remains unique among the ancient sources.

---

57. For studies on the text-critical issues regarding the variant datings in Flood chronology between MT, LXX, and 4Q252, see Longacre, "Charting the Textual Waters"; Hendel, "4Q252 and the Flood Chronology of Genesis 7–8."

58. Bernstein, "4Q252: From Re-Written Bible to Biblical Commentary," 8.

Qumran Interpretation of the Genesis Flood

Flood Event	MT	LXX	Jubilees	4Q252
Fountains broken up & windows of heaven opened (7:11)	2/17/600	2/27/600	2/17/600 (5:23–25)	2/17/600 First day of week (I:3–5)
Period of rainfall before ark lifted off ground (7:12, 17)	40 days/nights	40 days/nights	40 days/nights (5:25)	3/26/600 Fifth day of week (I:5–7)
Waters prevailed (7:24; 8:3)	150 days	150 days	150 days Five months (5:27–28)	7/14/600 Third day of week (I:8–9)
Waters subsided	—	—	—	Fourth and Fifth days of week (I:9)
Ark rested on mountains of Ararat (8:4)	7/17/600	7/27/600	—	7/17/600 Sixth day of week (I:9–10)
Waters subsided (8:5)	Until 10th month	Until end of 10th month	—	10/1/600 Fourth day of week (I:11–12)
Mountain tops visible (8:5)	10/1/600	11/1/600	10/1/600 (5:30)	After 40 days (I:12–13)
Noah opened the window of the ark (8:6)	After 40 days	After 40 days	—	11/10/600 First day of week (I:12–14)
First flight of dove (8:8)	—	—	—	— (I:14–15)
Second flight of dove (8:10)	After 7 days	After 7 days	—	11/24/600 First day of week (I:15–17)
Third flight of dove (8:12)	After 7 days	After 7 days	—	12/1/600 First day of week (I:18–20)
Waters dried up from the earth (8:13)	1/1/601	1/1/601	1/1/601 (5:31)	1/1/601 Fourth day of week (I:20–22)
Earth was dried up (8:14)	2/27/601	2/27/601	2/17/601 (5:31–32)	2/17/601 First day of week (II:1–3)
Ark opened/animals go out (8:14–19)	—	—	2/27/601 (5:32)	— (II:4–5)
Duration of the Flood	1 year, 10 days	1 year	1 year	1 year (364 days)

While the additional information provided in 4Q252 is not found in MT, LXX, or *Jubilees*, the additional dates are deduced from the biblical text itself. Further, the chronology of 4Q252 follows the chronology of the biblical text, except for the end date of the Flood. Drew Longacre observed that ". . . never are the dates invented or altered to have significant events occur on certain days of the week. It is true that in 4Q252 the Flood ends and begins on the same day, but that is a necessary phenomenon in the 364-day calendar."[59]

According to column II, lines 1–2, Noah exited the ark on 2/17/601, the same day the earth dried up. The text then explicitly states the number of days of the full solar year for the Flood's duration in II:2–3: "On that day, Noah went out of the ark, at the end of a complete year of three-hundred and sixty-four days."[60] The author further reinforces this as a major concern by reiterating that Noah exited the ark למועד שנה תמימה (at the appointed time of a complete year) (II:4–5). This language is attested in *Commentary on Genesis D* (4Q254a) which also states that Noah departed from the ark למועד (at the appointed time) (frag. 3, line 2).[61] The author of 4Q252 has already meticulously shown that no dated events during the Flood occurred on a seventh day (Sabbath) or a principal feast day. Coupled with this, the use of למועד (at the appointed time) appears to further indicate the divinely ordered nature of the Flood judgment.

In summary, several observations can be made concerning the chronology in this exegetical retelling of the Flood. First, the chronology of the Flood is framed around the life of righteous Noah (who was delivered). Second, the dates in the Flood narrative correspond to the solar calendar. Third, the author meticulously shows that no dated events occurred on a seventh day (Sabbath) or a principal day of a festival. Fourth, 4Q252 has resolved the chronological conundrum of the waters prevailing one hundred and fifty days and the ark landing on 7/17/600 by understanding them sequentially as two separate events. Last, just as the feasts and Sabbaths were appointed by God and kept during the Flood, so too the Flood itself ended at God's appointed time, precisely the length of a solar year.

---

59. Longacre, "Charting the Textual Waters."

60. The solar calendar is attested elsewhere in Qumran literature, being used explicitly in *Jubilees* and underlying the *Genesis Apocryphon* (1QapGen) and the *Temple Scroll* (11QTª).

61. 4Q254a, frag. 3, line 2 reads: נוח יצא מן התבה למועד ימים ימימה. The phrase ימים ימימה is a difficult reading as ימימה may be defective of תמימה (complete).

Flood Interpretation in 4Q252: Conclusions

It is clear that chronology is of primary concern in this retelling of the Flood in 4Q252. But the question regarding the purpose of the author's focus on chronology still remains on the table. Is the author just simply resolving exegetical issues concerning chronology or is this exegetical retelling of the Flood (I:1–II:5) conveying a particular message which is echoed in the work as a whole?

Due to the diversity of genres and interpretive methods employed in the various sections, Bernstein does not view 4Q252 as an integrated whole, but as a non-related collection of exegetical remarks on various passages from Genesis 6–49, with no intended unifying message(s) for the work as a whole.[62] Consequently, Bernstein has sought to understand the Flood section in isolation from the rest of the text. Thus, he concluded, "What the author has done is to write a chronological commentary on the biblical text of the flood story, taking into account both textual difficulties in the Bible and the calendar framework with which he is familiar."[63] It can be agreed upon that the author of 4Q252 sought to resolve exegetical difficulties concerning chronology in the biblical text and the calendar. However, examination of the Flood section itself and the literary shape of 4Q252 as a whole has revealed that the author attempted to present the reader with more than just solutions to exegetical difficulties concerning chronology in the biblical text.

The various exegetical sections of 4Q252 deal with the wicked and the righteous represented in consecutive periods of history. Further, the author composed this highly selective commentary through an alternating series of counterparts in which the wicked are destroyed or subjugated, while the righteous are rescued and/or inhabit the land.[64] Columns I–III form a historical sequence beginning with the Flood, in which the past is to be understood as determinative of the present for the author and his

---

62. Bernstein, "4Q252: From Re-Written Bible to Biblical Commentary," 25–26.

63. Ibid., 9.

64. I:1–3, The 120 years of Gen 6:3 as the determined (decreed) period until the Flood judgment; I:3–II:5, Chronology of the Flood (righteous Noah delivered); II:5–8, The curse of Canaan and subjugation to his brothers; II:8–13, Abram's entry into the land and God's covenant with him; III:1–6, Destruction of Sodom & Gomorrah; III:6–14, Abraham merits the covenant and Isaac's blessing; IV:1–3, The destruction of Amalek (a traditional enemy of Israel) "in the last days" (באחרית הימים); IV:3–VI:2, "The Blessings of Jacob"–the eternal, messianic rule of Judah.

community. Columns IV–V then deal with the future eschatological age when the wicked will be destroyed and the righteous delivered. Thus, the future messianic age is also anticipated in the present for the author and his community. Understood in its entirety, 4Q252 is an eschatological and messianic commentary, validating the possession of the land for the righteous (past, present, and future). The Flood section, which opens this work, is an integral part of this literary shaping and, hence, the purpose of 4Q252.

The opening lines (I:1–3) teach that the "120 years" of Genesis 6:3 do not refer to the shortened life-span of man, but to the period of time determined for wicked humanity until the Flood. In I:3–II:5 the author presents a meticulous chronology of the Flood based on the solar calendar in which no dated events occurred on a Sabbath or a principal day of a festival. After the land was dried up, righteous Noah exited the ark, entering the land למועד (at the appointed time) of an exact 364-day year (II:1–5). The focus on chronology in this retelling of the Flood indicates the divinely ordered nature of the destruction of the wicked from the land and the deliverance of the righteous during the Flood judgment. Further, the author's interest in timing and chronology is not limited to the Flood section.[65] Observing this, Daniel Falk succinctly confirmed the thematic purpose of the chronology in the Flood section:

> Comparison with the rest of 4Q252 shows that interest in timing and chronology run throughout many of the selections, especially with regard to expulsion of the wicked and/or possession of the land. In this section, it is likely that the 120 years until destruction and the meticulous chronology of the flood illustrate for the compiler that removal of the wicked from the land and God's deliverance of His people follow a divinely ordained timetable.[66]

---

65. For example, a fairly detailed chronology concerning Abram's entry into the land is presented in II:8–14. Thus, in the past the destruction of the wicked from the land (pre-Flood humanity and Sodom and Gomorrah) and the righteous inheritance of the land (Noah and Abram) have apparently been shown to follow a divine order. Columns IV and V shift this focus to the future. In IV:1–3, a specific time is spoken of concerning the eradication of Amalek (an enemy of Israel) from under the heavens באחרית הימים (in the last days), thus taking on eschatological implications. V:1–7 cites Genesis 49:10: "the scepter shall not depart from the tribe of Judah." Timing is again addressed: "While Israel has the dominion, there will not be cut off someone who sits on the throne of David. For the staff is the covenant of royalty, and the thousands of Israel are the standards *vacat* Until (עד) the Messiah of righteousness comes, the Branch of David" (V:1–4). Thus, as in the past, the future destruction of the wicked from the land and deliverance of the righteous will follow a divine timetable.

66. Falk, *The Parabiblical Texts*, 130.

Qumran Interpretation of the Genesis Flood

The retelling of the Flood, with its focus on chronology, provides an explicit historical illustration of the divinely ordered destruction of the wicked from the earth and deliverance of the righteous. Just as the Flood followed a divinely ordained timetable, so too, the reader could be assured that the future destruction of the wicked from the land and deliverance of the righteous would follow a divinely ordered timetable. In this manner, the explicit illustration of destruction and deliverance provided in this exegetical retelling of the Flood could also be understood as implicitly presenting the Flood as an eschatological archetype.

CHAPTER FOUR

AN ADMONITION BASED ON THE FLOOD
(4Q370)

Discovery of 4Q370

AN ADMONITION BASED ON the Flood (4Q370) is another intriguing manuscript concerning the Genesis Flood that was found among the thousands of scroll fragments (representing some 600 manuscripts) from Cave 4 in 1952. However, like many of the other scrolls from Cave 4, the publication of 4Q370 was significantly delayed. Over 35 years would pass from the time this text was discovered by Bedouin to the time it was revealed to the public in Carol Newsom's preliminary publication in 1988.[1] Then in 1995, over 40 years after its discovery, the official edition of 4Q370 was published by Newsom in volume 19 of the *Discoveries in the Judaean Desert* series.[2]

Physical Description of 4Q370

4Q370 consists primarily of a single fragment which measures 10 x 19 cm and preserves parts of two columns of text. This Hebrew text is written in the Second Temple period Jewish script. More specifically, according to paleographical analysis, 4Q370 is written in a late Hasmonean semi-formal

---

1. Newsom, "4Q370: An Admonition Based on the Flood," 23–43.
2. Newsom, "4QAdmonition Based on the Flood" (hereafter, DJD XIX), 85–97.

script, dating the manuscript to the second half of the first century B.C. (ca. 50–25 B.C.).[3]

This single fragment of 4Q370 preserves parts of two columns of text (Courtesy of The Leon Levy Dead Sea Scrolls Digital Library; IAA, photo: Shai Halevi)

The first column contains a significant portion of ten lines of text which describes the abundance of the antediluvian world and the Genesis Flood. Lines 8–10 are not as well preserved as the bottom part of the scroll is more deteriorated. Newsom observed that "the rest of the column is broken away,"[4] which is all that can be concluded from the PAM 42.506 image of 4Q370. Indeed, the lower left-hand portion of column I appears to preserve only the top edges of a few letters for line 10. However, the PAM 43.369 image contains an additional smaller fragment with letters from only a single word (ישראל) preserved at the top. Interestingly, the top edges of these letters are missing. The PAM 43.369 image shows this smaller fragment with letters from a single word preserved at the top fitted to the lower left-hand side of column I where only the tops of a few letters are preserved. If this reconstruction is correct, a blank section of the manuscript appears to be preserved beneath the tenth line of text. If the bottom margin of the manuscript is represented here, this would indicate that column I had only

---

3. Newsom, DJD XIX, 86; García Martínez, "Interpretations of the Flood," 95–96. To date, 4Q370 has not been subjected to radiocarbon testing.

4. Newsom, DJD XIX, 85.

ten lines of text. Ariel Feldman argues that the smaller fragment present in PAM 43.369 is likely not part of the same manuscript based on codicological and paleographic grounds.[5] Concerning the former, Feldman observed that a vertical line ruled by a pointed instrument is found near the right edge of the fragment, though it is not visible in the photographs. He argues that this ruled line appears to be a right margin mark, while the primary fragment of 4Q370 does not contain ruled lines or margins.[6] Concerning the latter, he notes that while the script in the small fragment resembles that of the large fragment, the possibility of a different scribal hand remains.[7]

The second column preserves the first several words of nine lines of text as the left side of the fragment is broken off at this point. Concerning the content, Newsom observed that ". . . enough text is preserved, however, to indicate that column ii did not contain more narrative but rather homiletical or admonitory remarks."[8]

Returning now to the question of the length of the columns, the content may provide additional insight. The references at the end of column I to the covenant and the rainbow (lines 7–8) indicate the Flood narrative was coming to a close at that point. Further, column II does not continue the Flood narrative found in Column I. Newsom concluded that ". . . one can assume that the transition from narrative to admonitory comment was accomplished in the now lost portion of column i."[9] Thus, according to both the physical and textual data, it appears that column I likely consisted of roughly ten to fifteen lines of text. However, due to the paucity of evidence, conclusions concerning the original length of columns remain tentative.

4Q370: A Qumran Composition?

Is 4Q370 a Qumran sectarian composition? If not, how can it be included in a study of *Qumran* interpretation of the Genesis Flood? It is readily

---

5. Feldman, "The Reworking of the Biblical Flood Story in 4Q370," 31–49, here 31–32.

6. Ibid., 31–32. Feldman also recognizes that, among the Qumran scrolls, ". . . some were not ruled at all, while in others irregular margins' ruling is found." Thus, the possibility would remain that if this fragment does belong to 4Q370, it would represent an otherwise unpreserved column of text, not part of column I.

7. Ibid., 32. See footnote 9.

8. Newsom, "4Q370: An Admonition Based on the Flood," 23; see Newsom, DJD XIX, 85.

9. Ibid., 38.

Qumran Interpretation of the Genesis Flood

apparent that 4Q370 is a *Jewish* composition. For example, 4Q370 is a *Hebrew* text found in Judea at Qumran. Further, it dates to the second half of the first century B.C., which places it during the period of sectarian writing at Qumran. Nonetheless, even though this manuscript was found at Qumran and dates to the second half of the first century B.C., doubts have been raised as to whether 4Q370 was actually composed at Qumran.

Newsom holds that it is unlikely that 4Q370 was composed at Qumran based on two major arguments. First, she noted that none of the themes or terminology found in distinctly sectarian texts such as the *Community Rule* (1QS), the *Hodayot* (1QH), or the *Pesharim* is found in 4Q370.[10] This may be the case. But how does this rule out 4Q370 as a Qumran composition with any certainty? The extant text of 4Q370 is *incomplete* and it is difficult to determine with absolute certainty whether or not the text originally would have had any sectarian terminology or not. Further, what terms or themes *must* be present in a text in order to determine that it came from the Qumran community? This can become rather arbitrary. Also, the literary use of historical examples in order to exhort readers for certain religious purposes is found not only in 4Q370, but also in the sectarian *Damascus Document* (CD). Second, Newsom argued that 4Q370 employs the Tetragrammaton (יהוה), while compositions which are indisputably from Qumran avoid it.[11] This may generally be the case. However, the *Habakkuk Pesher* (1QpHab), which is generally understood as a *sectarian* Qumran text, employs the Tetragrammaton. In the end, Newsom has raised legitimate issues and may even be correct in her assessment concerning the provenance of 4Q370. However, no definitive conclusion appears to be demonstrable at this point.

While 4Q370 may or may not have been composed by the Qumran community (יחד), it was certainly composed by Jews and found to be acceptable for study and use at Qumran. The theological teaching in the text may not be overtly sectarian, but it does coincide with Qumran thought quite nicely. Further, 4Q370 was found in Cave 4, which Sidnie White Crawford, among others, has shown gives evidence of having been a dwelling space directly connected to the Qumran site.[12] 4Q370 was likely present

---

10. Newsom, DJD XIX, 86.

11. Ibid.

12. Crawford, "A View from the Caves," 30–39, 69. Crawford sets forth a number of evidences showing that Cave 4 was a dwelling space connected to the Qumran site itself: 1) The cave lies within the Sabbath limit of 1,000 cubits from the Qumran site. 2) The cave was well lit and ventilated with flat floors and storage niches. 3) Storage jars, lamps, bowls, cooking utensils, and scrolls were found in the cave. 4) There were also trails

in the Qumran community before it was conveniently placed in this nearby cave as the Roman legion approached in A.D. 68. Thus, whether or not 4Q370 was composed at Qumran, its presence in Cave 4 indicates it was accepted and used by the Essenes at Qumran. Consequently, the inclusion of this text for understanding *Qumran* interpretation of the Genesis Flood is warranted.

View of Khirbet Qumran looking south, with Cave 4 in close proximity
(Photograph by Jeremy D. Lyon)

History of Research on 4Q370

The substantial delay in publishing the numerous Cave 4 fragments resulted in scholarly research on 4Q370 not being made available until the late-1980s. In the following decades since its initial publication, 4Q370 has not received as much attention as 1QapGen or 4Q252. Nonetheless, several scholarly treatments are particularly relevant concerning this current treatment on Qumran interpretation of the Genesis Flood.

---

leading from the Qumran site to the marl terrace caves (which include Cave 4).

Qumran Interpretation of the Genesis Flood

Carol A. Newsom

A preliminary publication of 4Q370 was produced by Carol Newsom in *Revue de Qumran* in 1988.[13] This article, simply titled "*4Q370*: An Admonition Based on the Flood," is a thorough introductory treatment that includes a brief general description of the text, a transcription of both columns of text, discussion on paleography, notes on the readings, discussion on orthography, a translation of the text, and detailed line-by-line comments on the entire text. Newsom's designation of 4Q370 as "An Admonition Based on the Flood" is because the first column provides an account of the Genesis Flood while the second column contains "homiletical or admonitory remarks."[14] In 1995, Newsom's official edition of 4Q370 was published in volume 19 of the *Discoveries in the Judaean Desert* series, where much of the material from the 1988 preliminary publication was reproduced.[15] Newsom's publications provided the foundation for 4Q370 studies.

Florentino García Martínez

In 1998, Florentino García Martínez published a chapter titled, "Interpretations of the Flood in the Dead Sea Scrolls," in which he provided a brief summary overview of allusions to the Flood in the Qumran texts and presented a more detailed discussion of 4Q252 and 4Q370.[16] García Martínez provided a brief introduction to the text, followed with a translation of column I and discussion of the text. In his discussion of 4Q370, García Martínez noted that the author did not intend to "re-write" or "paraphrase" the biblical text, but used the well-known Flood story for a didactic or moral purpose.[17] García Martínez concluded that 4Q370 "has not read the Flood story as a story of deliverance of a just man . . . but has interpreted it exclusively in terms of punishment for the rebellion against God."[18] García Martínez concluded his discussion of 4Q370 with only a few comments concerning column II, followed with a translation.

---

13. Newsom, "*4Q370*: An Admonition Based on the Flood," 23–43.
14. Ibid., 23.
15. Newsom, DJD XIX, 85–97.
16. García Martínez, "Interpretations of the Flood," 86–108.
17. Ibid., 97.
18. Ibid., 99.

Moshe Bernstein

In 1999, Moshe Bernstein produced a chapter, "Noah and the Flood at Qumran,"[19] in which he sought to evaluate the different ways the Flood story was employed at Qumran. In his discussion on 4Q370, Bernstein distinguished this text as taking a different posture than much of the Flood material at Qumran.[20] The selective nature of the Flood story in 4Q30 indicates "the moral dimension" of the story was the author's concern. According to Bernstein, 4Q370 does not tell the Flood story for the story's sake, but for the purpose of the admonitory message.[21] Bernstein's chapter only deals briefly with the Flood material in 4Q370, but provides insightful discussion on how the Flood story was used.

Ariel Feldman

The most detailed study on the Flood material of 4Q370 was published by Ariel Feldman in his 2007 article, "The Reworking of the Biblical Flood Story in 4Q370."[22] His article examines "the additions introduced by 4Q370 into the biblical Flood narrative" and "the various techniques employed in rewriting the biblical text."[23] Feldman addresses four major aspects of the first column of 4Q370: 1) the abundance of food in the antediluvian world and subsequent rebellion (lines 1–2), 2) judgment on the Flood generation (line 3), 3) a description of the Flood (lines 3–5), and 4) the list of those who died in the Flood, including the "strong ones" (line 6). Feldman's in-depth study of the Flood material (column I, lines 1–6) reveals the author's paradigmatic understanding of the Flood and admonitory purpose for that generation.

Dorothy Peters

In 2008, Dorothy Peters published her seminal work on Noah in the Qumran literature in *Noah Traditions in the Dead Sea Scrolls: Conversations*

---

19. Bernstein, "Noah and the Flood at Qumran," 199–231.
20. Ibid., 211.
21. Ibid., 211–12.
22. Feldman, "The Reworking of the Biblical Flood Story in 4Q370," 31–49. The Hebrew version was published as "Mikra and Aggada in 4Q370 (Admonition Based on the Flood)" [(4Q370) מקרא ואגדה בקטע תוכחה מקומראן], 219–36.
23. Ibid., 32.

and Controversies in Antiquity. Within this comprehensive analysis Peters includes a brief section discussing 4Q370. Her literary analysis of this text is once again insightful and relevant to understanding Flood interpretation in this current study.

Alex P. Jassen

Alex P. Jassen's treatment of 4Q370 appeared in 2013 in the multi-volume reference work, *Outside the Bible: Ancient Jewish Writings Related to Scripture*.[24] Preceding his discussion of the text itself, Jassen briefly introduces the text with a summary of the content, a discussion of its composition and history, and its significance in Second Temple period biblical interpretation. The primary value of Jassen's work is the line-by-line commentary on the text of 4Q370, accompanying the translation. In particular, the commentary relates the text of 4Q370 extensively with both biblical and Second Temple period texts.

Content and Literary Structure of 4Q370

The title, "Admonition Based on the Flood," was given by the manuscript's original editor because the first column provides a summary retelling of the Flood while the second column contains admonitory remarks based on this historical example. 4Q370 provides us with a good example of *how* the Flood narrative was used for admonitory or homiletic purposes during the Second Temple period.

The first column of 4Q370, containing nine lines of text, provides a narrative retelling of the biblical Flood account and the events that precipitated it. It is likely that the beginning of the text is not preserved, based on the context and syntax of the opening lines of column I.[25] Line 1 begins with a description of the agricultural abundance and blessing in the antediluvian world. In response, humanity was commanded to bless the Lord for this abundance. Line 2 records that humanity instead did evil and rebelled against God. Humanity's rebellion resulted in God judging them with the Flood. Lines 3–5 provide a selective description of the Flood while line 6 delineates all those who perished in the Flood judgment. The last few lines mention God's covenant and the rainbow. The author's selective summary

---

24. Jassen, "Admonition Based on the Flood," 263–71.
25. Newsom, "4Q370: An Admonition Based on the Flood," 30.

of the Flood, partially using the wording of the biblical text, implies the readers were likely also familiar with the biblical account.[26] It does not appear that the author intended to quote the biblical text exactly. Divergences from the biblical Flood text do not reflect a different text tradition nor do they appear to be exegetically motivated. Rather, as Newsom has noted, the author was likely citing the biblical text from memory.[27] García Martínez observed that the ". . . biblical text is still perceptible in the new text, but the author has transformed the concrete narrative into a general paradigm" wherein God's blessing of humanity is answered by human rebellion, which is followed by God's judgment.[28]

The second column is more fragmentary, with only a third of the text preserved, making it more difficult to discern the content and literary style with certainty. However, it is evident that the Flood narrative found in the first column does not continue in the second. Newsom noted that enough text is preserved to indicate that ". . . column ii does not contain more narrative but rather homiletical or admonitory remarks."[29] Feldman, however, sees in the second column *both* the admonitory remarks *and* some sort of narrative, though not the Flood narrative.[30] There is certainly a literary shift of some sort from the first to second column. The distribution of verbs used by the author further indicates a distinct literary shift between columns I and II. The Flood narrative in the first column is written in the framework of *wayyiqtol* (*waw* consecutive) and *qatal* (perfect) verbs, which are primary in narrating *past* events. The Flood narrative also includes some discourse (speech) embedded within, which is not uncommon. Column II then indicates a shift from the past to the future with *yiqtol* (imperfect) verbs: ידרשו "they will seek" (line 1) and יצדיק "[YHWH] will justify" (line 2).[31] Though fragmentary, the rest of the extant column II text continues with verbs indicative of some sort of discourse in which the author also admonished his contemporary readers to avoid the future judgment by not rebelling against the words of the LORD (line 9).

---

26. García Martínez, "Interpretations of the Flood," 96.
27. Newsom, DJD XIX, 87.
28. García Martínez, "Interpretations of the Flood," 99.
29. Newsom, "4Q370: An Admonition Based on the Flood," 23.
30. Feldman, "The Reworking of the Biblical Flood Story in 4Q370," 32.
31. Dorothy Peters reads ידרשו as ודרשו, a *weqatal* (*waw* + perfect) verb. García Martínez and Tigchelaar, Wise, and Jassen all appear to follow Newsom's reading of ידרשו.

Qumran Interpretation of the Genesis Flood

4Q370 Verb Distribution	
Column I – *The Past* Narrative of the Flood	**Column II** – *The Future* Discourse with Admonition
L1 ויעטר "and He crowned" ושפך "and poured down" השביע "He satisfied" עשה "do" יוכלו "will eat" וישבעו "and be satisfied" אמר "says [YHWH]" L2 ויברכו "and will bless" עשו "they have done" אמר "says [YHWH]" ויאמרו "and opposed" L3 וישפטם "and [YHWH] judged" וירעם "and He thundered" וינעו "and [foundations] shook" L4 נבקעו "[and waters] were broken up" נפתחו "[windows] were opened" ופצו "and [the depths] overflowed" L5 הריקו "poured out" [rain] ואבדם "and He destroyed them" L6 נמחו "was wiped out" וימת "and died" נמלטו "did not escape" L7 ויעש "and [God] made" נתן "[a rainbow] He gave" זכור "to remember" L8 יהיה "[never] will [the waters] be" יפתחו "[never] will be opened" L9 עשו "they made"	L1 ידרשו "they will seek" L2 יצדיק "[YHWH] will justify" L3 ויטהרם "and He will cleanse them" L5 יצמחו "they sprout" L6 ירחם "He will have compassion" L7 זכרו "remember" (imperative) L8 ותשמח "and let [your soul] rejoice" L9 [אל] תמרו "[do not] oppose"

AN ADMONITION BASED ON THE FLOOD

The general verbal distribution pattern supports a literary shift from the past (the Flood as an historical example) to the future (an admonition to contemporaries to avoid future judgment).

> 1. Because of iniquity they will seek (ידרשו) [ ] 2. Yahweh will make righteous (יצדיק) [ ] 3. And He will cleanse them (ויטהרם) from their iniquity [ ] 4. their evil, in their knowledge o[f good and evil ... like grass] 5. they spring up (יצמחו) and like a shadow are their days o[n earth ... from eternity] 6. to eternity He will have compassion (ירחם) [ ] 7. the strength of Yahweh; remember (זכרו) the won[ders ...] 8. because of the fear of Him; and let [your] so[ul] rejoice (ותשמח) [...] 9. those who follow you. Do not rebel (אל תמרו) against the word[s of Yahweh ...] (column II, lines 1–9)

Notably, column II contains no explicit references to the Flood. But references to the Flood are not necessary at this point since the historical paradigm, for the author's purposes, has already been established in the first column. Column II contains statements regarding human iniquity and justification (lines 1–4), followed by a remark on the transitory nature of human life (line 5). The extant text closes with an exhortation to not rebel against the words of the LORD (line 9). Due to the fragmentary nature of the second column, one can only speculate how the author may have further employed the paradigm, based on the Flood story in column I, for his readers. A basic conclusion, nonetheless, from the extant text is that the author used the historical paradigm for an admonitory purpose.

While the two columns differ in both their content and literary style, there are linguistic and contextual reasons to read them together as a literary unit. First, the Flood narrative in column I is employed as a historical example of the devastating consequences of human iniquity and rebellion against God. This historical example is reinforced in the second column by references to the transitory nature of human life (line 5).[32] The author then draws on this historical example to admonish his readers. Second, both columns make reference to historical examples as part of the author's appeal to the reader to not rebel against God. Column I refers to the Flood while column II likely makes a reference to the Exodus (line 7).[33] Third, the

---

32. Jassen, "Admonition Based on the Flood," 263.

33. Column II, line 7, reads: "the strength (mighty acts) of YHWH; remember the won[ders . . .]." The text is then lost at this point. Both Newsom and Jassen have observed the connection between 4Q370 (col. II, line 7) and 4Q185, which reads: "Draw wisdom from the might of God. Remember the wonders He did in Egypt and the portents [in the land of Ham]." Jassen commented on these references to historical examples: "The

two columns are linked lexically. The language of the admonition in column II, line 9, אל תמרו (do not rebel), draws the reader back to the human rebellion in column I, line 2, ויאמרו אל (and they rebelled against God), forming an *inclusio* around the text.³⁴ Last, the use of historical examples for the purpose of teaching and admonition is a literary device that is well attested in both biblical and ancient Jewish literature (cf. Deut. 1–4; Psalm 78, 105–106; Nehemiah 9; *3 Maccabees*; *Damascus Document*; Hebrews; *1 Clement*).³⁵ Newsom observed that the speaker/author of 4Q370 (col. II) is ". . . more like the anonymous didactic voice of Psalm 78 or the *Damascus Document*, using a well known historical example to instruct a general audience."³⁶

In summary, the author of 4Q370 employed the Flood narrative as a historical example in order to admonish his contemporary readers to avoid future judgment. This use of the Flood narrative for didactic and admonitory purposes is notable among the Qumran texts. It is within this overall literary shaping and context that the author recounts the Flood. From this unique text, several aspects of Qumran interpretation of the Flood can be discerned regarding the Flood's cause(s), archetypal description, and scope.

The Cause(s) of the Flood: The Nature of the Rebellion

The opening lines of the first column are concerned with what precipitated the Flood, opening with a brief description of the agricultural abundance provided by God to every living soul in the antediluvian world.

---

author of 4Q185 appeals to the historical example of the Exodus to compel the audience to follow God's will. This passage in 4Q185 reinforces the similar, more-developed appeal to the Flood example in column 1 of 4Q370." Jassen, "Admonition Based on the Flood," 270; see Feldman, "The Reworking of the Biblical Flood Story in 4Q370," 32.

34. Both columns warn of rebellion against God using the root term מרה. See Jassen, "Admonition Based on the Flood," 263; Feldman, "The Reworking of the Biblical Flood Story in 4Q370," 32.

35. Newsom, "4Q370: An Admonition Based on the Flood," 29; See DJD XIX, 85; See Jassen, "Admonition Based on the Flood," 263. For example, the opening chapters of Deuteronomy (1–3) recite historical examples before exhorting the reader in chapter 4ff to obey the Lord.

36. Newsom, DJD XIX, 85.

AN ADMONITION BASED ON THE FLOOD

[ו]יעטר הרים תנ[ובה ו]שפך אכל על פניהם ופרו טוב השביע כלנפש

[And] He crowned the mountains with pro[duce and po]ured out food upon them and with good fruit He satisfied every living being. (line 1a)

This description of the mountains overflowing with produce calls to mind a number of biblical texts,[37] but is not specifically attested in the Hebrew Bible.[38] This entire clause appears to be an adaptation from a passage in the *Hymn to the Creator*, a psalm-like composition found in 11QPs^a (XXVI, 9–15), which refers to God's works at creation: מעטר הרים תנובות אוכל טוב לכול חי (He crowns the mountains with produce *vacat* good food for all the living) (line 13). While Newsom, García Martínez, and Jassen view 4Q370 as dependent on the *Hymn to the Creator*,[39] Feldman suggests it is possible that both texts may work from an unknown common source.[40] Regardless of which text is dependent, there are striking parallels between 4Q370 (line 1) and the *Hymn to the Creator* (line 13):

Hymn (XXVI:13)   מעטר הרים תנובות
4Q370 (I:1a)   [ו]יעטר הרים תנובה

Hymn (XXVI:13)   אוכל טוב לכול חי
4Q370 (1:1a)   ושפך אכל על פניהם ופרו טוב השביע כלנפש

The author of 4Q370 appears to have cited the first phrase from line 13 of the *Hymn to the Creator* almost verbatim and then paraphrased and/or expanded the latter phrase from line 13. Jassen notably observed that the phrase "good food" (אוכל טוב) from the *Hymn to the Creator* (line 13) is reformulated in 4Q370 in such a way that "each of these words appears in a separate clause with its own verb of divine action."[41]

Hymn (XXVI:13) "good food (אוכל טוב) for all the living"

4Q370 (I:1a) "and He poured out (divine action) food (אכל) upon them"

4Q370 (I:1a) "and with good fruit (ופרו טוב) He satisfied (divine action) every living soul"

---

37. Cf. Ezekiel 36:8; Joel 3:18; Amos 9:13; Psalm 72:16.

38. Feldman, "The Reworking of the Biblical Flood Story in 4Q370," 33.

39. Newsom, "*4Q370*: An Admonition Based on the Flood," 30–31; García Martínez, "Interpretations of the Flood," 97–98; Jassen, "Admonition Based on the Flood," 265.

40. Feldman, "The Reworking of the Biblical Flood Story in 4Q370," 34.

41. Jassen, "Admonition Based on the Flood," 265.

Further, the literary context of line 13 in the *Hymn to the Creator* is that of a fuller description of God as Creator (lines 9–15). Thus, Newsom concluded that "... the use of the *Hymn to the Creator* suggests that the author of *4Q370* is describing creation."[42]

The depiction of mountains being crowned with produce is followed by further description of God's abundant provision: ושפך אכל על פניהם ופרו טוב השביע כלנפש (and He poured out food upon them and with good fruit He satisfied every living being) (line 1a). The term שפך ("to pour out") is used frequently in the Hebrew Bible, but is not used with אכל specifically. Rather, נתן אכל ("to give food") is found in the Hebrew Bible. Thus, Feldman regards the usage of שפך אכל in 4Q370 as emphasizing the abundance of food provided for the antediluvian world.[43] Further, the food is poured out by God על פניהם (lit. "upon their faces"), portraying the image of God pouring the food directly into their mouths.[44] The אכל (food) which God abundantly provided for the antediluvians is delineated as תנובה (produce) and פרו טוב (good fruit), which recall the provision of food in Genesis 1:29–30. Line 1 continues, stating that God's abundant provision השביע כלנפש (satisfied every living soul). The description of God's abundant provision upon every soul in the antediluvian world is followed by Divine speech:

כל אשר עשה רצוני יוכלו וישבעו אמר י[ה]וה ויברכו את שם [קדש]י

"Let all who do My will, eat and be satisfied," said Yahweh, "And let them bless My holy name." (lines 1b–2a)

This direct speech expresses God's expectations (commands) for humanity in response to His provision: "do My will" and "bless My holy name." Jassen has suggested that כל אשר עשה רצוני ("all who do My will") could be understood as modifying the preceding clause. In other words, the "all" (כל) who are satisfied in the preceding clause are now identified as *only* "all" (כל) who do God's will.[45] The next clause, יוכלו וישבעו (let them eat and be satisfied), is a supralinear insertion apparently added by the scribe due to an initial omission. Interestingly, the verbs יוכלו, וישבעו, and ויברכו ("eat, be satisfied, bless"; 4Q370, lines 1b–2a) echo Deuteronomy 8:10, the only

---

42. Newsom, "*4Q370*: An Admonition Based on the Flood," 30–31.
43. Feldman, "The Reworking of the Biblical Flood Story," 34.
44. Ibid.
45. Jassen, "Admonition Based on the Flood," 265.

other occurrence of those three verbs (eat, be satisfied, bless) in uninterrupted sequence.[46]

"Let all who do My will, eat (יוכלו) and be satisfied (וישבעו)," said Yahweh, "And let them bless (ויברכו) My holy name." (4Q370, I:1b–2a)

"When you have eaten (ואכלת) and are satisfied (ושבעת), then you shall bless (וברכת) Yahweh your God for the good land which He has given you." (Deut 8:10)

In Deuteronomy 8:10 these three verbs (eat, be satisfied, bless) are linked specifically to the giving of the "good land" to the Israelites. By linking 4Q370 with Deuteronomy, the author equates the Land of Israel to the earth at creation, in which both are filled with God's abundant agricultural provision.[47] The author of 4Q370 also expanded the biblical passage by adding the phrase: כל אשר עשה רצוני (all who do My will). This reworked version of Deuteronomy 8:10 indicates that: 1) doing God's will is a prerequisite for enjoying His abundant provision and 2) blessing God's holy name is the proper response to His provision.

The divine commands for the antediluvians to eat, be satisfied, and bless God (lines 1b–2a) are immediately followed by God's statement that something contrary has occurred. Thus, a sharp contrast is presented between God's abundant generosity and human ingratitude.[48]

והני הם אז עשו הרע בעיני אמר יהוה ויאמרו אל במ[אלי]ליהם

"But look, they have done what is evil in My eyes," said Yahweh. And they rebelled against God in their deeds. (line 2b)

The antediluvians did evil in God's eyes by not following His commands (lines 1b–2a) and properly acknowledging (blessing) God for His abundant provision. The context also indicates the phrase והני הם אז עשו הרע בעיני אמר יהוה in 4Q370 is an allusion to Genesis 6:5: וירא יהוה כי רבה רעת האדם בארץ (And Yahweh saw that the wickedness of man was great in the earth). The biblical text then only notes that the "intents of the thoughts

---

46. Newsom, DJD XIX, 92; "4Q370: Admonition Based on the Flood," 31. See García Martínez, "Interpretations of the Flood," 98; Feldman, "The Reworking of the Biblical Flood Story in 4Q370," 35; Peters, *Noah Traditions in the Dead Sea Scrolls*, 146; Jassen, "Admonition Based on the Flood," 266.

47. Jassen, "Admonition Based on the Flood," 266.

48. Newsom, DJD XIX, 92.

of his heart was only evil continually." However, 4Q370 further explains the evil of humanity as related to their acts: ויאמרו אל במ[א]לי[ליהם (and they rebelled against God in their deeds).

The link between 4Q370 (I:1b–2a) and Deuteronomy 8 provides insight into the nature of the rebellion spoken of in line 2b. God's commands to eat, be satisfied, and bless God in the good land given to them (Deut 8:10) are followed by a warning that those who enjoy abundance are prone to rebel against God and then suffer judgment:

> "Beware that you do not forget the LORD your God by not keeping His commandments, His judgments, and His statutes . . . lest, when you have eaten (תאכל) and are satisfied (ושבעת) . . . you forget the LORD your God . . . Then it shall be, if you by any means forget the LORD your God, and follow other gods . . . you shall surely perish. As the nations which the LORD destroys before you, so you shall perish, because you would not be obedient to the voice of the LORD your God." (Deut 8:11–14; 19–20)

The human rebellion appears to go beyond simply failing to bless God for His abundant provision (Deut 8:10). Jassen observed in Deuteronomy a progression in which failure to bless God would lead to a disregard for God (8:11–18) and following other gods (8:19), which would result in exile from the land filled with abundance (8:20).[49] Israel's failure to heed this warning did result in their exile from the land, which is described in Nehemiah 9:25–27.[50] Thus, the link between 4Q370 and Deuteronomy not only equates the Land of Israel to the earth at creation, but also the exile from the land to the Flood (exile from the abundant earth).

In 4Q370, lines 1b–2, human ingratitude and rebellion precipitated the divine judgment mentioned immediately afterwards in the first part of line 3:

וישפטם יהוה כ[כל]דרכיהם וכמחשבות יצר לבם ה[רע]

> And Yahweh judged them ac[cording to al]l their ways, and according to the thoughts of the [evil] inclination of their heart. (line 3a)

---

49. Jassen, "Admonition Based on the Flood," 266.

50. "So they ate (ויאכלו) and were satisfied (וישבעו) . . . and delighted in Your great goodness. Nevertheless, they were disobedient and rebelled (וימרו) against You . . . Therefore You delivered them into the hand of their enemies." The language of Nehemiah 9:25–27 parallels 4Q370 (I:b –2) and Deuteronomy 8:10–20.

God is justified in His response to human rebellion, judging the antediluvians "according to all their ways, and according to the thoughts of the evil inclination of their heart."⁵¹

In summary, 4Q370 begins with a vivid description of God's provision of agricultural abundance to the antediluvian world in which every soul was satisfied (line 1a). The following divine speech expresses God's expectations (commands) for humanity to respond properly to His provision by doing His will and blessing His holy name (lines 1b–2a). Instead, humanity did evil and rebelled against God, resulting in judgment for their ingratitude for God's provision (line 2b). The phrase עשו הרע בעיני (they have done what is evil in My eyes) (line 2b) refers to the רעת האדם (evil of man) (Gen 6:5), indicating that 4Q370 sought to explain the nature of the evil that led to the judgment upon humanity.⁵² The rebellion of the antediluvians is immediately followed by God's judgment (line 3a). The cause(s) of the Flood according to 4Q370 could be summed up: God's Abundance/Provision → Human Ingratitude/Rebellion → Flood Judgment. This particular tradition of what precipitated the Flood is not found in the biblical Flood narrative. The author used both biblical (e.g. Deut 8) and non-biblical (e.g. *Hymn to the Creator*) sources in presenting this tradition of the cause(s) of the Flood.

The Flood as Judgment

In 4Q370, the ingratitude and rebellion of humanity (I:1b–2) is directly followed by God's judgment: וישפטם יהוה כ[כל]דרכיהם וכמחשבות יצר לבם ה[רע] (And Yahweh judged them ac[cording to al]l their ways, and according to the thoughts of the [evil] inclination of their heart) (line 3a). This particular juxtaposition (lines 2–3) in 4Q370 is noteworthy in comparison to the biblical account. The phrase וישפטם יהוה (and Yahweh judged them) is not explicitly found in the biblical Flood narrative. The next two phrases allude to Genesis 6:5, 12. The phrase כ[כל]דרכיהם (according to all their ways) alludes to Genesis 6:12: כי־השחית כל־בשר את־דרכו על־הארץ (for all flesh had corrupted their way on the earth). The phrase וכמחשבות יצר לבם ה[רע] (and according to the thoughts of the [evil] inclination of their heart) alludes to Genesis 6:5: וירא יהוה כי רבה רעת האדם בארץ וכל־יצר מחשבת לבו רק רע כל־היום (Then Yahweh saw that the wickedness of man was great in the earth, and that every intent of the thoughts of his heart was only evil

---

51. This phrase reworks Genesis 6:5, 12.
52. Feldman, "The Reworking of the Biblical Flood Story in 4Q370," 40.

Qumran Interpretation of the Genesis Flood

continually). As noted already, the author previously alluded to Genesis 6:5 in line 2b: והני הם אז עשו הרע בעיני אמר יהוה. Notably, the first verse the author used from the biblical Flood narrative (6:5) comes immediately before the introduction of Noah, who "found grace in the eyes of the LORD" and "was a just man, perfect in his generations" (see Gen 6:8–10). An allusion is also made then to Genesis 6:12 in 4Q370. Strikingly, not only does 4Q370 omit the introduction of righteous Noah in this reworked Flood narrative, but as García Martínez observed, ". . . the author omits the warning of the Flood and all the preparations, the construction of the ark and Noah's entering into it with the animals, in order to link the announcement of the punishment with its realization as described in Genesis 7:11."[53]

Comparing the two Flood accounts, 4Q370 describes the human ingratitude, wickedness, and rebellion in line 2b (parallel to Gen 6:5), but then departs from the biblical narrative at this point. 4Q370 does not mention Noah or the construction and entry into the ark, but instead, moves directly to the judgment for this rebellion. Thus, 4Q370 (lines 2–3) speaks only of the Flood (described in lines 3–5) as God's judgment in response to human rebellion. Newsom concluded, "This selection and omission of detail suggests that the author is interested in the flood as a story of disobedience and punishment rather than e.g., a story of the deliverance of the righteous."[54] García Martínez also concluded that 4Q370 ". . . has not read the Flood story as a story of the deliverance of a just man, for example . . . but has interpreted it exclusively in terms of punishment for the rebellion against God."[55] The phrase וישפטם יהוה (and Yahweh judged them), not explicitly found in the biblical narrative, further supports the author's emphasis of the Flood as judgment against human rebellion. This emphasis on judgment continues in the following lines which describe the Flood.

---

53. García Martínez, "Interpretations of the Flood," 98.
54. Newsom, "4Q370: An Admonition Based on the Flood," 35; see DJD XIX, 88.
55. García Martínez, "Interpretations of the Flood," 99.

4Q370 (col. I)	Genesis Flood Narrative
Wickedness of Humanity	*Wickedness of Humanity*
"'But look, they have done what is evil in My eyes,' said Yahweh. And they rebelled against God in their deeds." (line 2b)	"Then the LORD saw that the evil of man was great in the earth, and that every intent of the thoughts of his heart was only evil continually" (Gen 6:5)
—	*Introduction of Righteous Noah in Contrast to Wicked Humanity* (Gen 6:6–12)
—	*Warning of the Flood* (Gen 6:13, 17)
—	*Ark Construction & Other Preparations* (Gen 6:13–22)
—	*Noah, His Family, and the Animals Enter the Ark* (Gen 7:1–10; cf. also vv. 13–17)
Flood Judgment	*Flood Judgment*
"And Yahweh judged them ac[cording to al]l their ways, and according to the thoughts of the [evil] inclination of their heart. And He thundered against them with [His] strength. [And] all the foundations of the ea[rth] shook, [and the wa]ters were broken up from the deeps. All the windows of the heavens were opened and all of the deeps overflowed [with] mighty waters. And the windows of the heavens p[our]ed out rain. And He destroyed them in the Flood [...] ... them all ... [...] (lines 3–5)	"In the six hundredth year of Noah's life, in the second month, the seventeenth day of the month, on that day all the fountains of the great deep were broken up, and the windows of heaven were opened." (Gen 7:11)

Qumran Interpretation of the Genesis Flood

The Flood as an Archetype of Eschatological Judgment

A number of Second Temple period texts understand the Flood in relation to the eschatological judgment[56] and 4Q370 also addresses this in a unique way. The description of the Flood itself immediately follows the statement in line 3 concerning Yahweh judging rebellious humanity:

וירעם עליהם בכחו וינעו כל סוסדי אר[ץ ימ]ים נבקעו מתהמות כל
ארבות השמים נפתחו ופצו כל תהמו[ת מ]מים אדרי⁵ וארבות השמים
ה[רי]קו מטר[ו]אבדם במבול[...].ים כלם ...[...]ה

> 3b. And He thundered against them with [His] strength. [And] all the 4. foundations of the ea[rth] shook, [and the wa]ters were broken up from the deeps. All the windows of the heavens were opened and all of the deeps overflowed [with] mighty waters. 5. And the windows of the heavens p[our]ed out rain. And He destroyed them in the Flood [ ] ... them all [ ] ... (column I, lines 3b–5)

The language of God's thundering and the foundations of the earth shaking (lines 3b–4a) are not found in the biblical Flood narrative. However, this language introduced into the Flood story of 4Q370 does occur in biblical poetic descriptions of Yahweh in His power and as Divine Warrior (cf. 1 Sam 2:10; Ps 18:8, 14, 16 [MT]; 29:3; 68:9 [MT]; Job 37:4–5).[57] Further, this language also occurs in descriptions of God's future war against the nations (Isa 24:18–20; 29:6; Joel 4:15–16 [MT]). Not surprisingly, this imagery of God thundering and the foundations of the earth shaking are found in Second Temple period literature describing the eschatological war.[58] For example, *Hodayot* (1QH^a) XI:34–35 reads: כיא ירעם אל בהמון כוחו...ויתמוגגו וירעדו אושי עולם (For God will thunder with the roar of His strength ... and the eternal foundations melt and shake).[59]

Jassen suggests that the use of this type of divine imagery in 4Q370 might indeed have been influenced by passages such as Psalm 29:3: "The

---

56. *1 Enoch* (90; 108); *Sibylline Oracles*; *Genesis Apocryphon* (1QapGen); *Commentary on Genesis* (4Q252); New Testament (Matthew 24:37–39; 2 Peter 3:3–7); Josephus (*Antiquities* 1.70–71).

57. Newsom, DJD XIX, 94; Feldman, "The Reworking of the Biblical Flood Story in 4Q370," 41.

58. Feldman, "The Reworking of the Biblical Flood Story in 4Q370," 42.

59. Text and translation is from García Martínez and Tigchelaar, *The Dead Sea Scrolls Study Edition*, 166–67.

voice of the LORD is over the waters; the God of glory thunders (הרעים); the LORD is over many waters."⁶⁰ Most notably though, the phrase וינעו כל מוסדי ארץ (and all the foundations of the earth shook) (lines 3b–4a) appears to allude to the future judgment spoken of in Isaiah 24:18–20: וירעשו מוסדי ארץ...נוע תנוע ארץ כשכור (and the foundations of the earth are shaken ... the earth shall reel to and fro like a drunkard).⁶¹ Further, the description of this future destruction of the earth in Isaiah 24:18–20 begins with the phrase "for the windows from on high are opened" (v. 18), alluding to the Flood narrative: "and the windows of heaven were opened" (Gen 7:11). In addition, the opening phrase of line 3, וישפטם יהוה (and Yahweh judged), immediately precedes the language of God thundering and the earth shaking, perhaps further indicating that the Flood story in 4Q370 was linked to future judgment.

4Q370 (col I, lines 3–5) *Eschatological language employed in Flood Judgment*	Isaiah 24:18–20 *Flood language employed in Eschatological Judgment*
"And Yahweh judged" (line 3) "And He thundered" (line 3) "and all the foundations of the earth shook" (lines 3b–4a)	"For the windows on high are open" (v. 18)
"and the waters were broken up from the deeps. All the windows of the heavens were opened and all of the deeps overflowed with mighty waters. And the windows of the heavens poured out rain. And He destroyed them in the Flood." (lines 4–5)	"And the foundations of the earth are shaken" (v. 18) "The earth shall reel to and fro like a drunkard" (v. 20)

The reworking of Genesis 7:11–12 in 4Q370 (lines 4–5) is introduced with eschatological language not found in the biblical Flood narrative, but linked to Isaiah 24:18–20. Feldman concluded, "Thus, while Is 24:18 describes the future catastrophe employing the language of the Flood

60. Jassen, "Admonition Based on the Flood," 267.

61. This connection was first noted in Newsom, "4Q370: An Admonition Based on the Flood," 36; DJD XIX, 94; cf. Feldman, "The Reworking of the Biblical Flood Story in 4Q370," 42; Peters, *Noah Traditions in the Dead Sea Scrolls*, 146; Jassen, "Admonition Based on the Flood," 267. Feldman has developed in most detail this connection between the Flood story in 4Q370 and Isaiah 24:18–20.

narrative, 4Q370 seems to introduce into its Flood story the elements of the eschatological war."[62]

The reworking of Genesis 7:11 in lines 4–5 also introduces new material to the Flood story. Newsom viewed the phrase, "and the waters were broken up from the deeps; all the windows of heaven were opened" (line 4), as a paraphrase of Genesis 7:11b. The next phrase, "and all of the deeps overflowed with mighty waters; and the windows of heaven poured out rain" (lines 4b–5a), was understood as an expansion of Genesis 7:11b, which also alluded to the "rain" in 7:12.[63] Jassen understood the first phrase as a reproduction of Genesis 7:11 and the following phrase as a two-fold account of the floodwaters that described how the same two sources poured out rain (7:12).[64] Feldman, however, viewed lines 4–5 as rewriting Genesis 7:11b twice, perhaps to emphasize the amount of water poured out on the wicked. The first reworking uses vocabulary directly from Genesis 7:11b, while the second introduces language from other biblical texts.[65] One phrase introduced in the second reworking stands out. The phrase מים אדרים (mighty waters) (line 4) appears to allude to the Song of the Sea in Exodus 15:10: "You blew with Your wind, the sea covered them; they sank like lead in the mighty waters (מים אדירים)." The use of this phrase in 4Q370 links the Flood account and the Song of the Sea, both of which speak of the watery destruction of the wicked and deliverance of God's people. This destruction of the wicked is confirmed in the following phrase in 4Q370: "and He destroyed them in the Flood" (line 5).

In addition to the description of the Flood (lines 3–5), the overall literary shaping of the text provides the necessary framework for understanding the purpose of the Flood story in 4Q370. While, the first column provides a retelling of the Flood and the events that precipitated it, the second column contains admonitory remarks based on this historical example. As noted, the verbal distribution in 4Q370 indicates a literary shift from *the past* in column I (the Flood as an historical example) to *the future* in column II (an admonition to contemporaries to avoid future judgment). Peters noted that column II ". . . effectively contemporized the primordial story of destruction and deliverance, containing instructions for how to be delivered from future judgment based on an implied understanding of how and why the

62. Feldman, "The Reworking of the Biblical Flood Story in 4Q370," 42.
63. Newsom, DJD XIX, 94.
64. Jassen, "Admonition Based on the Flood," 267.
65. Feldman, "The Reworking of the Biblical Flood Story in 4Q370," 43–44.

primordial Noah was delivered."⁶⁶ More specifically though, the language of the admonition in column II, line 9, אל תמרו (do not rebel) against the words of Yahweh, directly draws the reader back to the human rebellion in column I, line 2, which precipitated the Flood judgment: ויאמרו אל (and they rebelled against God). Just as the antediluvians rebelled against God and were judged by the Flood, so the author exhorts his contemporaries to avoid the future judgment by *not* rebelling against God. To conclude, both the eschatological language employed in lines 3–4 and the overall literary shape of the text indicates that the author presented the Flood as a *paradigm* of the eschatological judgment for admonitory purposes.

Those Who Perished in the Flood

After the description of the Flood (lines 3–5) the narrative continues in line 6 with the results of the destruction, a summary of all those who perished in the Flood:

עלכן נ[מחו] כל אש[ר ב]חרבה וי[מ]ת האדם ו[הבהמה וכל [צפר כל
כנף והג[בור]ים לוא נמלטו

> Therefore, all which was on dry ground was [wiped out,] and mankind, and [beasts and all] birds, every winged being, died. And the giants did not escape. (column I, line 6)

The author of 4Q370 appears to rework Genesis 7:21–23, summarizing and making additions to the biblical text.⁶⁷ The phrase כל אשר בחרבה (all which was on dry ground) echoes Genesis 7:22b, while the phrase האדם ו[הבהמה וכל [צפר כל כנף (mankind and [beasts and all] birds, every winged being) reworks 7:23. Reworking the list in 7:23, the author omits רמש (creeping thing), and substitutes עוף השמים (bird of the air) with וכל צפר כל כנף (and all birds, every winged being), adopted from Genesis 7:14 (כל צפור כל־כנף).⁶⁸ In addition, 4Q370 includes a group not mentioned in the bibli-

---

66. Peters, *Noah Traditions in the Dead Sea Scrolls*, 145.

67. Genesis 7:21–23: "And all flesh died that moved on the earth: birds and cattle and beasts and every creeping thing that creeps on the earth, and every man. All in whose nostrils was the breath of the spirit of life, all that was on the dry land, died. So He destroyed all living things which were on the face of the ground: both man and cattle, creeping thing and bird of the air. They were destroyed from the earth . . . "

68. Jassen, "Admonition Based on the Flood," 268; Feldman, "The Reworking of the Biblical Flood Story in 4Q370," 45.

cal text among those who perished in the Flood: הגבורים (the mighty ones). This is a reference to the offspring of the "sons of God" and "daughters of men" in Genesis 6:4: "There were giants (הנפלים) on the earth in those days, and also afterward, when the sons of God came in to the daughters of men and they bore children to them. Those were the mighty men (הגברים) who were of old, men of renown." Note that Genesis 6:4 also identifies הנפלים (*nephilim* "the giants") with הגברים (the mighty ones).

The reference to the giants perishing in the Flood in 4Q370 is a tradition commonly found in Second Temple period literature (*1 En* 89:5–6; *Sir* 16:7; CD II:18–21; *Wis* 14:6–7; *3 Macc* 2:4). For example, *3 Maccabees* 2:4 states: "You destroyed those who in the past committed injustice, among whom were even giants, who trusted in their strength and boldness, whom You destroyed by bringing upon them a boundless flood."[69]

Notably, the author of 4Q370 did not simply add the "mighty ones" to the list of those who perished, but rather, he supplied a separate clause: והג[בור]ים לוא נמלטו (and the giants did not escape). Perhaps, as Feldman has noted, this served to emphasize the death of the "mighty ones" in the Deluge.[70] But *why* does 4Q370 include, with such emphasis, the "mighty ones" among those who perished in the Flood? While much of the literature from the Second Temple period attests to the giants perishing in the Flood, there was also a tradition that some giants did escape the Deluge.[71] Thus, Peters understands the insertion of this clause as a polemic against the tradition claiming that the giants did escape the Flood.[72] This may partially explain the insertion of this clause in 4Q370. However, Jassen suggests that this insertion is addressing an exegetical problem raised in the description found in Genesis 7:21–23 of all humanity and earthly creatures perishing in the Flood. What about the offspring of the "sons of God" and the "daughters of men," those half-human, half-angelic giants?[73] With this insertion 4Q370 emphatically states that even the giants perished in the Flood. Further, the inclusion of the giants appears to buttress the teaching in 4Q370 of the Flood as judgment due to rebellion against God.

---

69. Translation from Johnson, "3 Maccabees," 2688–89.
70. Feldman, "The Reworking of the Biblical Flood Story in 4Q370," 46.
71. This tradition is found in Rabbinic literature as well.
72. Peters, *Noah Traditions in the Dead Sea Scrolls*, 146.
73. Jassen, "Admonition Based on the Flood," 268.

Flood Interpretations in 4Q370: Conclusions

The author of 4Q370 reworked the Flood story utilizing both biblical and non-biblical sources in various ways (e.g. expansions, omissions, allusions). Ultimately 4Q370 does not tell the Flood story for the story's sake, but presents the Flood as a *paradigm* of the eschatological judgment, reworking it for *admonitory* purposes. Within this reworked Flood story several aspects of Qumran Flood interpretation are addressed.

First, the cause of the Flood in 4Q370 is attributed to human ingratitude and rebellion in light of God's blessing the antediluvians with abundance (lines 1–3a). The author used both biblical (e.g. Deut 8) and non-biblical (e.g. *Hymn to the Creator*) sources to present this tradition not found in the biblical Flood narrative. Second, the author moved directly from the human rebellion to judgment, omitting any mention of righteous Noah or the construction and entrance into the ark found in the biblical Flood narrative (lines 3–6). Thus, 4Q370 selectively described the Flood, not as a story of deliverance of the righteous, but as God's judgment in response to human rebellion. Third, the addition of eschatological language (lines 3–4; cf. Isa 24:18–20) to the Flood story and the overall literary shape of the text indicates that the author presented the Flood as an archetype of the eschatological judgment. Last, though not included in Genesis 7:21–23, the author of 4Q370 included the "giants" among those who perished in the Flood (line 6; cf. CD II:18–21; *1 En* 89:5–6; *3 Macc* 2:4).

CHAPTER FIVE

PARAPHRASE OF GENESIS AND EXODUS
(4Q422)

Discovery of 4Q422

PARAPHRASE OF GENESIS AND *Exodus* (4Q422) is the third manuscript from Cave 4 dealing with the Genesis Flood. Though this intriguing fragmentary text was found in 1952, like 4Q252 and 4Q370, the publication of 4Q422 would be delayed. In fact, over forty years would pass before this manuscript was published in 1994 by Torleif Elgvin and Emanuel Tov in volume 13 of the *Discoveries in the Judaean Desert* series.[1] The portion of the manuscript dealing with Genesis was edited by Elgvin.

---

1. Elgvin and Tov, "4QParaphrase of Genesis and Exodus" (hereafter, DJD XIII), 417–41, Pl. XLII–XLIII.

Qumran Cave 4 (Photograph by Jeremy D. Lyon)

Physical Description of 4Q422

4Q422 is a poorly preserved manuscript consisting of thirty-three fragments.[2] Of these fragments, only eleven were reconstructed into three columns of text by Elgvin and Tov.[3] These columns contain what is often referred to as a "paraphrase" of Genesis (frags 1–9) and Exodus (frags 10a, e). Column I recounts creation and human rebellion (Genesis 1–3) while column II, consisting of six fragments (2–7), relates to the Flood (Genesis 6–9).[4] Column III reworks the first chapters of Exodus, including the plagues against Egypt. 4Q422 is a Hebrew text written in the Jewish script. Based on paleographical study, the scroll was written in an early Hasmo-

---

2. Feldman, "The Story of the Flood in 4Q422," 58. Here, I follow Feldman's count as he points out, "The DJD edition of 4Q422 counts thirty-four fragments. However, a small fragment joined to frag. 10e . . . was also edited there as an unidentified frg. P."

3. Elgvin and Tov, DJD XIII, 417–41, Pl. XLII–XLIII.

4. Fragments 8 and 9 possibly relate to the Flood, though the language could relate to the creation also. In addition, several of the 22 hitherto unassigned fragments appear to also contain language related to the Flood story (e.g. frags. C, D, G, L, P).

Qumran Interpretation of the Genesis Flood

nean hand, dating the scroll to the early part of the first century B.C. (c. 100–75 B.C.),[5] or perhaps as early as the latter part of the second century B.C. (c. 125–100 B.C.).[6]

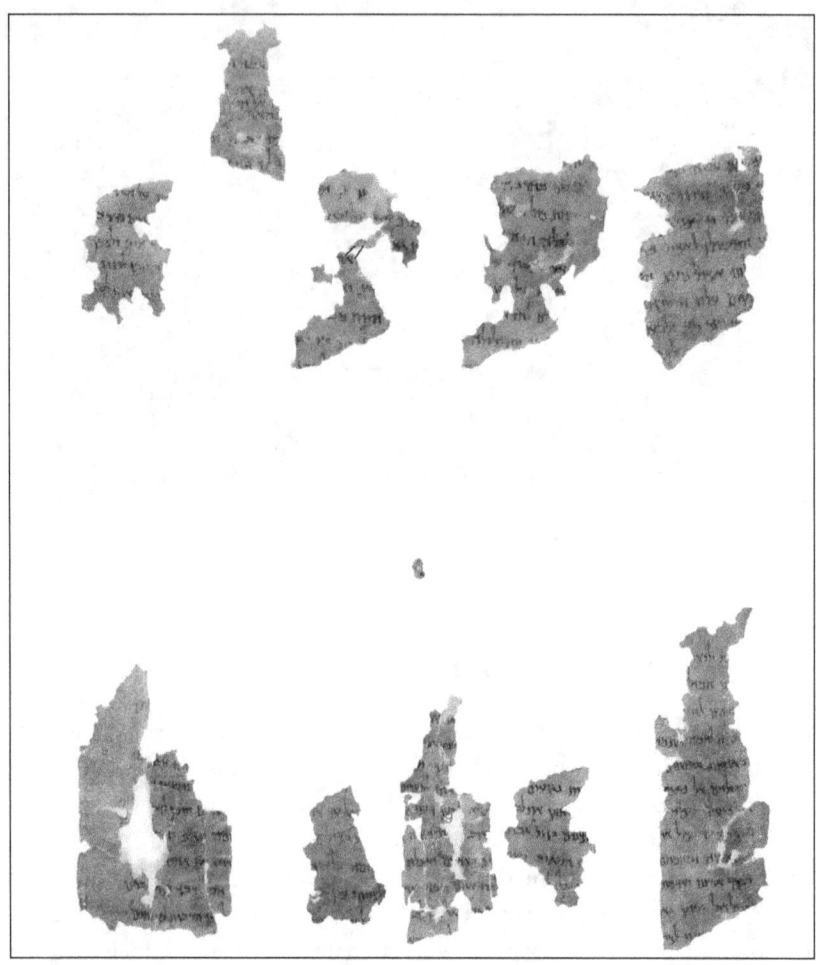

Fragments of 4Q422 (Courtesy of The Leon Levy Dead Sea Scrolls Digital Library; IAA, photo: Shai Halevi)

The opening lines (1–5) of column I, now missing, were likely the beginning of the manuscript since lines 6–13 (frag 1) cover the creation

---

5. Elgvin and Tov, DJD XIII, 420; Vermes, *The Complete Dead Sea Scrolls in English*, 478.

6. Elgvin, "The Genesis Section of 4Q422 (4QParaGenExod)," 196.

(Genesis 1–2) and humanity's rebellion (Genesis 3). Interestingly, the partially preserved left margin of column III (frag 10e) has stitching marks at the end of the sheet, indicating that another sheet likely followed.[7] The first sheet measured roughly 52 cm in length. Based on measurements and the rolling of the scroll, Elgvin estimated the missing second sheet was only about 17 cm, containing one column of text.[8]

Reconstruction of the fragmentary 4Q422 scroll is aided by several factors. The partial preservation of the margins between columns I and II, II and III, and the left margin of column III helps to provide a framework. The PAM 42.820 image of 4Q422 presents the fragments according to the four stacks in which they were found. Each horizontal row represents several fragments which were stuck together. Studying the shapes of these fragments which were stuck together is helpful in reconstructing this fragmentary scroll since the similar shape between fragments indicates close relationship. According to the scroll's editors, the matching shapes of these various fragments show that they "... represent layers of the original scroll which were rolled immediately upon one another."[9] This is further shown by a number of fragments (2, 3, 4, 8, 10d, 10e, and E) which reveal an additional layer of writing where ink from one layer has left an imprint on the backside of the scroll layer above it.[10] For example, only traces of ה and ב remain from the word המבול in fragment 4 (line 4), which are imprinted on the backside of fragment 10a. Thus, 4Q422 has been partially reconstructed based on a number of factors including the partial preservation of several margins, the similar shapes of fragments found stuck together in stacks, and the ink from the writing on one layer imprinted on the backside of another layer. Nonetheless, uncertainties remain as more of the text is missing than is extant. Also, a number of fragments remain unplaced in the reconstructed text. Thus, caution is prerequisite in studying the text of 4Q422.

4Q422: A Qumran Composition?

It is apparent that 4Q422 is a *Jewish* composition, since it is: 1) a Hebrew text found in Judea at Qumran, 2) dates to the Hasmonean period (placing

---

7. Elgvin and Tov, DJD XIII, 417. Stitching marks are clearly visible in the PAM 42.820 image.

8. Ibid., 420.

9. Elgvin, "The Genesis Section of 4Q422," 181.

10. Ibid., 183.

it in the period of sectarian writing at Qumran), and 3) relates to and paraphrases texts from the Hebrew Bible. But, is 4Q422 a *Qumran* sectarian composition? If not, should it be included in this study of *Qumran* interpretation of the Genesis Flood?

Elgvin acknowledges that 4Q422 has "no clear signs of sectarian theology," but then mentions several elements which may indicate that 4Q422 was composed within the Qumran community.[11] He points out several phrases occurring in both 4Q422 and sectarian texts (רוח קודשו "His Holy Spirit," מועדי יום ולילה "the set times of day and night," דורות עולם "generations of eternity" I:7; II:10–12; III:7), the use of the Divine name אל instead of יהוה in paraphrasing Genesis 7:16 (II:5) and Exodus 9:12 (III:11), the interchange (the Masoretic יֶרֶק of Ex 10:15 with ירוק in 4Q422 II:11) attested in 1QIsa[a] (indicating Qumran scribal practice since 1QIsa[a] was copied at Qumran), and links with the sectarian *Sapiential Work* (4QInstruction).[12] In other words, 4Q422 is not overtly a sectarian manuscript, but it might be, based on numerous affinities with sectarian literature. However, Feldman views 4Q422 strictly as a non-sectarian text and is doubtful that Elgvin's observations demonstrate otherwise.[13] In particular, Feldman does not see any of the observations linking 4Q422 to sectarian writings as being strictly sectarian in nature, but as common within Second Temple period Judaism.[14] While a sectarian provenance for 4Q422 may not be demonstrable at this point, it remains possible and plausible since it was found at Qumran (cave 4) and does display several affinities with sectarian writings (though not necessarily exclusive to sectarian literature).

Whether or not 4Q422 was composed at Qumran, it was certainly written by Jews during the Hasmonean period. While overtly sectarian theology may be absent, the content of 4Q422 is not inconsistent with Qumran ideology. Further, 4Q422 appears to have been acceptable for study and use at Qumran. This text was found in cave 4, a dwelling space directly connected to the Qumran site. Thus, it is likely that 4Q422 was present in the Qumran community before it was conveniently placed in this nearby cave as the Romans approached Qumran in A.D. 68. Whether or not 4Q422 was written at Qumran, its presence in cave 4 indicates that it

---

11. Ibid., 196.
12. Ibid.
13. Feldman, "The Story of the Flood in 4Q422," 57.
14. Ibid.

was probably accepted and used at Qumran. Therefore, the study of 4Q422 for understanding *Qumran* Flood interpretation is necessary.

History of Research on 4Q422

The publication of 4Q422 and the subsequent research on this text did not commence until the mid-1990s, over forty years after its discovery. This survey of the history of research on 4Q422 will focus on selected studies directly relevant to the current discussion on Flood interpretation. Several scholars have made significant contributions to the study of the Flood story in 4Q422.

Torleif Elgvin

The official edition of 4Q422 was published in 1994 in volume 13 of the *Discoveries in the Judaean Desert* series by Torleif Elgvin and Emanuel Tov,[15] with the Genesis section of 4Q422 (cols. I and II) edited by Elgvin. This edition included a physical description of the text, discussion on the reconstruction of the fragmentary columns, paleographical and orthographical notes, a transcription and translation of the text, notes on the readings, line-by-line comments on the text, and plates of the text. In 1994, Elgvin also published an article titled, "The Genesis Section of 4Q422 (4QParaGenExod)," in the journal *Dead Sea Discoveries*.[16] Here, much of the same material was published and Elgvin provided some concluding remarks on the text. Elgvin's editorial work on this text is foundational and remains the standard for 4Q422 studies.

Moshe Bernstein

In 1999, Moshe Bernstein published a chapter titled "Noah and the Flood at Qumran," in which he discussed the various ways the Flood story was employed in the Qumran literature.[17] He provides only a brief discussion on 4Q422, but it is nonetheless insightful. He understands the text as a paraphrase, but notes its selective use of themes from the biblical text in

---

15. Elgvin and Tov, DJD XIII, 417–41, Pl. XLII–XLIII.
16. Elgvin, "The Genesis Section of 4Q422," 180–96.
17. Bernstein, "Noah and the Flood at Qumran," 199–231.

this retelling. Bernstein also views 4Q422 much like 4Q370: "Neither one tells the story for the story's sake, but for its message."[18]

Dorothy Peters

In Dorothy Peters's 2008 work, *Noah Traditions in the Dead Sea Scrolls: Conversations and Controversies of Antiquity*, she included a brief section discussing 4Q422.[19] Peters's major contribution is the literary analysis of the Flood material, which provides insight into this current study of Flood interpretation in 4Q422.

Ariel Feldman

In 2009, Ariel Feldman published "The Story of the Flood in 4Q422" as a chapter in *The Dynamics of Language and Exegesis at Qumran*.[20] While Elgvin laid the foundation for 4Q422 studies and others have discussed this text subsequently, this chapter is perhaps the most detailed study of the Flood material in 4Q422 to date. Since problems related to the Flood column were still unresolved and the exegetical techniques employed had not been fully analyzed, Feldman sought to address these issues. Thus, he provided: 1) a new edition of column II, 2) a detailed commentary on this column, and 3) a "... fresh examination of the interpretive methods and literary strategies employed while reworking the biblical text."[21]

Literary Genre of 4Q422

4Q422 is usually labeled as a "paraphrase" of Genesis and Exodus, but that may not fully describe the genre of this composition for several reasons. First, the text is highly selective and does not appear to include a significant number of other stories from Genesis and Exodus.[22] Second, as Peters con-

---

18. Ibid., 212.
19. Peters, *Noah Traditions in the Dead Sea Scrolls*: 139–44.
20. Feldman, "The Story of the Flood in 4Q422," 57–77.
21. Ibid., 58.
22. Cf. Elgvin and Tov, DJD XIII, 426. Perhaps more passages were selected from Exodus on the missing sheet. Even if this were the case, the point remains that 4Q422 is a highly selective text which is not a paraphrase of *the whole book* of Genesis or *the whole book* of Exodus.

tends, the Flood narrative in 4Q422 is "... more complex and exegetically developed than a simple paraphrase would allow."[23] 4Q422 reworks in detail the Flood story, interweaving new biblical material and often differing in its order. This rewritten text also introduces material not found in the biblical text. While Elgvin views 4Q422 as a paraphrase, he recognizes that theological interpretations were woven into the paraphrases of these biblical texts.[24] This was more the case in the retelling of Genesis than of Exodus. Third, the Flood story in 4Q422 appears to be employed for hortatory or homiletic purposes, much like 4Q370 used it for admonitory purposes.[25] Elgvin even suggested that the Genesis section could be characterized as a "homiletic paraphrase."[26]

For the aforementioned reasons, among others, the label of "paraphrase" to describe 4Q422 does not appear to be sufficient. Martin Abegg understood this text as another example of "rewritten Bible," a popular method of biblical interpretation during the Second Temple period.[27] Feldman also understood 4Q422 as reworking the biblical narratives.[28] It is suggested here that 4Q422 is better described as a selective reworking of Scripture employing paraphrase, as well as insertions of other biblical material and additions not found in the biblical text, for didactic or homiletic purposes.

Content and Literary Structure of 4Q422

As reconstructed, 4Q422 consists of three fragmentary columns which contain a selective retelling of the opening chapters of Genesis (frags 1–9) and Exodus (frags 10a, e). Column I recounts creation and humanity's rebellion (Genesis 1–3) while column II relates to the Flood story (Genesis 6–9). Column III reworks the opening chapters of Exodus, including the plagues against Egypt.

---

23. Peters, *Noah Traditions in the Dead Sea Scrolls*, 140.
24. Elgvin, "The Genesis Section of 4Q422," 195.
25. Bernstein, "Noah and the Flood at Qumran," 212.
26. Elgvin, "The Genesis Section of 4Q422," 195.
27. Wise et al., *The Dead Sea Scrolls: A New Translation*, 495.
28. Feldman, "The Story of the Flood in 4Q422," 70–75.

Qumran Interpretation of the Genesis Flood

Column I (Creation, Eden, and Human Rebellion)

The first five lines of column I are missing and, based on the content in lines 6–13, were likely the opening lines introducing the creation story. Lines 6–8 recount the creation story in Genesis 1:1–2:4. Line 6 records that God made (עשה), by His word (בדברו),[29] the heavens and the earth.[30] In line 7, the phrase מלאכתו אשר עשה (His work which He had done) is taken from Genesis 2:2. The following phrase, ורוח קודשו (and His Holy Spirit), includes the role of God's Holy Spirit in the act of creating.[31] Line 8 refers to כול הנפש החיה והרמשת על הארץ (every living creature and what moves on the earth), echoing Genesis 1:28 (ובכל־חיה הרמשת על־הארץ) in which the context is humanity's dominion over the animals. Lines 9–10 speak of Adam in the Garden of Eden, whom God caused to have dominion/rule (המשילו) over the fruit of the ground (line 9), along with a warning not to eat from the tree of the knowledge of good and evil (line 10; cf. Gen 2:16–17). Lines 11–13 speak of humanity's rebellion: "[. . . and] he rose up against Him and they forgot [. . .] . . . with an evil inclination and for work[s of wickedness." The placement of the human rebellion immediately after line 10, which refers to Genesis 2:16–17, strongly suggests that this human rebellion in line 11 relates to Genesis 3–4.[32] The phrase ביוצר רע (with an evil inclination) (line 12) alludes to Genesis 6:5: וכל־יצר מחשבת לבו רק רע כל־היום (and every inclination of the thoughts of his heart was only evil continually) (cf. also 8:21).[33] Thus, the phrases "with an evil inclination" and "works of wickedness" in line 12 appear to serve as a literary bridge from Genesis 3–4 to the Flood story in 4Q422.

29. García Martínez and Tigchelaar do not include the reconstructed בדברו in their transcription. See García Martínez and Tigchelaar, *The Dead Sea Scrolls Study Edition*, 884–85.

30. If the reconstruction of בדברו is correct, an emphasis on the role of God's word in creating the heavens and the earth is present. Cf. Psalm 33:6; John 1:1, 3.

31. בדברו is used in line 6 and רוח קודשו is used in line 7. These terms are used together in reference to God's creative acts in Psalm 33:6: בדבר יהוה שמים נעשו וברוח פיו כל־צבאם. However, In the case of Psalm 33:6 רוח is understood as "breath" as the phrase וברוח פיו "and by the breath of His mouth" parallels the previous phrase, בדבר יהוה "by the word of the Lord." Accordingly, Elgvin sees in 4Q422 more importance assigned to the role of God's Holy Spirit in the acts of creating than in Genesis 1:1 and Psalm 33:6 (cf. "The Genesis Section of 4Q422," 186; DJD XIII, 422).

32. Elgvin and Tov, DJD XIII, 423.

33. Elgvin notes that the use of יצר (inclination) in reference to Genesis 3, rather than the Flood generation, indicates that the author of 4Q422 was emphasizing the beginning of sin on the earth with Adam (cf. Rom 5:12–18). DJD XIII, 423.

Column II (The Flood)

The second column of 4Q422 is concerned with retelling the Flood story. Line 1 begins with what appears to be a description of God seeing the wickedness of man as described in Genesis 6:5.[34] If this is the case, then the opening line of column II began the Flood story. Line 2a then reads "[righteous in] his generation up[on the earth]." The reading ב[דורו] (in his generation) led to Elgvin's reconstruction of צדיק ב[דורו].[35] This reconstruction seems likely in light of Genesis 6:9: נח איש צדיק תמים היה בדרתיו (Noah was a righteous man, perfect in his generations).

Lines 2(a)–6 refer to the deliverance (נצלו; line 3) of Noah and his family in the ark. The last phrase of line 2a, [א]תו אל חיה, has been read by Elgvin as "to an animal"[36] and by Bernstein as "to living creatures."[37] However, Feldman has proposed reading אל as "God" (instead of "to") and חיה as "kept alive" (instead of "animal" or "living creature"). Feldman's reading, "with him God kept alive," seems to fit better with the context of נצלו (they were delivered) in line 3 and the following lines.[38] Line 4, taken from Genesis 7:7, refers to Noah's sons, his wife, and his sons' wives, who were delivered from "the waters of the Flood" (מי המבול).[39] The next line states, [ויס]גור אל בעדם (and God shut behind them), which echoes Genesis 7:16: ויסגר יהוה בעדו (and Yahweh shut him in). Notice here the substitution of the Divine name יהוה for אל in 4Q422, which is a common scribal practice at Qumran. The next phrase of line 5, [צו]העליו את כ[ו]ל, appears to refer to God giving commands to Noah, while Genesis 6:22 and 7:5–6 records that Noah did all God had commanded.

Lines 6–8 describe the Flood itself, employing biblical language. The phrase [כול] אשר בחרבה כל א[שר] (all that was on the dry ground all which) (line 6) is likely taken from Genesis 7:22.[40] The phrase ארובות השמי[ם] נפ[ת]חו (the windows of heaven were opened) (line 6) is taken from Genesis 7:11. Interestingly, the missing text preceding this phrase in 4Q422

34. 4Q422 II:1: [...]ו. רבה כיא אל כי[וירא]; Cf. Gen 6:5: וירא יהוה כי רבה רעת האדם בארץ.
35. Elgvin, "The Genesis Section of 4Q422," 189.
36. Ibid., 190; cf. DJD XIII, 426.
37. Bernstein, "Noah and the Flood at Qumran," 212.
38. Feldman, "The Story of the Flood in 4Q422," 63, 71.
39. 4Q422 II:4: [...]ומ[מי המבול] מפני בניו ושי[ואת בניו א]שתו נוח את [...]; Cf. Gen 7:7: ויבא נח ובניו ואשתו ונשי־בניו אתו אל־התבה מפני מי המבול.
40. Gen 7:22: כל אשר נשמת־רוח חיים באפיו מכל אשר בחרבה מתו (All in whose nostrils was the breath of the spirit of life, all that was on the dry land, died).

may be represented by the phrase עינות רבה [מ] (great fountains), preserved in the unplaced fragment D.[41] The phrase תחת כול השמ[ים] (under all the heavens) alludes to Genesis 7:19 where the waters prevailed exceedingly upon the earth, covering all the high hills "under all the heavens" (תחת [ארבעים] יום וארב[עים] לילה היה ה[גשם] על [הארץ], כל השמים). In lines 7–8, (forty days and forty nights there was rain upon the earth) is adopted from Genesis 7:12.[42] The latter part of line 8 and the beginning of line 9 departs from the biblical Flood narrative, providing the purposes behind the Flood: "8. [the water]s were migh[ty] upon [the earth in order to] cleanse sin and in order to 9. make known the glory of the Mo[st High . . .]."

Lines 9–13 paraphrase Genesis 9, describing the post-Flood situation in language similar to Genesis 8–9 and even Genesis 1. The remaining few lines of column II are no longer extant.

There is not a lot of space in this single column for a detailed retelling of the biblical Flood account. The author was selective and, as far as one can tell from this fragmentary text, omitted numerous details such as the building of the ark, the landing of the ark on the mountains of Ararat, and the sending out of the birds. The author reworked or alluded to a number of biblical passages in this retelling of the Flood.

---

41. Elgvin, "The Genesis Section of 4Q422," 191; see Feldman, "The Story of the Flood in 4Q422," 68.

42. Gen 7:12: ויהי הגשם על־הארץ ארבעים יום וארבעים לילה (And the rain was on the earth forty days and forty nights).

PARAPHRASE OF GENESIS AND EXODUS

4Q422 (column II) The Flood Story	Biblical Passage Reworked or Alluded to in 4Q422 (col. II)
1 [...וי]רא אל כיא[רבה ו.] [...]	Genesis 6:5a
2 [...]ב את ה[...]	
2a צדיק ב[ ]דורו ע[ל הארץ ...א[תו אל חיה	Genesis 6:9, 19
3 [...] נצלו על [הארץ ...ע[ל הארץ כיא [ ]	Ezekiel 14:14–16; Genesis 6:17; 7:4
4 [... את נוח]ואת בניו א[שתו ונשי בניו מפני [מי המבול ומ[...]	Genesis 7:7
5 והע[וף ויס]גור אל בעדם [... צו[ ]העליו את כ[ו]ל [...] [ ] ... כול	Genesis 7:16b; 6:22; 7:5–6
6 אשר בחרבה כל א[שר]ארובות השמי[ם] נפ[ת]חו ח.[. ... גשם הרי[קו על	Genesis 7:22; 7:11–12 Ecclesiastes 11:3
7 תחת כול השמ[ים ... ל[עלות מים על האר[ץ ... ארבעים] יום וארב[עים]	Genesis 7:19; cf. Ezekiel 26:3; Genesis 7:12
8 לילה היה ה[גשם ... ע[ל הארץ ... המי[ם גב]רו [ ] על [הארץ ... למען]טהר חיט ולמען	Genesis 7:12; Ezekiel 39:12; Habakkuk 2:14
9 דעת כבוד על[יון ...את[...] הגיש לפניו	Habakkuk 2:14; Numbers 24:16
10 ויאר על [ה]שמ[ים ... הא[רץ וא[...]ימה אות לדור[ות]	Genesis 1:15, 17; 9:12–13
11 עולם לחרא[... ולוא עוד] היות מבול[לשחת הארץ ...]	Genesis 9:11–12, 15
12 [מו]עדי יום ולילה [... מאורות להאיר ע[ל שמים וא[רץ ...]	Genesis 1:14–15; 8:22
13 [הארץ ומ[ו]ל[ו]אה [...]הכו[ל נתן] לאדם]	Genesis 9:2–3

The author not only reworked or alluded to a number of passages from the biblical Flood narrative, but also likely alluded to passages from other biblical books. This column also reworks some of the Flood passages in a different order than the biblical narrative.

Column III (Exodus)

The third column of 4Q422 contains a paraphrase of the first part of the book of Exodus, covering the plagues and a few of the events prior to them. Lines 1–7 briefly mentions a few events leading up to the plagues: the two midwives (line 2), the Israelite sons thrown into the Nile (line 3), the sending of Moses to the people (line 4), possibly God's burning bush appearance (line 4), the sending of Moses and Aaron to Pharaoh (line 6), and the hardening of Pharaoh's heart (line 7). The author moved rapidly through these events using only a few words for each. Lines 7–12 (half the column) then describe the plagues in more detail.[43] But why does the author focus on the plagues in column III, immediately following the retelling of the Flood story in column II? Peters suggested, "Its very juxtaposition with the creation and flood narratives highlights a thematic reversal of creation."[44] In addition, both the Flood and plagues narratives describe well known examples of God's judgment upon the wicked and deliverance of God's people.

General Structure of 4Q422

A general description of the content of 4Q422 leads to discerning at least some literary patterns which make up this composition. Though fragmentary, a working general outline of 4Q422 may be proposed:

---

43. Tov, "The Exodus Section of 4Q422," 197–209. The list of plagues in 4Q422 III:7–12 includes all of those mentioned in the biblical narrative except for the plague of boils. Tov observes that the sequence of the plagues is close to that of the Exodus account and Psalm 105. Concerning the author's employment of biblical texts, Tov notes that ". . . in the description of the plagues, the wording of 4Q422 depends in the first place on the historical Psalm 78, second on Psalm 105, and third on the account in Exodus" (197).

44. Peters, *Noah Traditions in the Dead Sea Scrolls*, 140.

Outline of 4Q422		
Column I (Creation, Eden, Human Rebellion)	**Column II** (The Flood Story)	**Column III** (Book of Exodus, the Plagues)
• Creation (6–8) • Adam's rule in Eden (9–10) • Human rebellion (11–13) • ביוצר רע (with an evil inclination) **Gen 6:5**	• Human wickedness (1) **(Gen 6:5)** • Righteous Noah and family delivered in the ark (2a–6) • Flood judgment (6–8) • Purposes of the Flood (8–9) למען (in order to) • Post-Flood covenant (9–13)	• The two midwives (2) • Israelite sons thrown into the Nile (3) • Moses sent to the people (4) • Moses and Aaron sent to Pharaoh (6) • Pharaoh's heart hardened (7) Purpose: למען (in order to) • Plagues judgment (7–12)
Creation → Human Rebellion ←	→ Human Rebellion → Judgment	Human rebellion → Judgment

Column I covers creation, Eden, and human rebellion. Interestingly, in column I the author employed the biblical phrase ביוצר רע (with an evil inclination) (line 12) in reference to the human rebellion in Genesis 3–4 (lines 10–12). The phrase ביוצר רע is adopted from Genesis 6:5 which originally referred to the antediluvian rebellion. Thus, the author links the human rebellion in Genesis 3–4 to the Flood story. Column II then opens with human rebellion (antediluvians) with a likely reference to Genesis 6:5 and then the Flood judgment. Column III then also mentions human rebellion (Pharaoh), followed by the plague judgments. In addition, there is an important lexical link between columns II (Flood judgment) and III (judgment with plagues), as both provide the purpose of judgment, introduced with למען (in order that). These "purpose" statements are central to understanding the author's message in 4Q422.

The Flood as Judgment: The Sin–Judgment Cycle

The juxtaposition of the Flood story (column II) with the preceding Eden story (column I) and the following plagues story (column III) is quite telling in regard to the overall message of 4Q422. Column I, lines 8–9, describes Adam's dominion over the earth, alluding to Genesis 1:28–30 and 2:15–16.

Line 10, in reference to Genesis 2:17, then describes the warning not to eat from the tree that gives knowledge of good and evil: ל[ב]לתי אכול מעץ [... הד]עת (with the [excep]tion of eating from the tree of kn[owledge ...]). Interestingly, 4Q422 adds לבלתי, which is not found in the prohibition in Genesis 2:17. Esther Chazon has suggested that the formulation of Adam's prohibition in line 10, employing לבלתי, foreshadows the language of God's accusation in judgment of Adam in Genesis 3:11: המן העץ אשר צויתיך לבלתי אכל־ממנו אכלת ("Have you eaten from the tree of which I commanded you that you should not eat?").[45] Lines 11–12 then speak of the first human rebellion, relating to Genesis 3. As noted, line 12 provides a notable transition between the Eden story (column I) and the Flood story (column II). Line 12 uses the phrase ביוצר רע (with an evil inclination) in reference to Adam's rebellion (Genesis 3). This phrase is adopted from Genesis 6:5, which refers to the antediluvian rebellion. In this way, the author links the Eden and Flood stories, applying the "evil inclination" (Gen 6:5) to both, Adam's fall and the antediluvian rebellion. This literary juxtaposition of Adam's sin and fall (column I) with the antediluvian sin and consequent Flood judgment (column II) highlights one of the primary themes of 4Q422: the sin–judgment cycle.[46]

The Flood story in column II is also linked to the plagues story in column III. Both narratives describe well known examples of God's judgment of the wicked and deliverance of His people. Both columns (II and III) contain statements regarding the purpose of those judgments, introduced by למען (cf. II:8–9; III:7). Further, the theme of a sin–judgment cycle in columns I an II is reinforced in column III, where Pharaoh's heart was hardened to sin (line 7), immediately followed by the plague judgments (lines 7–12).

In addition to the sin–judgment cycle in which the Flood narrative is employed, 4Q422 may possibly highlight the nature of the Flood as judgment. While *An Admonition Based on the Flood* (4Q370) highlights the judgment aspect of the Flood by omitting any mention of deliverance for righteous Noah, 4Q422 does make reference to the deliverance of Noah and his family in the ark. However, Peters pointed out an important link between the Flood and plagues stories that could emphasize the judgment nature of the Flood in another way.[47] Virtually all of the language in

45. Chazon, "The Creation and Fall of Adam in the Dead Sea Scrolls," 16.
46. Ibid., 17.
47. Peters, *Noah Traditions in the Dead Sea Scrolls*, 139–41. Concerning the link

column III comes from Exodus, Psalm 78, or Psalm 105,[48] except for one particular phrase in line 7, where Pharaoh's heart was hardened to sin "... in order to make known (למען דעת) [the glory (כבוד) of] God for eternal gener[ations] (דורות עולם)." This phrase appears to combine the Flood and plagues stories. In Exodus 7:5 and 14:4, the purpose of the judgments was for God to gain glory (כבוד) and for the Egyptians to know (ידע) that He is the LORD. Note, that "eternal generations" is absent. In Genesis 9:12, the sign of the covenant (the rainbow) is given for eternal generations (לדרת עולם). The author of 4Q422 likely adopted this phrase from Genesis 9:12 (the only occurrence in the Hebrew Bible),[49] and so, links the plagues judgments to the Flood in this way. This is not unreasonable to propose, considering the literary juxtaposition of these two stories in 4Q422. The plagues story is further linked to the Flood story through parallel language. In column II, "the waters were mighty upon the earth ... in order to make known (למען דעת) the glory (כבוד) of the Most High" (lines 8–9) and the rainbow "illuminated the heavens and the earth" as a "sign for eternal generations (דורות עולם)" (lines 10–11; cf. Gen 9:12).

Column II:8–11 (Flood Judgment)	Biblical Passages	Column III:7 (Plague Judgments)
II:8–9 [המי]ם גב[רו [על] הארץ ...ולמען דעת כבוד על[יון]	Gen 9:12 ויאמר אלהים זות אות־ הברית אשר־אני נתן... לדרת עולם	III:7 למען דעת א[ת כבד [אל עד דו[רות]עולם
II:10–11 ויאר על [ה]שמ[ים ... הא[רץ וא]...[ימה אות לדור[ות] עולם	Exod 7:5 וידעו מצרים כי־אני יהוה Exod 14:4 ואכבדה בפרעה ובכל־חילו וידעו מצרים כי־אני יהוה	

What is the exegetical purpose of 4Q422 weaving these two stories from the biblical narratives in this way? The linking of II:8–11 and III:7

---

between II:8–11 and III:7, Dorothy Peters first made the argument that 4Q422 "incorporates judgment into its definition of covenant" (p. 139). Thus, this immediate discussion is largely dependant upon her original observations.

48. Tov, "The Exodus Section of 4Q422," 197.
49. Cf. Isaiah 51:9 (דרות עולמים); Elgvin and Tov, DJD XIII, 427.

adds to the meaning of the sign of God's covenant in a subtle way. In the biblical Flood narrative, the rainbow served as a sign to eternal generations that God would never again destroy the whole earth with a Flood (Gen 9:15). However, in 4Q422, the sign of the covenant for eternal generations (column II) is also linked to further judgment (column III). Peters noted that the rainbow "... becomes a 'post-judgment sign' announcing to 'eternal generations' that God had the power to destroy His enemies."[50] Not only would God never again destroy the earth with a Flood, but the sign of the covenant now contains more emphasis on judgment. The sign of the covenant warns future generations that God not only *has* judged the wicked in the past, but *will* judge the wicked in the future, as reinforced by the plague judgments.[51] To conclude, the literary juxtaposition of the Flood story with the Eden and plagues stories highlights a unifying theme of the sin-judgment cycle in 4Q422, while the literary links between II:8–11 and III:7 subtly add a new emphasis of judgment with the sign of the covenant.

The Flood as a Reversal and Renewal of Creation

The juxtaposition of the Eden, Flood, and plagues stories in 4Q422 may also emphasize a theme of creation, reversal of creation, and renewal of creation. 4Q422 links the Flood directly to creation through the distinct juxtaposition of the stories, which are also linked by the reference to "evil inclination" (col. I, line 12). Thus, it seems likely that the creation and Flood stories are to be read together as a literary unit. In the biblical Flood narrative the entire earth is destroyed, being covered by water (cf. Gen 6:17; 7:19–20), which recalls the earth covered by water at the beginning of creation week (cf. Gen 1:2). In 4Q422, the juxtaposition and linking together of the Flood and plagues narratives, immediately after the creation narrative, appears to highlight the Flood and plagues as reversals of creation. Both stories involve God's judgment upon the wicked, which involves destruction/reversal of the natural order.

In addition, column II, lines 9–13, appears to describe the post-Flood situation in language similar to Genesis 1, perhaps viewing the Flood as a re-creation or renewing of creation.[52] Line 10 reads, ... ויאר על [ה]שמ[י]ם

50. Peters, *Noah Traditions in the Dead Sea Scrolls*, 141.

51. Ibid.

52. Cf. Elgvin and Tov, DJD XIII, 427; Peters, *Noah Traditions in the Dead Sea Scrolls*, 143–44; Feldman, "The Story of the Flood in 4Q422," 74.

הא[רץ (and it [rainbow] shined on the heavens and the earth). The verb אור (to shine), coupled with השמים (the heavens), is found in Genesis 1:15, 17, where God set the sun, moon, and stars in "the firmament of the heavens (השמים) to give light (להאיר) on the earth." *Jubilees* also makes reference to the sun, moon, and stars being set ". . . in the firmament of heaven so that they might give light upon the whole earth" (cf. 4QJub[a]).[53] Line 12 reworks Genesis 8:22 with the phrase, [מו]עדי יום ולילה [...מאורות להאיר ע]ל שמים וא[רץ ...] ([the fixed ti]mes of day and night [. . . luminaries to illuminate] heaven and ear[th . . .]). However, 4Q422 introduces the idea of מועדי (fixed times), which was likely adopted from Genesis 1:14: "Then God said, 'Let there be lights in the firmament of the heavens to divide the day (היום) from the night (הלילה); and let them be for signs and seasons (ולמועדים), and for days and years.'" Thus, 4Q422 introduces creation language into the post-Flood covenant description to emphasize that the seasons (מועדים) established at creation were reestablished in the post-Flood world.[54] The following extant phrase in line 12, "[o]n heaven and ear[th]," was reconstructed by Elgvin as,[מאורות להאיר ע]ל שמים וא[רץ] (luminaries to illuminate heaven and earth), which may allude to Genesis 1:15.[55] This presentation of the Flood story in language connected to creation also fits with the biblical understanding of the Flood as a re-creation or renewal of creation.[56]

---

53. Translation from Kugel, "Jubilees," 290.

54. Peters, *Noah Traditions in the Dead Sea Scrolls*, 143–44.

55. Elgvin and Tov, DJD XIII, 427; cf. Feldman, "The Story of the Flood in 4Q422," 74.

56. The biblical Flood narrative parallels the creation account in numerous ways: 1) God creates the heavens and the earth in 1:1 and in 6:13ff He destroys the earth with water. 2) The earth was covered in water at the beginning of creation week (1:2) and the earth was covered in water during the Flood (6:17; 7:19–20). 3) The dry land appeared out of the water on day three of creation week (1:9) and the dry land (mountains) appeared out of the Flood waters (8:5). 4) The creation of the different kinds of land animals in 1:24–25 is paralleled by the preservation of the different kinds of land animals on the ark (6:18–22; 7:1–16). 5) God creates humanity in 1:26–27 and preserves humanity from destruction in 6:13ff. 6) God blessed Adam and Eve and commanded them to "be fruitful and multiply, and fill the earth" in 1:28 and He also blessed Noah and his sons, commanding them to "be fruitful and multiply, and fill the earth" in 9:1. 7) God's provision of food (every herb that yields seed . . . every tree whose fruit yields seed) for humanity in 1:29 is paralleled by God's provision of food ("I have given you all things, even as the green herbs") for humanity in the post-Flood world in 9:3.

Qumran Interpretation of the Genesis Flood

The Purpose of the Flood

Certainly, one of the major purposes of the Flood was to judge the earth because of the rampant wickedness. However, 4Q422 provides additional details concerning the purpose(s) of the Flood. Column II, lines 6–8, describes the Flood itself, employing biblical language. However, at the end of line 8, 4Q422 departs from the biblical narrative, which goes on to describe the subsiding of the waters, the landing of the ark, and the departure from the ark. Interestingly, these aspects of the biblical narrative are all omitted in 4Q422. Instead, at this point, 4Q422 introduces new material to the Flood story pertaining to its purposes.

[המי]ם גב[רו] על [הארץ ... למען]טהר חיט ולמען דעת כבוד על[יון]

> 8. the water]s were migh[ty] upon [the earth in order to] cleanse sin and in order to 9. make known the glory of the Mo[st High] (col. II, lines 8–9)

The phrase "in order to cleanse sin" (line 8) indicates that the Flood was viewed as a purifying bath. The term טהר (to cleanse, purify) is often employed in the Hebrew Bible in reference to ceremonial or moral cleansing.[57] In the case of 4Q422, the Flood waters could be understood as a "baptism" of the earth from sin. This idea of the Flood cleansing or purifying the earth from sin is also attested elsewhere in Second Temple period literature. For example, *1 Enoch* 10:20–22 states:

> 20. And You, cleanse the earth from all wrong, and from all iniquity, and from all sin, and from all impiety, and from all the uncleanness which is brought about on the earth; remove them from the earth. 21. And all the sons of men shall be righteous, and all the nations shall serve and bless Me, and all shall worship Me. 22. And the earth will be cleansed from all corruption, and from all sin, and from all wrath, and from all torment; and I will not again send a Flood upon it for all generations forever.[58]

---

57. For the use of טהר in reference to ceremonial cleansing, cf. Gen 35:2; Lev 11:32; 13:6, 34; 14:8–9; 15:13, 28; 17:5; 22:4, 7; Num 8:6–7; 19:12, 19; 31:23; Ezek 43:26; Ezra 6:20; Neh 12:30; 13:22. For moral cleansing, cf. Lev 16:30; Jer 13:27; 33:8; Ezek 24: 13; 36:25, 33; 37:23; Mal 3:3; Job 4:17.

58. Translation from Brand, "1 Enoch," 1374. Brand's translation is taken from Michael Knibb's translation, based primarily on a single Ethiopic text thought to be superior.

This tradition found in *1 Enoch* was also likely known at Qumran, where numerous fragmentary copies of this book were found.[59] However, it is difficult to determine if 4Q422 was dependant upon this tradition found in *1 Enoch*. This understanding of the Flood as a "baptism" of the earth from sin is also attested in 1 Peter 3:20–21.[60]

The phrase "and in order to make known the glory of the Mo[st High]" (lines 8–9) teaches that another purpose of the Flood was to reveal God's glory. Certainly, God's judgment of the whole earth, through such a catastrophic Flood, displayed His glory and power as the Most High. Interestingly, the juxtaposed narrative of Pharaoh's hardened heart and plague judgments (column III, line 7) echoes this notion of judgment revealing God's glory: עולם] דו[רות עד אל] כבוד א[ת דעת למען ל]חטוא ל[ב]ו את יחזק[ו] ("[And] He hardened [his] heart [to] sin in order to make known [the glory of] God for eternal gener[ations]").[61] Thus, this idea of God's glory being revealed through His judgments appears to be a central message of 4Q422.

To conclude, the purpose of the Flood, according to 4Q422, was not simply to judge the earth due to wickedness, but to cleanse the earth from sin and to reveal God's glory. This understanding of the Flood's purposes also appears to play an important role in the meaning of 4Q422.

Flood Interpretation in 4Q422: Conclusions

Due to the fragmentary nature of 4Q422, it must be noted that any conclusions maintain a degree of tentativeness. Nonetheless, 4Q422 appears to bring to light several aspects of Flood interpretation from Qumran. First, the literary juxtaposition of the Eden, Flood, and plagues stories highlights a

---

59. Twelve copies, in fragmentary form, of *1 Enoch* were found at Qumran (eleven from Cave 4 and one from Cave 7).

60. 1 Peter 3:19–21: "... He [Christ] went and preached to the spirits in prison, who formerly were disobedient, when once the Divine longsuffering waited in the days of Noah, while the ark was being prepared, in which a few, that is, eight souls, were saved through water. There is also an antitype which now saves us–baptism (not the removal of the filth of the flesh, but the answer of a good conscience toward God), through the resurrection of Jesus Christ."

61. Feldman, "The Story of the Flood in 4Q422," 73. I am following Feldman's reconstruction. From an understanding of the physical remains, his reconstruction of the text appears just as plausible as other reconstructions (א[נשי] דעת למען ל]חטוא ל[ב]ו את יחזק[ו] ישר[אל עד דו[רות] עולם cf. Elgvin and Tov, DJD XIII, 199; García Martínez and Tigchelaar, *The Dead Sea Scrolls Study Edition*, 886–887). Notably, Feldman also points out that his reconstruction is "... in line with 4Q422 ii 8–9."

recurring theme of sin, followed by judgment. In addition, the literary links between II:8–11 and III:7 provide a new emphasis of judgment to the post-Flood sign of the covenant. Second, the juxtaposition and linking together of the Flood and plagues narratives, immediately after the creation narrative, emphasizes the Flood as a reversal of creation. Not only this, column II, lines 9–13, imports creation language into the description of the post-Flood situation, presenting the Flood also as a re-creation or renewing of creation. Last, the purpose of the Flood was not simply to judge the earth due to wickedness, but to cleanse the earth from sin and to reveal God's glory.

Though often labeled a "paraphrase," 4Q422 is another example of rewritten Bible in the Second Temple period. The author selectively reworked biblical passages, juxtaposing the creation, Flood, and plagues narratives, for homiletic purposes. In particular, the Flood and plagues judgments are linked by statements concerning their purposes, introduced with למען (in order to). As Feldman concluded, "It is therefore clear that the author selected several biblical stories exemplifying God's power and justice and reworked them, presumably, with a didactic or admonitory purpose in view."[62] Indeed, a recurring theme in 4Q422 is the judgment upon the wicked so that the power and glory of God would be revealed.

---

62. Ibid., 75.

CHAPTER SIX
CONCLUSION

AT FIRST GLANCE, SUCH fragmentary ancient texts as 1QapGen, 4Q252, 4Q370, and 4Q422 may not appear to be a treasure trove for gleaning information about how the Genesis Flood was understood at Qumran. However, upon closer examination, these individual manuscripts have proven to contain a wealth of information for understanding Qumran interpretation of the Genesis Flood. Not only do the scrolls reveal various aspects of *what* the Qumran community believed concerning the Flood, but they also provide unique examples of *how* the Flood story was employed during the Second Temple period.

In 1QapGen, the author skillfully linked together the Noah (cols. 0–XVII) and Abram (cols. XVIII–XXII) narratives, indicating that a primary purpose of the text was to present Noah and Abram as righteous archetypes who inherited the land. In 4Q252, the selective retelling of the Flood is part of a complex messianic and eschatological "commentary," involving various genres, which validates the possession of the land for the righteous (past, present, and future). 4Q370 does not tell the Flood story for the story's sake, but presents the Flood as a paradigm of the eschatological judgment, reworking it for admonitory purposes. In 4Q422, the author selectively reworked biblical passages, juxtaposing the creation, Flood, and plagues narratives, for homiletic or paraenetic purposes. Within these various literary contexts and purposes, 1QapGen, 4Q252, 4Q370, and 4Q422 reveal various aspects of Flood interpretation. The following will synthesize, in summary form, the findings from these manuscripts.

Qumran Interpretation of the Genesis Flood

The 120 Years in Genesis 6:3 as the Period before the Flood

The opening lines of 4Q252 sought to resolve a dispute in antiquity concerning Genesis 6:3: "And the LORD said, 'My Spirit shall not strive with man forever, for he is indeed flesh; yet his days shall be one hundred and twenty years.'" Do the "120 years" refer to the shortened lifespan of man or the period of time remaining for humanity until the Flood?

4Q252 (column I, lines 1–3) teaches that the "120 years" of Genesis 6:3 refer to the period of time remaining for man until the Flood. The reference to the 480th year of Noah's life in line 1 places God's statement to him in that same year (lines 2–3), 120 years before the 600th year of Noah's life when the Flood came (lines 3–4). God's statement to Noah (in the 480th year) is rather conclusive: "My Spirit will not reside in man forever. Their days shall be fixed at one hundred and twenty years until the end of the waters of the Flood" (lines 2–3). The final phrase, עד קץ מי מבול (until the end of the waters of the Flood), explicitly identifies the 120 years as the period of time determined for man until the Flood. The use of the phrase ויחתכו ימיהם (their days shall be fixed), which fits with deterministic Qumran ideology, coupled with the lack of any references to repentance, indicates that the 120 year period was not understood as an opportunity for repentance.

The Cause(s) of the Flood

In Second Temple period literature, the cause of the Flood is usually attributed to 1) the wickedness of the "sons of God" (cf. Gen 6:1–4), often understood as fallen angels known as the "Watchers" (e.g. *Jubilees*; *1 Enoch*), 2) the wickedness of humanity (cf. Gen 6:5–7, 11–13), or 3) a combination of both, the wickedness of the Watchers and humanity. Both 1QapGen and 4Q370 address the cause(s) of the Flood, but in different ways, discussing different aspects for the suited purposes of each text.

1QapGen does not present a single cause for the Flood, but instead, presents multiple interwoven issues connected to a single story. Columns 0–I deal with God's angry response to the wickedness of humanity and the illicit relationships between the "Watchers" and the "daughters of men" (cf. Gen 6:1–4) before the Flood. Columns II–V cover the birth of Noah, dealing with Lamech's concern about the legitimate conception of Noah and his connection to the story of the Watchers. Enoch's speech (columns III–V) confirms that the child Noah is truly Lamech's seed, not the seed

CONCLUSION

of the Watchers. Thus, the birth of Noah, the righteous seed who would be delivered from the coming Flood, is directly linked to the story of the Watchers. In columns VI-VII, Noah's righteousness is contrasted with the illicit relationships of the "Watchers" and the "daughters of men," which violated "the law of eternal statutes which the Lord of eternity gave to the sons of man" (VI:8-9). Then, in a vision, Noah saw all the wicked conduct of the "sons of heaven" (Watchers) (VI:11-VII:5), which would result in the Flood. Thus, 1QapGen attributes the cause(s) of the Flood to both, wicked humanity and the Watchers, in which the story of the Watchers is central.

While 1QapGen attributes the cause of the Flood to wicked humanity and the Watchers, 4Q370 focuses on the nature of the human rebellion that caused the Flood.[1] Column I opens with a description of the agricultural abundance provided by God to the antediluvian world (line 1a). Instead of responding properly to God's provision by doing His will and blessing His holy name (lines 1b-2a), the antediluvians did evil and rebelled against God, resulting in judgment for their ingratitude (line 2b). This particular description of the nature of human rebellion in lines 1-2 is immediately followed by God's judgment in line 3a. Thus, according to 4Q370, the cause of the Flood was human ingratitude and rebellion in response to God's abundance/provision. The author employed Deuteronomy 8 and the non-biblical source, *Hymn to the Creator*,[2] to present this tradition not found in the biblical Flood narrative.

The Chronology of the Flood

The Flood narrative in 4Q252 (I:3–II:5) gives attention only to biblical passages related to Flood chronology (Gen 7:11-12; 17, 24; 8:3-6, 8-14). The biblical narrative dates the events of the Flood according to days of months, while 4Q252 dates not only according to days of months, but also days of weeks. 4Q252 also explicitly dates other events that are more vaguely dated in the biblical account.

Concerning the chronology of the Flood in 4Q252, several conclusions can be made. First, the chronology is framed around the life of Noah

---

1. עשו הרע בעיני (they have done what is evil in My eyes) (line 2b) refers to רעת האדם (the evil of man) in Genesis 6:5, indicating that 4Q370 sought to clarify the nature of the evil of humanity that precipitated their judgment.

2. *Hymn to the Creator* is a psalm-like composition attested at Qumran in 11QPs^a (XXVI, 9-15).

(a righteous archetype), who was delivered from the Flood. Second, the dates used in 4Q252 correspond to the 364-day solar calendar. Third, the author sought to demonstrate that no dated events occurred on a Sabbath day or a principal day of a festival. Fourth, 4Q252 resolved the chronological conundrum of the waters prevailing one hundred and fifty days (the waters began to decrease after 150 days; cf. Gen 8:2–3) and the ark landing on 7/17/600 (Gen 8:4) by understanding them sequentially as two separate events. Fifth, just as the Sabbaths and feasts were appointed by God and kept during the Flood, so too, the Flood ended at God's appointed time (למועד), precisely the length of a solar year (364 days).[3] In other words, the Flood was divinely ordered. Last, in view of the literary context of 4Q252 as a whole, the author presented the chronology of the Flood for a greater purpose–to serve as a divinely ordered archetype of eschatological judgment (see below "The Flood as an Archetype of Eschatological Judgment").

Those Who Perished in the Flood

4Q370 (column I, line 6) reworks Genesis 7:21–23, summarizing all those who perished in the Flood. Interestingly, 4Q370 includes a group not mentioned in the biblical text among those who died in the Flood: הגבורים (the mighty ones).[4] Genesis 6:4 identifies הגברים (the mighty ones) with הנפלים (the giants), the offspring of the "sons of God" (fallen angels) and the "daughters of men." Thus, 4Q370 addresses an exegetical question raised from the description in Genesis 7:21–23 of all humanity and earthly creatures perishing in the Flood. What happened to the *offspring* of the "sons of God" and the "daughters of men"? 4Q370 emphatically affirms that even the giants (mighty ones) did not escape the Flood. Though this insertion is not found in the biblical Flood narrative, the tradition of the giants perishing in the Flood is common in Second Temple period literature.[5]

---

3. The duration of the Flood in *Jubilees* and LXX is also exactly one year. 4Q252, *Jubilees*, and LXX, differ from MT (one year, ten days).

4. The author did not just add "the mighty ones" to the list of those who perished, but provided a separate clause for "the mighty ones," emphasizing their death: והג[בור]ים לוא נמלטו (and the giants did not escape).

5. Cf. *1 En* 89:5–6; *Sir* 16:7; CD II:18–21; *Wis* 14:6–7; *3 Macc* 2:4.

CONCLUSION

The Landing of the Ark

The Bible only states that "... the ark rested ... on the mountains of Ararat (הרי אררת)" (Gen 8:4), leaving the exact location or mountain the ark rested upon unspecified. As a result, Second Temple period literature sought to provide more specific locations.[6] The Qumran literature also contributed to this discussion. While 4Q252 (I:10) only mentions הרי הוררט (the mountains of Ararat), 1QapGen (X:12; XII:13; cf. *Jubilees* 5:28; 7:1), 4Q244 (frag 8), and 6Q8 provide the name of the specific mountain as לובר (Lubar). However, 1QapGen is interested in more than just providing geographical information concerning the landing place of the ark.

In 1QapGen, the author employed the geographical information as a literary device, linking the Noah and Abram narratives for a theological purpose. The narrative of the landing of the ark (column X, lines 12–18) and Noah's subsequent survey of that land (column XI, lines 1, 9–15) intentionally links the land of righteous Noah to the Promised Land of Abram (column XXI, lines 9–14), with the intended purpose of legitimizing the right of the righteous seed to the land. The Qumran community understood themselves as the righteous seed who would be delivered from the eschatological judgment (as righteous Noah was delivered from the Flood), while the wicked would be removed from the land (as the wicked were removed in Noah's day). Thus, the mountain upon which the ark rested, and the land subsequently surveyed by Noah from that mountain, were understood as an archetype for the Promised Land.

The Purpose of the Flood

4Q422 introduces details not found in the biblical narrative concerning the purposes of the Flood: "... the waters were mighty upon the earth in order to (למען) cleanse sin and in order to (למען) make known the glory of the Most High" (column II, lines 8–9). The idea of the Flood as a "baptism," cleansing the earth from sin, is attested elsewhere in Second Temple period literature.[7] The idea of God's glory being revealed through His judgments is echoed in the plagues narrative (column III, line 7) and appears to be a

---

6. The *Sibylline Oracles* (1.261–74) placed the ark's landing in Phrygia and Josephus (*Antiquities* 1.92) mentioned Armenia. *Jubilees* (5:28), which was also a popular book at Qumran, specified Mount Lubar as the mountain the ark rested upon.

7. Cf. *1 Enoch* 10:20–22; 1 Peter 3:19–21.

central message of 4Q422.[8] Thus, according to 4Q422, the purpose of the Flood was not only to judge the earth due to wickedness, but to cleanse the earth from sin and to reveal God's glory.

The Flood as Judgment

4Q370 selectively described the Flood, not as a story of deliverance of the righteous, but as God's judgment in response to human rebellion. The rebellion of humanity (I:1b–2) is immediately followed by a statement of God's judgment: "And Yahweh judged them ac[cording to al]l their ways, and according to the thoughts of the [evil] inclination of their heart" (line 3a; cf. Gen 6:5, 12). With this juxtaposition, 4Q370 departs from the biblical narrative, intentionally omitting the introduction of righteous Noah, the warning of the Flood, and the construction and entry into the ark, in order to highlight the Flood (described in I:3–5) as *judgment*. The phrase "And Yahweh judged them," not found in the biblical narrative, further highlights this emphasis on the Flood as judgment.

Unlike 4Q370, the author of 4Q422 discusses the deliverance of Noah and the inhabitants of the ark from the Flood (II:2a–5) and makes reference to God's covenant (II:9b–13). Nonetheless, an emphasis on judgment is expressed as 4Q422 juxtaposes the Flood story (column II) with the Eden (column I) and plagues (column III) narratives, highlighting a sin-judgment cycle. Also, the literary links between II:8–11 and III:7 (cf. Gen 9:12; Exod 7:5; 14:4) subtly add a new emphasis of judgment with the sign of the covenant. Thus, 4Q370 and 4Q422 both emphasize the nature of the Flood as *judgment*, but in remarkably different ways.

The Flood as a Reversal and Renewal of Creation

4Q422 juxtaposes the Eden, Flood, and plagues stories, emphasizing a theme of creation, reversal of creation, and renewal of creation. The Flood story (column II) is linked directly to the Eden story (cf. column I, line 12) resulting in these stories constituting a literary unit. The Flood story is also linked in various ways to the following plagues narrative in column III, forming a literary untiy across all three narratives. The juxtaposition

8. Col. III, line 7: [ו]יחזק את לב[ו] ל[ח]טוא למען דעת א[ת כבוד [אל עד דו]רות [עולם ([And] He hardened [his] heart [to] sin in order to make known [the glory of] God for eternal gener[ations]).

and linking together of the Flood and plagues stories, immediately after the creation narrative, highlights the Flood and plagues as reversals of creation. Both stories record God's judgment upon the wicked, which involves destruction/reversal of the natural order. In addition to presenting the Flood as a reversal of creation, 4Q422 also introduces creation language (cf. Gen 1:14–18) into the description of the post-Flood covenant (II:9–13), presenting the Flood as a re-creation or renewal of creation.

The Flood as a Restoration of Eden and Anticipation of the Promised Land

1QapGen presents the Flood as ushering in a new creation with Noah as a new Adam (columns XI–XII). First, the author depicts Noah's survey of the land in an Eden-like paradise (XI:11–12). Second, the author reworked Genesis 9:1–3 in order to show that the dominion mandate of Genesis 1:28–30 was restored to Noah (XI:16–17). Third, the description of Noah planting a vineyard on Mount Lubar recalls the Garden of Eden (XII:13; cf. XI:11–12). 1QapGen also links Noah and Abram, tying the land Noah surveyed (column XI) to the land promised to Abram (column XXI). Thus, the Flood narrative appears to be understood as an important link, restoring Eden and anticipating the Promised Land.

The Flood as an Archetype of Eschatological Judgment

Numerous works from the Second Temple period attest to the understanding of the Flood as an archetype of eschatological judgment.[9] The Qumran literature is no exception as 1QapGen, 4Q252, and 4Q370 each present the Flood as an archetype of eschatological judgment in various ways.

In 1QapGen (columns 0–XV), the author introduces, repeats, and weaves together themes, linking the Flood judgment with the eschatological fiery judgment.[10] 1QapGen presents Noah as a righteous archetype of

---

9. Cf. *Sibylline Oracles*, *1 Enoch* (90; 108), the New Testament (Matthew 24:37–39; 2 Peter 3:3–7), and Josephus (*Antiquities* 1.70–71).

10. Columns 0–I introduce recurring themes such as חמת (heat), נור (fire), and תקף (strength), which anticipate both the imminent Flood judgment and the eschatological judgment. Columns II–V present Noah as the righteous "seed" who would be delivered, not as the seed of the wicked who would be judged in the Flood. The author recalls themes such as heat and fire from columns 0–I and introduces themes (e.g. the righteous

deliverance for the righteous seed in the last days. Just as Noah, the true seed and righteous planting, was delivered while the wicked were judged in the Flood, so too Noah's seed, the righteous planting, would be delivered while the wicked are thrown onto the fire in the eschatological judgment.

In 4Q252, the focus on chronology in the retelling of the Flood (I:1–II:5) points to the divinely ordered nature of the destruction of the wicked from the land and the deliverance of the righteous during the Flood. The literary composition of 4Q252 as a whole[11] indicates that the author presented the Flood as a divinely ordered archetype of eschatological judgment. Just as the Flood followed a divinely ordered timetable, so too, the future destruction of the wicked from the land and deliverance of the righteous would follow a divinely ordered timetable.

In 4Q370, the author reworked the Flood story, invoking eschatological language not found in the biblical Flood narrative (I:3–5; cf. Isa 24:18–20).[12] Also, the admonition, אל תמרו (do not rebel) against Yahweh (II:9), is based upon the antediluvian rebellion which resulted in the Flood: ויאמרו אל (and they rebelled against God) (I:2). Thus, 4Q370 presents the Flood as a historical paradigm of the eschatological judgment, reworking it for admonitory purposes.

1QapGen, 4Q252, and 4Q370 each understand the Flood as an archetype of eschatological judgment, but present this in various ways. In each case, the Flood is understood to provide the historical basis for the deliverance of the righteous and destruction of the wicked in the eschatological judgment.

---

planting) later occuring in relation to Noah's vision of imminent judgment (VI–VII) and his vision of eschatological judgment (XIII–XV). The language in Noah's first vision (VI–VII) echoes previous columns and anticipates the eschatological vision (XIII–XV). In Noah's eschatological vision, the destiny of his seed as an eternal righteous planting (לנצבת קושט) and the wicked being thrown onto the fire (נור), recalls language from previous columns (0–I, II–5, and VI–VII), further connecting the two judgments.

11. 4Q252 is an eschatological and messianic commentary, validating the possession of the land for the righteous (past, present, and future). Columns I–III contain a historical sequence beginning with the Flood, in which the past is viewed as determinative of the present for the author and the community. Columns IV–V deal with the eschatological age in which the wicked will be destroyed and the righteous delivered.

12. The language of God thundering and the foundations of the earth shaking is used elsewhere in descriptions of Yahweh in His power and as Divine Warrior (1 Sam 2:10; Ps 18:8, 14, 16 [MT]; 29:3; 68:9 [MT]; Job 37:4–5) and descriptions of God's future war against the nations (cf. Isa 24:18–20; Joel 4:15–16 [MT]). This language is also in Second Temple period texts describing the eschatological war (e.g. 1QH^a).

CONCLUSION

Qumran Interpretation of the Genesis Flood: Concluding Remarks

This study of 1QapGen, 4Q252, 4Q370, and 4Q422 has brought to light various aspects of Flood interpretation among the Dead Sea Scrolls. Further, these Qumran texts display each author's affinity for intertextual exegesis, demonstrating their keen familiarity with the Hebrew Bible as a whole and various theological traditions during the Second Temple period. As a result, a more comprehensive picture of the methods and beliefs that constitute a "Qumran Flood Theology" is beginning to emerge. One major challenge to arriving at more definitive conclusions concerning the various Qumran interpretations of the Flood is the fragmentary nature of these texts. Looking ahead, further physical analysis of these fragmentary manuscripts (e.g. reconstruction methods; imaging techniques) could potentially refine, or perhaps modify, some of the more tentative conclusions of this study. Nonetheless, these fragmentary texts have provided priceless insights into Flood interpretation during the Second Temple period. In particular, Qumran interpretation of the Genesis Flood provides ancient Jewish precedent for understanding the text today in lieu of modern tendencies.

Appendix A
Text and Translation of Columns 0–XII of Genesis Apocryphon
(1QapGen)[1]

---

1. Text and translation is adapted from Fitzmyer, *The Genesis Apocryphon of Qumran Cave 1* (1Q20); Machiela, *The Dead Sea Genesis Apocryphon*.

TEXT AND TRANSLATION OF COLUMNS 0–XII OF GENESIS APOCRYPHON

Column 0

1 [	...ל .כא.[ ] ....
2 [	די בכול נקבל גיור[
3 [	]ד *vacat*
4 [	]כו[ל די חמ]ד [
5 [	]ם רגזך תתקף ותתקיאם ומן הוא
6 די[	*vacat*]ם חמת רגזך *vacat*
7 [	]תיא וכביא ושפליא דאלין וזאעין
8 [	]וכען הא אנחנא אסירין
9 [	]תא [ ]..[ ]ל[
10 [	].[ ]רגז[ט]ישח[.ן *vacat*
11 [	]ברגזך ...מן די נהך לבית נש[קד]ישא רבא
12 [ ]	וכען קריבה ידך לממחה ק.ד א[ ]ולאעדיא כול
13 [ ]	]בעד מלוהי סאף [עד]א די אסרנא[ ]נור די אתחזי
14]ל[ ]ל[	]שמ.[ ]קוד[ם]ש.
15 [	]ל ומתמחין מן אחיהון ול[א]עוד
16 [	] *vacat*
17 [	]אן מתחתנין ו...ן ... למא
18 [	*vacat* קודם מרה עלמא [.
19 [	]ל[ ]ל[]ל[ ]ל

1 [   ].k' l...
2 [   ]for in every (way) we shall become an adulterer
3 [   ]k (vacat)
4 [al]l that he de[sired]
5 [   ]m You will intensify Your anger and will be sustained. But who is there
6 [who can withstand   ]m the heat of Your anger. (vacat)
7 [   ]ty' and kby'; and the lowly ones (are) trembling and shuddering
8 [   ]. And now, look we are prisoners
9 [   ]
10 [   ]n Your anger will dest[roy]
11 [ ]in Your anger ... from the time that we go to the house of ns[ ] the great [Ho]ly One.
12 [   ] And now Your hand (is) near to strike [   ] and to remove all
13 [ ] because of his words the [time] of our imprisonment is coming to an end[ ] fire which is seen
14 [ ]l[ ]l[   ]s. befor[e   ]sm.
15 [   ]l and they are being smitten by their brothers and n[o] longer
16 [   ] (vacat)
17 [   ]'n that they would not ally themselves by marriage w...n... why
18 [   ]. before the eternal Lord.
19 [   ]

TEXT AND TRANSLATION OF COLUMNS 0–XII OF GENESIS APOCRYPHON

Column I

1 [	]...א נחו.ן ועם נקבתא
2 [	].ואף רז רשעא די
3 [	].תין ורזא די
4 [	].שתון לא מדעין
5 [	]...
6 [	]א עד
7 [	]
8 [מ	]אנון ..[
9 [	יום ד]י
10 [	כול ...ין] [
11 [	סמין כשפין וח[רשין]...
12 [	ארעא תר.ע ..ל.] על]
13 [	עובדא די עבד]ו [
14 [	ובישתא למק..] [
15 [	והא כול] [
16 [	] [
17 [	] [
18 [	] [
19 [	אלפא ..ן]
20 [	].. [....
21 [	] [vacat
22 [	]...נין אסיר תקיף
23 [	]רין פ..דין ובש.ין א.ן[
24 [	] [
25 [	]...א.. ולקלל לכול בשרא
26 [	].רה ובמשלחן לכון שלח הוא
27 [	]לארעא ולמחת לה אינ..עמא
28 [	לא יד]עין מא למעבד אנשא לארעא
29 [	]להון עבד ואף לכול בשרא
30 [	].ל.. ....

1   [   ]...*n* and with the women
2   [   ].. Moreover, the mystery of evil which
3   [   ].*tyn* and the mystery which
4   [   ]... not known (?)
5   [   ]
6   [   ].... until
7   [   ]
8   *m*[   ].. them
9   a day wh[ich   ]
10 all ...*yn* [   ]
11 medicines, magicians, and sooth[sayers   ]
12 the earth *tr.'..l*[about]
13 the deed which [they] did [   ]
14 and the evil for *mq*..[   ]
15 and look, all[   ]
16 [   ]
17 [   ]
18 [   ]
19 [   ]the thousand ..*n*
20 [   ].. ....
21 [   ] *vacat*
22 [   ]*nyn* a strong prisoner
23 [   ]*ryn p..dyn wbs.yn '.n*
24 [   ] ....
25 [   ]...'.. and as a shame for all flesh
26 [   ].*rh* and by messengers he sent to you
27 [   ]to the earth, and go down (to it) ... the people
28 [not kno]wing what to do. Mankind to the earth
29 [   ] he did to them, and also to all flesh.
30 [   ] .*l*.. ....

Column II

1 הא באדין חשבת בלבי די מן עירין הריאתא ומן קדישין זרעא ולנפיל[ין]
2 ולבי עלי משתני על עולימא דנא
3 באדין אנה למך אתבהלת ועלת על בתאנוש אנ[תתי ואמרת לה]
4 [   ]אנא ועד בעליא במרה רבותה במלך כול ע[למים   מן]
5 [הד] בני שמין עד כולא בקושטא תחויני הן
6 [בקושט] תחויני ולא בכדבין הדא ב[   ]   בעליא במרה רבותא[
7 במלך כול עלמים עד בקושט עמי תמללין ולא בכדבין]
8 אדין בתאנוש אנתתי בחלץ תקיף עמי מללת וב[כת
9 ואמרת יא אחי ויא מרי דכרלך על עדינתי א]
10 [בחו]ם ענתה ונשמתי לגו נדנהא ואנה בקושט כול[א אחוינך
11 מ]ולדא ושגי לבי עלי אדין אשתני [   ]
12 וכדי חזת בתאנוש אנתתי די אשתני אנפי עלי]
13 באדין אנסת רוחהא ועמי תמלל ולי תאמר יא מרי ויא אחי [דכרלך]
14 עדינתי יאמיא אנה לך בקדישא רבא במלך ש[מיא
15 די מנך זרעא דן ומנך הריונא דן ומנך נצבת פריא[דן
16 ולא מן כול זר ולא מן כול עירין ולא מן כול בני שמ[י]ן למא צלם]
17 אנפיך כדנא עליך שנא ושחת ורוחך כדן עליבא[ארי אנה]
18 בקושט ממללא עמך   vacat   ]
19 באדין אנה למך רחיט על מתושלח אבי וכולא לה חו[ית די יהך על חנוך]
20 אבוהי וכולא מנה ביצבא ינדע בדי הוא רחים ור[גיג אלהא ועם קדישיא]
21 עדבה פליג ולה מחוין כולא vacat וכדי שמע מתושל[ח אבי מלי]
22 [רט] על חנוך אבוהי למנדע מנה כולא בקושטא]   [
23 רעותה ואזל לארך מת לפרוין ותמן אשכחה לחנו]ך אבוהי   [
24 ו]אמר לחנוך אבוהי יא אבי ויא מרי די אנה לך את]ית   [
25 [ ] ל[ ] ואמר לך דאל תרגז עלי די לתנא אתית ל]ך   [
26 דחיל לעליד]ך   [

1   Behold then, I thought in my heart that the conception was from the Watchers and the seed from the Holy Ones, and (belonged) to Nephil[im]
2   and my heart within me was upset because of this child.
3   Then I, Lamech, was frightened, and I went to Bitenosh, my wi[fe and said to her, ...]
4   [Behold, I adjure you by the Most High, by the Majestic Lord, by the King of all A[ges]
5   [with one of] the sons of heaven, that in truth you make everything known to me, whether [ ]
6   [in truth] you must tell me and without lies whether this [... swear by the Most High, the Majestic Lord]
7   by the King of all Ages that you are speaking to me in truth and without lies [ ].
8   Then Bitenosh, my wife, spoke to me very harshly and [ ]
9   and she said, "O my brother and my lord, remember my (sexual) pleasure [ ]
10 [in the heat] of the time, and the gasping of my breath in my breast. For [I shall tell you] everything in truth [ ]."
11 [the b]irth. And my heart was much changed within me. [ ]
12 When Bitenosh, my wife, realized that my countenance had changed [ ]
13 then she suppressed her anger, speaking to me and saying to me, "O my lord and [my brother, remember]
14 my (sexual) pleasure. I swear to you by the Great Holy One, by the King of h[eaven]
15 that this seed is from you, that this conception comes from you, and from you the planting of [this] fruit [ ]
16 and not from any stranger, or from any of the Watchers, or from any of the sons of hea[ven. Why is the expression]
17 of your face so changed and distorted, and your spirit so depressed? [Behold I]
18 speak to you in truth.   vacat   [ ]
19 Then I, Lamech, ran to Methuselah my father and I to[ld] him everything [that he might go to Enoch]
20 his father and would know everything for certain from him, for he is beloved and a fa[vorite of God and with the Holy Ones]

Column III

]ל[...ן ולא לאורכא	2
]ארי ביומי ירד אבי[	3
]ין בני[	4
] [	5
]ם[..	6
]ולד להון[	7
] [	8
] ... על ארעא כולהא[	9
] [............ארעא לימא דן	10
] ..מן...... ל..... ...ישים ארעא[..	11
] ארעא[... וכען אזל	12
] הואא בקשוט די לא בכדבין[	13
] [............................	14
] [	15
] [	16
] פלג כול ארעא ..ם ....ן[	17
] א ולעמלהון[	24

21 his inheritance is found and they everything known to him. When Methusela [h my father] heard [my words]
22 [he ran] to Enoch, his father, in order to learn everything from him in truth [ ]
23 his will. And he went through the length of the land to Parvaim, and there he found Eno[ch, his father].
24 [And] he said to Enoch, his father, "O my father and my lord, since I have co[me] to you [ ]
25 [ ] And I say to you, do not be angry with me because I came here to [you]
26 fear/reverence (?) before you [   ]

2 [   ]*l...n* and not for length
3 [   ] for in the days of Jared, my father
4 [   ]*yn* sons of
5 [   ]
6 [   ]*m*
7 [   ]and they will be to you
8 [   ]
9 [   ].... Upon all the land
10 [   ]the land to this sea
11 [   ].. from ..... to .... he will put the land
12 [   ]the land ... ... and now go
13 [   ] *hw"* in truth without lies
14 [
15 [
16 [
17 [   ]he divided all the earth ..*m* ....*n*

24 [   ]' and for their effort

Column IV

1]מן[ ].ו יהרגשון
2]א..ושו [
3] [.ד לכול עלמים   באישתא

11 חזית למעבד דין ..[ ].ן שם
12] [רבא וקץ [ ] ע[ל אנפי ארעא
13] [
14] [עליהון

1   From [   ] they will stir up
2   wšw ..'[   ]
3   [   ].d for all ages   the evil

11 you saw (fit) to mete out justice[   ]..n he put
12 the great and the end of[o]n the face of the earth
13 [   ]
14 [   ] upon them

Column V

1 וכתב ..ל[ ]   [
2 vacat ולד מתושלח ב[רי   ]ל די עולימא
3 דן הא כדי אנה חנוך]   [ולא מן בני
4 שמין להן מן למך ברד[ ]   [
5 ומדמא לא הווא ..]   [
6 אלא]   [מן
7 חזוה דחל למדברד[ ]   [
8 בקושט מהימן די .... vacat
9 וכען לצ{א} אנה אמר ברי ולך אנה מחוה אדין בקושט ....]   [
10 אזל אמר ללמך ברך]   [
11 ורמוהי בארעא וכול עובד [בני שמין] ..פל וה..   [
12 לאנפוהי נסבא בי ודנחא עינוהי כשמ[שא   [
13 עולימא דן נור והוא ל...]   [
14] [[
15 ...]   [
16 הא באדין אשתבשון ואתכלו[ן]   [
17 עלמא יהבין בש...]   [
18 עבדין חמס שגיא יעבדון עד די]   [
19 וסלקין וכול שבילי]   [
20 וכען לך אנה [מ]חוה ברי ....]   ללמד[
21 ברך אחוי ברזא דנא ...]   [
22 ביומוהי .ת עובד והא ..]   [
23 מברך למרה כולא ה.]   [
24 וכדי שמע מתושלח ל[מליא אלן   [
25 ועם למך ברה ברי מלל]   [
26 וכדי אנה למך ..[ ].]   אנה[
27 חזי די מני אנפיק מ..]   [
28 vacat
29 [פרשגן] כתב מלי נוח]   [

TEXT AND TRANSLATION OF COLUMNS 0–XII OF GENESIS APOCRYPHON

1 and he wrote ..*l*[   ]
2 *vacat* and to you Methuselah, [my] s[on] of this child.
3 Behold, when I, Enoch [   ] and not from the sons of
4 heaven, but from Lamech, your son [   ]
5 and he did not resemble ..[   ]
6 but [   ] because of (?)
7 Lamech, your son, feared his appearance [   ]
8 in truth trust that *vacat*
9 And I tell you, my son, and to you I make known in truth [ ]
10 Go, tell Lamech, your son [   ]
11 and they tossed it on the earth and every deed of [the sons of heaven] ..*pl wh*..[
12 his face has lifted to me and his eyes shone like the su[n   ]
13 this child is a flame and he *l*..[   ]
14 [   ]
15 .... [   ]
16 Then they were confounded and were held back [of]
17 eternal they give [   ]
18 doing much violence, they will do until [   ]
19 and are mounting up, and all the paths of [   ]
20 and now to you I [ma]ke known, my son, [to Lamech]
21 your son, make known about this mystery [   ]
22 in his days .*t* a work, and behold [   ]
23 blessing the Lord of all, *h*[   ]
24 And when Methuselah heard [these words   ]
25 and with Lamech, his son, he spoke about a mystery [   ]
26 And when I, Lamech [   ]
27 that he has brought forth from me *m*..[   ]
28   *vacat*
29 [A copy of] the book of the words of Noah [   ]

Column VI

1 מן עול ובכור הורתי יעית לקושט וכדי נפקת מן מעי אמי לקושט נציבת
2 וקושטא כול יומי דברת והוית מהלך בשבילי אמת עלמא ועמי קדיש[א] הוא
3 ᵛᵃᶜᵃᵗמסלי אוחת קושט ולאזהרותני מן נתיב שקר די אזלן לחשון עלמא א....
4 [ ]ל.[].א וחצי אסרת בחזון קושטא וחכמתא במעיל א... ....
5 [ ]ל[].. כול שבילי חמס   vacat
6 בא[ד]ין הוית אנה נוח גבר ואחדת בקושטא ואתקפת ב.... א......
7 [בר]קיאל ולאמזרע ברתה לי לאנתה נסבת והרת מני וילדת לי בנין ת[לת]ה [ובנן]
8 [נקבן]באדין לבני נשין נסבת מן בנת אחי ובנתי לבני אחי יהבת כדת חוק עלמא
9 [די יהב]ה עליא לבני אנשא vacat וביומי כדי שלמו לי לחשבון די חשבת
10 [ ]..[ ]..א יובלין עשרה באדין שלם לבני למסב להון נשין לאנתו
11 [ ]. שמיא בחזיון חזית ואחואת ואודעת בעובד בני שמין ומא כול
12 [ ]. שמיא וטמרת רזא דן בלבבי ולכול אנוש לא אחויתה   vacat
13 [ ]..עלי בעירא רבא ᵛˡⁱ בציר ובמשלחת קדישא [רבא]
14 [ ].... ובחזיון עמי מלל ולקובלי קם ....
15 [ ] במ[שלחת קדישא רבא לי קל אשמע לך אמרין יא נוח
16 [ ].רמו וחשבת בי כול לכת בני ארעא ידעת וחוית כול]
17 [ ] [.]..........[].קל יצלחון ובחר. .אנון
18 [ ] שבועין תרין ובאדין מסתם י]הוה
19 [ ] מעיו. דמא די אשדו נפיליא שפית וקוית ᵛᵈⁱ ᵠ[
20 [ ] קדישין די עם בנת אנו]ש [
21 [ ] ק.ס.א א] [.]ן וא.לן..[
22 [ ] [
23 [ ] ואש[כחת אנה נוח חן רבו וקושט...] [
24 [ ] [.]ן .ל[ ]ל. [עליא יום ק.ל] [
25 [ ] [...][ ]לך [עד תרעי שמיא ..] [
26 [ ] ... לאנשא ולבעירא ולחיותא לעופא ו] [
27 [ ] [...... ......] [

TEXT AND TRANSLATION OF COLUMNS 0–XII OF GENESIS APOCRYPHON

1. from iniquity; and in the womb of her who bore me I came forth for truth/uprightness; an when I came forth from my mother's womb, I was planted for truth/uprightness.
2. And all my days I have practiced truth/uprightness and I have been walking along the paths of eternal truth; and with me the Holy One
3. on my tracks truth/uprightness was settled, and to warn me against the path of falsehood which leads to darkness ……..'.
4. [ ]l.[ ]' And I girded my loins in a vision of truth/uprightness and wisdom. In a robe ……..
5. … all the paths of violence *vacat*
6. Then I, Noah, became a man and I clung to truth/righteousness and strengthened myself in ……
7. [Ba]raqiel, and I took Imzera (Amzara), his daughter, as my wife, and she conceived from me and bore me th[re]e sons [and daughters]
8. … I took wives for my sons from the daughters of my brothers, and I gave my daughters to the sons of my brothers, according to the eternal law
9. [which] the Most High gave to the sons of man *vacat* And in my days, when there had been completed for me, according to the calculation by which I reckoned,
10. [ ]..[ ]… ten jubilees, then my sons completed taking for themselves women in marriage,
11. [ ]. the heavens. In a vision I saw and was shown and informed of the deed/conduct of the sons of heaven and how all
12. [ ]. the heavens. And I hid this mystery in my heart and to no person did I make it known. *vacat*
13. [ ] to me by a great Watcher, to me by a messenger and by an emissary of the Holy One
14. [ ] and in visions he spoke with me, and he was standing before me …
15. [an e]missary of the great Holy One, a voice called out to me: "'Io you, O Noah, they say, …"
16. [ ].*rmw* and I considered within me all the conduct of the sons of the earth, and I knew and made known to all [ ]
17. [ ]………[ ]*ql* they will split, and he chose … them …
18. [for] two weeks, and then from what w[ill be] hidden [ ]
19. [ ]*m'yw*. the blood which the Nephilim shed. And I waited until [ ]
20. [ ] the holy ones who were with the daughters of m[en].
21. [ ].*qs*.' '[ ].*n w'.ln* ..[ ]

Column VII

1] ... [תשלט] עליהון ארעא וכול די עליהא בימיא ובטוריא
2] [... ..דא כול מזלת שמיא שמשא שהרא וכוכביא ועיריא
3] [ל] [שנין] [מן
4] [לך ל] [עליהון
5] [. יקר ואגרי אנה משלם לך ..
6] [vacat
7] [... קדישא רבא וחדית למלי מרה שמיא ואציחת
8] [...[לכולא] ת על דנה
9] [...[... vacat
10] [מללת] [

17] [........] [............
18] לחד שפירא[
19 שמיא לחדא וקצי] להעדותני ולמבנה[
20] [.למת] שכלותא[
21] ...ת כול ע.[
22] [לל] [לי ל..ל א] [כול
23] [ל.[צ.איין וכנישת

TEXT AND TRANSLATION OF COLUMNS 0–XII OF GENESIS APOCRYPHON

22 [   ]
23 [And] I Noah [fou]nd grace, greatness, and truth/uprightness [   ]
24 [   ].*n.l*[   ] the Most High a day of *q.l* [   ]
25 [   ]… to you [   ] unto the gates of heaven [   ]
26 [   ]… to mankind and to the cattle and to beasts, to the birds and [   ]
27 [   ]…. ……[   ]

1 …[you shall rule] over them, the earth, and all that is upon it, in the seas and on the mountains
2 [   ]… ..*d'* all the constellations of the heavens, the sun, the moon, and the stars. And the Watchers
3 [   ]*l*[   ] years [   ] from
4 [   ] to you *l*[   ] on them
5 [   ]. glory, and my reward I give to you
6 [   ]
7 [   ] the Great Holy One. And I was happy at the words of the Lord of heaven and I called out
8 [   ]… … for all of it [   ]*t* about this
9 [   ]… … *vacat*
10 [   ] I spoke [   ]

17 [   ]……..[   ]………[   ]
18 [   ] very beautiful
19 the heavens very much, and the ends of [   ] to remove me and to build
20 [   ].*lmt*[   ] the insight
21 [   ].*t* all …
22 [   ]*ll*[   ] to me *l..l* '[   ] all
23 [   ]*l*[   ].*ṣ.'yyn* and the gathering of

167

Column VIII

1 אנתתה בתרה ח..] [ן. רה והואת
2 [ ] [
3 [ ] [
4 עלמא] [

9 ובכול מש] [

Column X

1 רבה *vacat* באדין ב..ל.ת כולא די בני מן ...ל ושלם..........
2 לנוח .. בליליא דן .... לל.. ...
3 בליליא ל.. ל.. ל...] [..........

8 ......ן והללו ושבחו ... ...ד ברכא ....
9 ... ... ודי כול ..ה ... ושקיט ....כולכון למרכון ...
10 למלך כול עלמיא לעלם ולעד עד כול עלמים   *vacat*
11 באדין ..א על ארעא ..... ונסב מן ....
12 משכח ארי ב.......ט..... על ...] [..תבותא נחת חד מן טורי הוררט ונור עלמא
13 [ ] לק..............] [ועל כול ארעא כולהא כפרת וראיש .תה ...
14 [שעיר]א לקדמין ובתרה אתה ל..] [.. ותרבא על נורא אקטרת ותניאיא
15 ... ל...לון דמהון ל^איסוד מדבחא אשד[ת] וכול בשרהון על מדבחא אקטרת ותליתי א לבני שפנינא
16 [ ]ן על מדבחא קרבנא ....הון עליה יהבת סולת נשיפא פילא במשח עם לבונא למנחא
17 [ ]ן מ..........ס בכלהון מלחא הוית יהב ורח מקטורתי ל[ש]מיא סלק   *vacat*
18 באדין עליא ....ל. ל...] [

TEXT AND TRANSLATION OF COLUMNS 0–XII OF GENESIS APOCRYPHON

1 his wife after him *ḥ*..[   ]*n.rh* and she was
2 [   ]
3 [   ]
4 the world [   ]

9 and in all the *mš*[   ]

1 great vacat Then I *b..l.t* all of my sons from ...*l* and it came to pass (?)
2 to Noah ...in this night ... . *ll..* ...
3 in the night *l.. l.. l.. l.*...[   ]...............

8 ....*n* and they praised and glorified ...*k* a blessing ....
9 ... ... and what all ..*h* ... and quiet........... you all to your Lord
10 to the King of all Ages, forever and ever, for all eternity. Vacat
11 Then ..' on the earth ..... and he took from ....
12 finding, for on .... Upon ...[   ] the ark rested [on] one of the mountains of Ararat. And eternal fire
13 [ ] .... *lq*..........[   ] and I atoned for all the whole earth, and the head of .*th* ....
14 the [he-goat] first, and after it there came .[   ].. and I burned the fat upon the fire; and secondly ...
15 ... ..*l* ...*lwn* their blood at the base of the altar [I] poured out, and I burned all their flesh on the altar; and thirdly the young turtledoves
16 [ ]*n* upon the altar as an offering ....*hwn* on it I put fine flour, mixed in oil together with frankincense, as a meal-offering
17 [ ]*n m*..........*m* on all of them I placed salt, and the scent of my burnt-offering rose to heaven vacat
18 Then the Most High .... [   ]

Column XI

1 [ ]אנה נוח הוית בתרע תיבותא באירא לק...............

5 [ ].א...בריא..........הון].......   [

9 [ ]....א לטוריא ומדבריא לעובריא ודא......ל.[.......]ה לא

10 [ ]..[.]ארבע. vacat

11 [אדי]ן אנה נוח נפקת והלכת בארעא לאורכהא ולפותיהא [   ]..ל......ן

12 [ ]...עליהא אדן בעליהון ובאנבהון וארעא כולהא מליא דתא ועשב ועבור אדין ברכת למרה

13 [שמיא די] שבח עבר לעלם הוא ולה תשבחתא ותבת וברכת די רחם על ארעא ודי אעדי ואבד מנהא

14 כול עבדי חמסא ורשעא ושקרא ופלט לגבר א צדיקא ל....... לכול קנה בדילה

15 [ואתחזי] לי [מרה] שמיא מלל עמי ולי אמר אל תדחל יא נוח עמך אנה ועם בניך די להון כואתך לעלמים

16 ....ל. ארעא ושלט בכולהון ימיהא ובמדבריהא ובטוריהא ובכול די בהון והא אנה

17 [י]הב לך ולבניך כולא למאכל בירקא ועשבא די ארעא ברם כול דם לא תאכלון אימתכון ודחלתכון

18 [ ]....לעלמים אמ......................

19 [ ]אנה לך [די] ישנין בניך [[

TEXT AND TRANSLATION OF COLUMNS 0–XII OF GENESIS APOCRYPHON

1 [ ] I, Noah, was at the door of the ark. The spring *lq*.... ......

5 [ ]...' ...*bry*' ....*hwn* ......[   ]

9 [ ]....' The mountains and the deserts and the thickets and *d*'... ..*l*.
   [ ]......*h* not
10 [ ]..[   ] four. *vacat*
11 [Then] I, Noah, went out and walked on the land through its length and its breadth [ ] .. *l*..........*n*
12 [ ] upon it. (There was) pleasure in their leaves and in their fruits. And all the earth (land) was filled with grass, herbs, and grain. Then I blessed the Lord of
13 [heaven], whose praise endures forever, and to whom (be) glory! And I blessed Him again because He had mercy on the earth (land), because He removed and destroyed from it
14 all workers of violence, evil, and deceit, and has saved (rescued) the righteous man for .... He acquired all for His sake. *vacat*
15 [And there appeared] to me the [Lord of] heaven ... spoke with me and said to me, "Do not be afraid, O Noah! I am with you and all of your sons, who will be like you forever.
16 ......*l*.. of the earth, and rule over all of them, its seas and its deserts and its mountains, and over all that is in them. Behold, I
17 give all of it to you and to your children to eat of the greenery and the and herbs of the earth (land). But you are not to eat any blood. The fear and dread of you
18 ..... forever. '*m*... ....
19 [   ] I am for you [who] your sons *yšnyn* [   ]

Column XII

1	[ ]הא קשתי [בענן י]הבת והואת לי לאת בעננא ולמהוה ..את
2	[ ].................[על א]רעא
3	[ ]שגיאן ב.ש אתחזיאת לי
4	[ ].....................[ ]למל....ל.........ת
5	[ ]
6	[ ]ן[vacat
7	[ ].................................בטורי [הוררט]
8	[ ]....ת כרם בטורי הוררט ומן בתר כן נחתת לשפולי טורא דן אנה ובני ובני בני
9	[ ] ... ארי צדותא הואת שגיא בארעא וילידו ל[בני בני]ן [וב]נן מן בתר מבולא
10	[לשם] ברי רבא יליד לה בר לקדמין ארפכשד תרתין שנין בתר מבולא [והוו]א כול בני שם כולחון
11	vacat [עיל]ם ואשור ארפכשד לוד וארם ובנן נקבן חמש ו[בני חם כוש ומצרי]ן ופרט וכנען ובנן
12	נקבן שבע vacat ובנ[י] יפת גומר ומגוג ומדי ויואן ותובל ומשוך ותירס ובנן נקבן ארעא vacat
13	[ו]שרית אנה ובני כולהון למפלח בארעא ונצבת כרם רב בלובר טורא ולשנין ארבע עבד לי המר
14	שגיא וכול חמרא אהתת vacat וכדי אתא רגלא קדמיא ביום חד לרגלא קדמיא די בחודשא
15	[קדמיא].........[די כרמי כומרא דן פתחת ושרית למשתיה ביום חד לשתא חמישיתא [מן]
16	[בתר מב]ולא ביומא דן קרית לבני ולבני בני ולנשי בני ולנשי בניהון ואתכנשנא כחדא ואזלנא
17	[לאתר מדבח]א והוית מברך למרה שמיא לאל עליון לקדישא רבא די פלטנא מן אבדנא
18	[ ].....הי די אבוהי שתיו ואש...[ולכול.....
19	[ ] מן ..ני ושפכת על ...בי וחמרא [
20	[ ]
21	[ ]סיר[
27	[ ].......ל... כול שנה ול....

1 [   ] .... Look, I have put My bow [in the cloud]." And it became for Me a sign in the cloud and (was) to be ... a sign
2 [on] the [ea]rth
3 [   ] many, .bs was revealed to me
4 [   ]..................[ ]lml ...l.....................t
5 [   ]..
6 [   ]n vacat
7 [   ] ....on the mountains of [Ararat]
8 [   ]m in the mountains of Ararat (Hurarat); and afterwards I went down to the base of this mountain, I and my sons and my grandsons.
9 [ ] ... for desolation was great in the earth. [Son]s [and daugh]ters were born to [my sons] after the Flood.
10 [To Shem], my oldest son, was born first Arpachshad two years after the Flood. All the sons of Shem, all of them, wer[e]
11 [El]am, Asshur, Arpachshad, Lud and Aram, and five daughters vacat And [the sons of Ham (were) Cush and Mizrai]n, and Put and Canaan, and seven
12 daughters. vacat The son[s] of Japeth (were) Gomer and Magog, Madai and Javan, Tubal and Meshech, and Tiras, and four daughters.
13 [And] I, with all my sons, began to till the earth. I planted a large vineyard on Mount Lubar, and in the fourth year it produced wine for me
14 and I brought down all the wine vacat And when the first feast came, on the first day of the first feast, which is in the
15 [first] month .... of my vineyard. I opened this vessel and began to drink it on the first day of the fifth year
16 [after the Fl]ood. On that day I invited my sons and my grandsons, and all our wives and their daughters. And we gathered together and went
17 [to the place of] the [altar], and I blessed the Lord of heaven, God Most High, the Great Holy One, who saved (delivered) us from destruction.
18 [   ] and for all ... ...hy of his father; they drank and š̆...
19 [   ]... from ..ny and I poured out upon ...by and the wine [   ]
20 [   ]
21 [   ]syr

27 [   ]......l... every year and l....

Appendix B

Text and Translation of Columns I–II:5 of Commentary on Genesis (4Q252)[1]

---

1. Text and translation is adapted from García Martínez and Tigchelaar, *The Dead Sea Scrolls Study Edition*; Brooke, "The Thematic Content of 4Q252," 33–59.

Column I

1 [ב]שנת ארבע מאות ושמונים לחיי נוח בא קצם לנוח ואלוהים
2 אמר לא ידור רוחי באדם לעולם ויחתכו ימיהם מאה ועשרים
3 שנא עד קץ מי מבול ומי מבול היו על הארץ   בשנת שש מאות שנא
4 לחיי נוח בחודש השני באחד בשבת בשבעה עשר בו ביום ההוא
5 נבקעו כול מעינות תהום רבה וארבות השמים נפתחו ויהי הגשם על
6 הארץ ארבעים יום וארבעים לילה עד יום עשרים וששה בחודש
7 השלישי יום חמשה בשבת ויגברו המים על הארץ חמשים מאות יום
8 עד יום ארבעה עשר בחודש השביעי בשלושה בשבת ובסוף חמשים
9 ומאת יום חסרו המים שני ימים יום הרביעי ויום החמישי ויום
10 הששי נחה התבה על הרי הוררט ה[וא יו]ם שבעה עשר בחודש השביעי
11 והמים הי[ו] הלוך וחסור עד החודש [הע]שירי באחד בו יום רביעי
12 לשבת נראו ראשי ההרים ויהי מקץ ארבעים יום להראות ראשי
13 ההר[ים ויפ]תח נוח את חלון התבה יום אחד בשבת יום עשרה
14 בעש[תי עשר] החודש וישלח את היונה לראות הקלו המים ולוא
15 מצאה מנוח ותבוא אליו [אל] התבה ויחל עוד שבעת ימים א[חרים]
16 ויוסף לשלחה ותבוה אליו ועלי זית טרף בפיה [הוא יום עשרים]
17 וארבעה לעשתי עשר החודש באחד בשב[ת וידע נוח כי קלו המים]
18 מעל הארץ   ומקץ שבעת ימים אחר[ים שלח א]ת ה[יונה ולוא]
19 יספה לשוב עוד הוא יום א[חד לשנים עשר] החודש [באחד]
20 בשבת ומקץ שלוש[ים יום לשלח את היונ]ה אשר לוא יספ[ה]
21 שוב עוד חרבו המ[ים מעל הארץ ו]יסר נוח מכסה התבה
22 וירא והנה [חרבו יום רביעי לשבת] באחד בחודש הריאשון

1 [In] the year four hundred and eighty of Noah's life, Noah reached the end of them. And God
2 said, "My Spirit will not reside in man forever. Their days shall be fixed at one hundred and twenty
3 years until the end of the waters of the flood. And the waters of the flood burst over the earth. In the year six hundred
4 of Noah's life, in the second month, on the first (day) of the week, on its seventeenth (day), on that day
5 all the fountains of the great deep were broken up and the windows of heaven were opened and rain fell upon
6 the earth forty days and forty nights, until the twenty-sixth day of the third
7 month, the fifth day of the week. One hundred and fifty days did the waters hold sway over the earth,
8 until the fourteenth day in the seventh month, the third (day) of the week. At the end of
9 one hundred and fifty days, the waters came down two days, the fourth day and the fifth day, and the
10 sixth day, the ark rested in the mountains of Hurarat (Ararat), it was the seventeenth day of the seventh month.
11 And the waters continued diminishing until the tenth month, on its first (day), the fourth day
12 of the week, the peaks of the mountains began to be visible. And at the end of forty days, when the peaks of the mountains had become visible,
13 Noah opened the window of the ark the first day of the week, which is the tenth day
14 of the eleventh month. And he sent out the dove to see whether the waters had diminished , but it did not
15 find a place of rest and returned to him, to the ark. And he waited yet another seven days
16 and again sent it out, and it returned to him, and in its beak was a newly plucked olive leaf. It was day twenty
17 four of the eleventh month, the first (day) of the week. And Noah knew that the waters had diminished
18 from upon the earth. And at the end of another seven days, he sent the dove out, but it did not
19 come back again. It was the first day of the twelfth month, the first day

Column II:1–5

1 באחת ושש מאות שנה לחיי נוח ובשבעה עשר יום לחודש השני
2 יבשה הארץ באחד בשבת ביום ההוא יצא נוח מן התבה לקץ שנה
3 תמימה לימים שלוש מאות ששים וארבעה באחד בשבת בשבעה
4 אחת ושש נוח מן התבה למועד שנה
5 תמימה ויקץ נוח נוח מיינו וידע את אשר עשה

20 of the week. And at the end of the thirty days, after having sent out the dove which did not return
21 again, the waters dried up from upon the earth and Noah removed the cover of the ark
22 and looked, and behold, they had dried up on the fourth day of the week, on the first (day) of the first month

1 in the year six-hundred and one of Noah's life. On the seventeenth day of the second month
2 the land dried up, on the first (day) of the week. On that day, Noah went out of the ark, at the end of a complete
3 year of three-hundred and sixty-four days, on the first (day) of the week. On the seventh
4 … one and six… Noah from the ark, at the appointed time of a complete
5 year. *vacat* And Noah awoke from his wine and knew what

Appendix C

Text and Translation of *An Admonition Based on the Flood*

(4Q370)[1]

---

1. Text and translation is adapted from Newsom, DJD XIX, 85–97; García Martínez and Tigchelaar, *The Dead Sea Scrolls Study Edition*.

TEXT AND TRANSLATION OF AN ADMONITION BASED ON THE FLOOD

Column I

1 [ו]יעטר הרים תנ[ובה ו]שפך אכל על פניהם ופרו טוב השביע כלנפש כל אשר עשה רצוני יוכלו וישבעו אמר י[ה]וה

2 ויברכו את שם [קדש]י והני הם אז עשו הרע בעיני אמר יהוה ויאמרו אל במ[אלי]ליהם

3 וישפטם יהוה כ[כל]דרכיהם וכמחשבות יצר לבם ה[רע]וירעם עליהם בכח[ו וי]נעו כל

4 סוסדי א[רץ ימ]ים נבקעו מתהמות כל ארבות השמים נפתחו ופצו כל תהמו[ת מ]מים אדרים

5 וארבות השמים ה[רי]קו סטר[ו]אבדם במבול[...].[...ים כלם ...][...]ה

6 עלכן נ[מחו]כל אש[ר ב]חרבה וי[מ]ת האדם ו[הבהמה וכל]צפר כל כנף והג[בור]ים לוא נמלטו

7 ו[...][...] ויעש אל [... וא]ת קשתו נתן[בענן ל]מען יזכור ברית

8 [... ולוא יהיה עוד]מי המבול ל[שחת ולוא יפ]תחו המון מים

9 [...]ם עשי ושחקים [...] למים [...]

10 [...]...[...]

TEXT AND TRANSLATION OF AN ADMONITION BASED ON THE FLOOD

1. [And] He crowned the mountains with pro[duce and po]ured out food upon them and with good fruit He satisfied every living being. "Let all who do My will eat and be satisfied," said Yahweh,
2. "And let them bless My holy name. But look, they have done what is evil in My eyes," said Yahweh. And they rebelled against God in their deeds.
3. And Yahweh judged them ac[cording to al]l their ways, and according to the thoughts of the [evil] inclination of their heart. And He thundered against them with [His] strength. [And] all the
4. foundations of the ea[rth] shook, [and the wa]ters were broken up from the deeps. All the windows of the heavens were opened and all of the deeps overflowed [with] mighty waters.
5. And the windows of the heavens p[our]ed out rain. And He destroyed them in the Flood [...] ... them all ... [...]
6. Therefore, all which was on dry ground was [wiped out,] and mankind, and [beasts and all] birds, every winged being, died. And the giants did not escape
7. And [...] and God made [...and] He placed His rainbow [in the clouds to] remember the covenant
8. [...and never again will] the waters of the Flood [come] for [destruction, or will the tumult of the waters [be op]ened
9. [...] they made and clouds [...] for water
10. [...] ... [...] ... [...]

Column II

1 מעון ידרשו .[...]
2 יצדיק יהוה ש[...]
3 ויטהרם מעונם [...]
4 רעתם בדעתם בי[ן טוב לרע ... כחציר]
5 יצמחו וכצל ימיהם ע[ל הארץ ... מעולם]
6 ועד עולם הוא ירחם [...]
7 גבורת יהוה זכרו נפל[אות ...]
8 מפני פחדו ותשמח נפ[שכם ...]
9 משניכם אל תמרו דבר[י יהוה ...]

TEXT AND TRANSLATION OF AN ADMONITION BASED ON THE FLOOD

1 Because of iniquity they will seek […]
2 Yahweh will make righteous […]
3 And He will cleanse them from their iniquity […]
4 their evil, in their knowledge o[f good and evil … like grass]
5 they spring up and like a shadow are their days o[n earth … from eternity]
6 to eternity He will have compassion […]
7 the strength of Yahweh; remember the won[ders …]
8 because of the fear of Him; and let [your] so[ul] rejoice […]
9 those who follow you. Do not rebel against the word[s of Yahweh …]

Appendix D
Text and Translation of Paraphrase of Genesis and Exodus
(4Q422)[1]

---

1. Text and translation is adapted from García Martínez and Tigchelaar, *The Dead Sea Scrolls Study Edition*; Feldman, "The Story of the Flood in 4Q422," in Dimant and Kratz, eds., *The Dynamics of Language and Exegesis at Qumran*, 57–77.

Column I

1–5 [...]
6 [...] השמים והארץ וכול [צבאם עשה בד.[...]
7 [...] מלאכתו אש[ר עשה ורוח קודש]ו ...
8 [...] כול הנפ[ש החיה והרמש]ת על הארץ [...]
9 [...] ע[ץ המשילו לאכול פר]י האדמה]
10 [...] [ל]ב[ל]תי אכול מעץ הד[עת ...
11 [...] ו[י]קום עליו וישכחו[ן ...]
12 [...][ביוצר רע ולמעש]י רשעה]
13 [...][שלו]ם ...]

Column II

1 [...ו]ירא אל כי א[רבה ו.[...]
2 [...]ב את ה[...]
2ᵃ [...צ]דיק ב[ד]ורו ע[ל הארץ ... א]תו אל חיה
3 [...] נצלו על [הארץ ... ע]ל הארץ כי א[...]
4 [... את נוח]ואת בניו א[שתו ונשי בניו מפני]מי המבול ומ[...]
5 והע[וף ויס]גור אל בעדם [... צו]העליו את כ[ו]ל [...] [... כול]
6 אשר בחרבה כֿלֿ א[שר   ]ארובות השמי[ם]נפ[ת]חו ח.[... גשם הרי]קו על הארץ
7 תחת כול השמ[י]ם ... ל]עלות מים על האר[ץ ... ארבעים יום וארב]עים]
8 לילה היה ה[גשם ע]ל הארץ ... המי[ם גב]רו] על [הארץ ... למען]טהר חיט ולמען
9 דעת כבוד על[יון ...][את]...[הגיש לפניו
10 ויאר על [ה]שמ[י]ם ... הא[רץ וא[...]ימה אות לדור[ות]
11 עולם לחרא[... ולוא עוד] היות מבול] לשחת הארץ [...]
12 [מו]עדי יום ולילה [... מאורות להאיר ע[ל שמים ואר[ץ ...]
13 [הארץ ומ[ל]ו]אה ... הכו]ל נתן] לאדם

1–5 [...]
6 [... the heavens and the earth and all] their host He made by ... [...]
7 [... His work whi]ch He had done and [His] Holy Spirit [...]
8 [... every] living [creat]ure and what moves [on the earth ...]
9 [...tr]ee, He gave him dominion to eat the frui[t of the ground]
10 [...] with the [excep]tion of eating from the tree of kn[owledge ...]
11 [... and] he rose up against him and they forgot [...]
12 [...] with an evil inclination and for work[s of wickedness]
13 [...] peace [...]

1 [...and God saw that] great, and [...]
2 [...] ... the [...]
2ª [... righteous in] his generation up[on the earth ... with]him God kept alive
3 [...] were saved on [the earth ... o]n the earth for [...]
4 [... Noah] and his sons, [his] w[ife and the wives of his sons from] the waters of the Flood and [...]
5 and the bir[ds ... and] God [sh]ut behind them [... commanded] him a[l]l [...] [all]
6 which was on dry ground all [...] the windows of heaven were opened ... [and] they [pou]red out [rain] on the earth
7 under all the heaven[s ... to] raise water upon the ear[th ...forty] days and for[ty]
8 nights there was [rain] up[on the earth ... the water]s were migh[ty] upon [the earth in order to] cleanse sin and in order to
9 make known the glory of the Mo[st High ...] ... [...] He placed before him
10 and it illuminated [the] heav[ens ... the ea]rth and [...] ... a sign for the generation[s of]
11 eternity, to ... [... and no more] will there be a Flood [to destroy the earth ...]
12 [the fixed ti]mes of day and night [... luminaries to illuminate] heaven and ear[th...]
13 [the earth and] its [fu]ll[ne]ss [...everythi]ng He gave [to mankind]

Column III

1 [...]ת ולוא [...]
2 [ש]תי המיל[דות ... וישליכו את]
3 [ב]ניהם ליוא[ר ...]...[...] א[ותם
4 [ו]ישלח להמה את מו[שה ...]במראת[...]
5 באותות ומופתים [...]תמכו וע[...]אחי חבר עמי
6 וישלחם אל פרעוה [...].ות נגועים [...]נפ[ל]אות למצרים[...] ויביאו דברו
7 אל פרעוה לשלח א[ת עמם ו]יחזק את לב[ו ל]חטוא למען דעת א[ת כבד]אל עד דו[רות]עולם ויפך לדם[מימ]יהמה
8 הצפרדעים בכול אר[צם] וכנים בכול גבול[ם ו]ערוב [בב]תיהסה ו[היה נג]ע בכול פ[...]הסה ויגוף בדב[ר את]
9 מקניהסה ובהמתם ל[מו]ת הסגיר ישי[ת חו]שך בארצם ואפלה ב[בתי]הסה בל ירא[ה] איש את אחיו [ויד]
10 בברד ארצם ואדמת[ם ב]חנמל לה[אביד כו]ל פרי אוכ[ל]ם ויבא ארבה לכסות עין הא[רץ] חסל כבד בכול גבולם
11 לאכול כול ירוק בא[רצם] ל[...]ם ויח[זק]אל את לב [פרעו]ה לבלתי [ש]לח[ם]ולמען הרבות מופתים
12 [ויק בכורם] רשית לכו[ל] אונם ...[...]...[...]

1   [...] and not [...]
2   the two mid[wives ... and they threw]
3   their sons into the Nil[e ...] ... [... t]hem
4   [and] He sent Moses to them [...] in the vision of [...]
5   with signs and wonders [...] ... and ... [...] my brother, as a companion with me.
6   And He sent them to Pharaoh [...] ... plagues [...] wo[nd]ers to Egypt [...] and they reported His word
7   to Pharaoh, to let [their people] go. [And] He hardened [his] heart [so that he would] sin in order to make known [the glory of] God for eternal gener[ations] and He turned their [water] into blood.
8   Frogs were in all [their] lan[d], and lice in all [their] territory, [and] gnats (?) [in] their hou[ses], and [there was afflict]tion in all their [...] and He struck with pestil[ence]
9   their livestock, and their animals He delivered to [dea]th. He pla[ced dark]ness in their land, and dimness in their [houses] so that no-one could see his brother. [And He struck]
10 their land with hail, and their ground [with] frost to de[story al]l the fruit which they ea[t]. And He brought locusts to cover the face of the ea[rth], heavy locust in all their territory
11 to eat all the vegetables in [their] l[and ...] and God har[dened] the heart of [Pharao]h so that he would not [let them] go, and in order to multiply wonders.
12 [And He struck their firstborn,] the firstfruits of al[l their manhood ...] ... [...]

Bibliography

Abegg Jr., Martin G. with James E. Bowley and Edward M. Cook, in consultation with Emanuel Tov. *The Dead Sea Scrolls Concordance: The Non-Biblical Texts from Qumran.* Vol. 1. Leiden: Brill, 2003.

Abegg Jr., Martin, Peter W. Flint, and Eugene Ulrich. *The Dead Sea Scrolls Bible.* San Francisco: HarperSanFrancisco, 1999.

Alexander, P., and Geza Vermes. *Qumran Cave 4, XIX: 4Q Serekh Ha-Yahad and Two Related Texts.* Discoveries in the Judaean Desert XXVI. Oxford: Clarendon, 1998.

Allegro, J. M., with A. A. Anderson. *Qumran Cave 4, I (4Q158–4Q186).* Discoveries in the Judaean Desert V. Oxford: Clarendon, 1968.

Avigad, Nahman, and Yigael Yadin. *A Genesis Apocryphon: A Scroll from the Wilderness of Judaea: Description and Contents of the Scroll, Facsimiles, Transcription and Translation of Columns II, XIX–XXII.* Jerusalem: Magnes and Heikhal Ha-Sefer, 1956.

Baillet, M. *Qumran Grotte 4, III (4Q482–4Q520).* Discoveries in the Judaean Desert VII. Oxford: Clarendon, 1982.

Baillet, M., J. T. Milik, and Roland de Vaux. *Les 'Petites Grottes' de Qumran.* Discoveries in the Judaean Desert III. Oxford: Clarendon, 1962.

Barthelemy, D., and J. T. Milik. *Qumran Cave 1.* Discoveries in the Judaean Desert I. Oxford: Clarendon, 1955.

Baumgarten, Joseph M. "The Calendar of the Book of Jubilees and the Bible." In *Studies in Qumran Law,* 101–14. SJLA 24; Leiden: Brill, 1997.

———. *Qumran Cave 4, XIII: The Damascus Document (4Q266–273).* Discoveries in the Judaean Desert XVIII. Oxford: Clarendon, 1996.

Baumgarten, J., et al. *Qumran Cave 4, XXV: Halakhic Texts.* Discoveries in the Judaean Desert XXXV. Oxford: Clarendon, 1999.

Bekkum, Wout J. van. "The Lesson of the Flood: מבול in Rabbinic Tradition." In *Interpretations of the Flood,* edited by Florentino García Martínez and Gerard P. Luttikhuizen, 124–33. Themes in Biblical Narrative 1. Leiden: Brill, 1998.

Benoit, P., J. T. Milik, and Roland de Vaux. *Les grottes de Murabbaat.* Discoveries in the Judaean Desert II (IIa). Oxford: Clarendon, 1961.

Bernasconi, Rocco. "A Literary Analysis of the *Genesis Apocryphon*." *Aramaic Studies* 9.1 (2011) 139–62.

Bernstein, Moshe J. "4Q252: From Re-Written Bible to Biblical Commentary." *Journal of Jewish Studies* 45 (1994) 1–27.

———. "4Q252: Method and Context, Genre and Sources: A Response to George J. Brooke." *The Jewish Quarterly Review* 85.1–2 (July–October 1994) 61–79.

———. "4Q252 i 2 לא ידור רוחי באדם לעולם: Biblical Text or Biblical Interpretation?" *Revue de Qumran* 16 (1994) 421–27.

———. "Contours of Genesis Interpretation at Qumran: Contents, Context, and Nomenclature." In *Studies in Ancient Midrash*, edited by James L. Kugel, 57–85. Cambridge, MA: Harvard University Press, 2001.

———. "Divine Titles and Epithets and the Sources of the *Genesis Apocryphon*." *Journal of Biblical Literature* 128.2 (2009) 291–310.

———. "From the Watchers to the Flood: Story and Exegesis in the Early Columns of the *Genesis Apocryphon*." In *Reworking the Bible: Apocryphal and Related Texts at Qumran. Proceedings of a Joint Symposium by the Orion Center for the Study of the Dead Sea Scrolls and Associated Literature and the Hebrew University Institute for Advanced Studies Research Group on Qumran, 15–17 January 2002*, edited by Esther G. Chazon, Devorah Dimant, and Ruth A Clements, 39–63. Studies on the Texts of the Desert of Judah 58. Leiden: Brill, 2005.

———. "Is the Genesis Apocryphon a Unity? What Sort of Unity Were You Looking For?" *Aramaic Studies* 8.1–2 (2010) 107–34.

———. "Noah and the Flood at Qumran." In *The Provo International Conference on the Dead Sea Scrolls: New Texts, Reformulated Issues, and Technological Innovations*, edited by Donald W. Parry and Eugene C. Ulrich, 199–231. Leiden: Brill, 1999.

———. "Re-Arrangement, Anticipation and Harmonization as Exegetical Features in the Genesis Apocryphon." *Dead Sea Discoveries* 3.1 (1996) 37–57.

Bernstein, M., and G. Brooke, with the assistance of J. Høgenhavn. *Qumran Cave 4, I: 4Q158–186*. Discoveries in the Judaean Desert V(a). Rev. ed. Oxford: Clarendon.

Bonani, Georges, Susan Ivy, Willy Wölfli, Magen Broshi, Israel Carmi, and John Strugnell. "Radiocarbon Dating of Fourteen Dead Sea Scrolls." *Radiocarbon* 34.3 (1992) 843–49.

Brooke, George J. "4Q252 as Early Jewish Commentary." *Revue de Qumran* 65–68.17 (November 1996) 385–401.

———. "Commentary on Genesis A." In *Outside the Bible: Ancient Jewish Writings Related to Scripture*. Vol. 1, edited by Louis H. Feldman, James L. Kugel, and Lawrence H. Schiffman, 211–15. Philadelphia: Jewish Publication Society, 2013.

———. "From Bible to Midrash: Approaches to Biblical Interpretation in the Dead Sea Scrolls by Modern Interpreters." In *Northern Lights on the Dead Sea Scrolls: Proceedings of the NordicQumran Network 2003–2006*, edited by Anders Klostergaard Petersen, Torleif Elgvin, Cecilia Wassen, Hanne von Weissenberg, Mikael Winninge, and assistant editor Martin Ehrensvärd, 1–19. Studies on the Texts of the Desert of Judah, 80. Leiden: Brill, 2009.

———. "The Genre of 4Q252: From Poetry to Pesher." *Dead Sea Discoveries* 1.2 (August 1994) 161–79.

———. "Some Remarks on 4Q252 and the Text of Genesis." *Textus* 19 (1998) 1–25.

———. "Thematic Commentaries on Prophetic Scriptures." In *Biblical Interpretation at Qumran*, edited by Matthias Henze, 134–57. Studies in the Dead Sea Scrolls and Related Literature. Grand Rapids, MI: Eerdmans, 2005.

———. "The Thematic Content of 4Q252." *The Jewish Quarterly Review*, 85.1–2 (July–October 1994) 33–59.

Brooke, G. J., J. Collins, P. Flint, J. Greenfield, E. Larson, C. Newsom, E. Puech, L. H. Schiffman, M. Stone, and J. Trebolle Barrera, in consultation with J. VanderKam. *Qumran Cave 4, XVII: Parabiblical Texts, Part 3*. Discoveries in the Judaean Desert XXII. Oxford: Clarendon, 1996.

Broshi, M., E. Eshel, J. Fitzmyer, E. Larson, C. Newsom, L. Schiffman, M. Smith, M. Stone, J. Strugnell, and A. Yardeni, in consultation with J. C. VanderKam. *Qumran Cave 4, XIV: Parabiblical Texts, Part 2*. Discoveries in the Judaean Desert XIX. Oxford: Clarendon, 1995.

Brown, Francis., S. R. Driver, and Charles A. Briggs. *The Brown-Driver-Briggs Hebrew and English Lexicon*. Peabody, MA: Hendrickson, 2001.

Charlesworth, James H., ed. *The Old Testament Pseudepigrapha*, 2 vols. New York, NY: Doubleday, 1985.

Chazon, Esther G. "The Creation and Fall of Adam in the Dead Sea Scrolls." In *The Book of Genesis in Jewish and Oriental Christian Interpretation: A Collection of Essays*, edited by Judith Frishman and Lucas Van Rompay, 13–24. Traditio exegetica Graeca 5. Leuven: Peeters, 1997.

Collins, John J. and Daniel C. Harlow, eds. *The Eerdmans Dictionary of Early Judaism*. Grand Rapids, MI: Eerdmans, 2010.

Cotton, H. M. and A. Yardeni. *Aramaic, Hebrew, and Greek Documentary Texts from Nahal Hever and Other Sites, with an Appendix Containing Alleged Qumran Texts*. Discoveries in the Judaean Desert XXVII. Oxford: Clarendon, 1997.

Crawford, Sidnie White. *Rewriting Scripture in Second Temple Times*. Grand Rapids, MI: Eerdmans, 2008.

———. "A View from the Caves: Who Put the Scrolls in There?" *Biblical Archaeology Review* 37.5 (September/October 2011) 30–39, 69.

Cross, Frank Moore. *The Ancient Library of Qumran and Modern Biblical Studies*. New York, 1958; 3rd ed. Sheffield, 1996.

———. "The Development of Jewish Scripts." In *The Bible and the Ancient Near East: Essays in Honor of William Foxwell Albright*, edited by G. E. Wright, 133–202. Garden City, NY: Doubleday, 1961; Anchor, reprint 1965.

Cross, Frank M., D. W. Parry, and Eugene Ulrich. *Qumran Cave 4, XII: 1-2 Samuel*. Discoveries in the Judaean Desert XVII. Oxford: Clarendon, 2002.

Crouse, Bill, and Gordon Franz. "Mount Cudi – The True Mountain of Noah's Ark." *Bible and Spade* 19.4 (Fall, 2006) 99–111.

Davies, Philip R. "Calendrical Change and Qumran Origins: An Assessment of VanderKam's Theory." *The Catholic Biblical Quarterly* 45 (1983) 80–89.

de Vaux, Roland. *Archaeology and the Dead Sea Scrolls*. The Schweich Lectures, 1959. Rev. ed. London: Oxford University Press, 1973.

de Vaux, Roland and J. T. Milik. *Qumran Grotte 4, II: I. Archeologie; II. Tefillin, Mezuzot et Targums (4Q128–4Q157)*. Discoveries in the Judaean Desert VI. Oxford: Clarendon, 1977.

Dimant, Devorah. "Noah in Early Jewish Literature." In *Biblical Figures Outside the Bible*, edited by Michael E. Stone and Theodore A. Bergren, 123–50. Harrisburg, PA: Trinity International, 1998.

———. *Qumran Cave 4, XXI: Parabiblical Texts, Part 4: Pseudo-Prophetic Texts*. Discoveries in the Judaean Desert XXX. Oxford: Clarendon, 2001.

Dimant, Devorah, ed. *Scripture and Interpretation: Qumran Texts that Rework the Bible.* Beihefte zur Zeitschrift für die alttestamentliche Wissenschaft 449. Berlin: De Gruyter, 2014.

Dimant, Devorah, and Reinhard Kratz, eds. *The Dynamics of Language and Exegesis at Qumran.* Forschungen zum Alten Testament 2, Reihe 35. Tübingen: Mohr Siebeck, 2009.

Eisenman, Robert, and Michael Wise. *The Dead Sea Scrolls Uncovered.* New York: Barnes & Noble, 1994.

Elgvin, Torleif. "The Genesis Section of 4Q422 (4QParaGenExod)." *Dead Sea Discoveries* 1.2 (August, 1994) 180–96.

Eshel, Esther. "Genesis Apocryphon." In *The Eerdmans Dictionary of Early Judaism,* edited by John J. Collins and Daniel C. Harlow, 664–67. Grand Rapids, MI: Eerdmans, 2010.

———. "The Genesis Apocryphon: A Chain of Traditions." In *The Dead Sea Scrolls and Contemporary Culture: Proceedings of the International Conference held at the Israel Museum, Jerusalem (July 6-8, 2008),* edited by Adolfo D. Roitman, Lawrence H. Schiffman, and Shani L. Tzoref, 181–94. Studies on the Texts of the Desert of Judah, 93. Leiden: Brill, 2011.

———. "Hermeneutical Approaches to Genesis in the Dead Sea Scrolls." In *The Book of Genesis in Jewish and Oriental Christian Interpretation: A Collection of Essays,* edited by Judith Frishman and Lucas Van Rompay, 1–12. Traditio exegetica Graeca, 5. Leuven: Peeters, 1997.

Falk, Daniel. "Anatomy of a Scene: Noah's Covenant in Genesis Apocryphon XI." In *Northern Lights on the Dead Sea Scrolls: Proceedings of the NordicQumran Network 2003–2006,* edited by Anders Klostergaard Petersen, Torleif Elgvin, Cecilia Wassen, Hanne von Weissenberg, Mikael Winninge, and assistant editor Martin Ehrensvärd, 21–39. Studies on the Texts of the Desert of Judah, 80. Leiden: Brill, 2009.

———. *The Parabiblical Texts: Strategies for Extending the Scriptures among the Dead Sea Scrolls.* Companion to the Qumran Scrolls, 8. Library of Second Temple Studies, 63. New York: T. & T. Clark, 2007.

Feldman, Ariel. "The Reworking of the Biblical Flood Story in 4Q370." *Henoch* 29 (2007) 31–49.

———. "The Story of the Flood in 4Q422." In *The Dynamics of Exegesis and Language at Qumran,* edited by Devorah Dimant and Reinhard Kratz, 57–77. Forschungen zum Alten Testament 2, Reihe 35. Tübingen: Mohr Siebeck, 2009.

———. "פרשת המבול המקראית במגילות קומראן" (1Q19, 4Q370, 4Q422, 4Q464 and 4Q577)." PhD diss., University of Haifa, 2007.

Feldman, Louis H., James L. Kugel, and Lawrence H. Schiffman, eds. *Outside the Bible: Ancient Jewish Writings Related to Scripture.* 3 vols. Philadelphia: Jewish Publication Society, 2013.

Fishbane, Michael. "Use, Authority and Interpretation of Mikra at Qumran." In *Mikra: Text, Translation, Reading & Interpretation of the Hebrew Bible in Ancient Judaism & Early Christianity,* edited by Martin Jan Mulder, 339–77. Peabody, MA: Hendrickson, 2004.

Fitzmyer, Joseph A. "Genesis Apocryphon." In vol. 1 of *Encyclopedia of the Dead Sea Scrolls,* edited by Lawrence Schiffman and James C. Vanderkam, 302–4. 2 vols. Oxford: Oxford University Press, 2000.

———. *The Genesis Apocryphon of Qumran Cave 1 (1Q20): A Commentary.* Biblica et Orientalia, 18b. 3rd ed. Rome: Pontificio Istituto Biblico, 2004.

———, consulting editor. *Qumran Cave 4, XV: Sapiential Texts, Part 1*. Discoveries in the Judaean Desert XX. Oxford: Clarendon, 1997.

———, consulting editor. *Qumran Cave 4, XXIV: Sapiential Texts, Part 2, 4QInstruction: 4Q415 ff*. Discoveries in the Judaean Desert XXXIV. Oxford: Clarendon, 1999.

Flint, Peter W. and Eugene Ulrich. *Qumran Cave 1, II: The Isaiah Scrolls*. Discoveries in the Judaean Desert XXXII. Oxford: Clarendon, 2010.

Frishman, Judith, and Lucas Van Rompay, eds. *The Book of Genesis in Jewish and Oriental Christian Interpretation: A Collection of Essays*. Traditio exegetica Graeca 5. Leuven: Peeters, 1997.

Fröhlich, Ida. "'Narrative Exegesis' in the Dead Sea Scrolls." In *Biblical Perspectives: Early Use and Interpretation of the Bible in Light of the Dead Sea Scrolls. Proceedings of the First International Symposium of the Orion Center for the Study of the Dead Sea Scrolls and Associated Literature, 12–14 May 1996*, edited by Michael E. Stone and Esther G. Chazon, 81–99. Studies on the Texts of the Desert of Judah, 28. Leiden: Brill, 1998.

———. "Themes, Structure, and Genre of Pesher Genesis: A Response to George J. Brooke." *The Jewish Quarterly Review* 85.1–2 (July-October 1994) 81–90.

García Martínez, Florentino. *The Dead Sea Scrolls Translated: The Qumran Texts in English*. Leiden: Brill; 2nd ed. Grand Rapids, MI: Eerdmans, 1996.

———. "Interpretations of the Flood in the Dead Sea Scrolls." In *Interpretations of the Flood*, edited by Florentino García Martínez and Gerard P. Luttikhuizen, 86–108. Themes in Biblical Narrative 1. Leiden: Brill, 1998.

García Martínez, Florentino, and Gerard P. Luttikhuizen, eds. *Interpretations of the Flood*. Leiden: Brill, 1998.

García Martínez, Florentino, and Eibert J. C. Tigchelaar. *The Dead Sea Scrolls Study Edition*, 2 vols. Leiden: Brill, 1997, 1998.

García Martínez, F., Eibert J. C. Tigchelaar, and A. S. van der Woude. *Qumran Cave 11, II: 11Q2–18, 11Q20–31*. Discoveries in the Judaean Desert XXIII. Oxford: Clarendon, 1998.

Geist, Andrew, and James C. VanderKam. "The Four Places That Belong to the Lord (Jubilees 4.26)." *Journal for the Study of the Pseudepigrapha* 22.2 (2012) 146–62.

Gropp, D.M. *Wadi Daliyeh II: The Samaria Papyri from Wadi Daliyeh*; James C. VanderKam and M. Brady, consulting editors. *Qumran Cave 4, XXVIII: Miscellanea, Part 2*. Discoveries in the Judaean Desert XXVIII. Oxford: Clarendon, 2001.

Grossman, Maxine L., ed. *Rediscovering the Dead Sea Scrolls: An Assessment of Old and New Approaches and Methods*. Grand Rapids, MI: Eerdmans, 2010.

Hendel, Ronald S. "4Q252 and the Flood Chronology of Genesis 7–8: A Text-Critical Solution." *Dead Sea Discoveries* 2 (1995) 72–79.

———. *The Text of Genesis 1–11: Textual Studies and Critical Edition*. New York: Oxford University Press, 1998.

Henze, Matthias, ed. *Biblical Interpretation at Qumran*. Studies in the Dead Sea Scrolls and Related Literature. Grand Rapids, MI: Eerdmans, 2005.

Herbert, Edward D., and Emanuel Tov, eds. *The Bible as Book: The Hebrew Bible and the Judaean Desert Discoveries*. London: British Library and New Castle: Oak Knoll in association with Grand Haven: Scriptorium, 2002.

Jassen, Alex P. "Admonition Based on the Flood." In *Outside the Bible: Ancient Jewish Writings Related to Scripture*. Vol. 1, edited by Louis H. Feldman, James L. Kugel, and Lawrence H. Schiffman, 263–71. Philadelphia: Jewish Publication Society, 2013.

———. "A New Suggestion for the Reconstruction of 4Q370 1 i 2 and the Blessing of the Most High (*Elyon*) in Second Temple Judaism." *Dead Sea Discoveries* 17 (2010) 88–113.

Jastrow, Marcus. *Dictionary of the Targumim, the Talmud Babli and Yerushalmi, and the Midrashic Literature*. Peabody, MA: Hendrickson, 2006.

Jaubert, A. "Le Calendrier des Jubiles et de la Secte de Qumran. Ses Origines Bibliques." *Vetus Testamentum* 3 (1953) 250–64.

Jull, A. J. Timothy, Douglas J. Donahue, Magen Broshi, and Emanuel Tov. "Radiocarbon Dating of Scrolls and Linen Fragments from the Judean Desert." *Radiocarbon* 37.1 (1995) 11–19.

Kugel, James L. "Jubilees." In *Outside the Bible: Ancient Jewish Writings Related to Scripture*. Vol. 1, edited by Louis H. Feldman, James L. Kugel, and Lawrence H. Schiffman, 272–465. Philadelphia: Jewish Publication Society, 2013.

Kutsch, Ernst. "Der Kalender des Jubiläenbuches und das Neue Testament." *Vetus Testamentum* 11 (1961) 39–47.

Kutscher, E.Y. "Dating the Language of the Genesis Apocryphon." *Journal of Biblical Literature* 76 (1957) 288–92.

———. "The Language of the 'Genesis Apocryphon': A Preliminary Study." In *Aspects of the Dead Sea Scrolls*, edited by Chaim Rabin and Yigael Yadin, 1–35. Jerusalem Scripta hierosolymitana, 4. Jerusalem, 1958.

Leith, M. J. W. *Wadi Daliyeh I: The Wadi Daliyeh Seal Impressions*. Discoveries in the Judaean Desert XXIV. Oxford: Clarendon, 1997.

Lewis, Jack P. *A Study of the Interpretation of Noah and the Flood in Jewish and Christian Literature*. Leiden: Brill, 1968.

Lim, Timothy H. "The Chronology of the Flood Story in a Qumran Text (4Q252)." *Journal of Jewish Studies* 43.2 (1992) 288–98.

Lim, Timothy H., and John J. Collins, eds. *The Oxford Handbook of the Dead Sea Scrolls*. Oxford: Oxford University Press, 2010.

Longacre, Drew G. "Charting the Textual Waters: Textual Issues in the Chronology of the Genesis Flood Narrative." In *Grappling with the Chronology of the Genesis Flood*, edited by Steven W. Boyd and Andrew A. Snelling, 231–96. Green Forest, AR: Master, 2014.

Machiela, Daniel A. *The Dead Sea Genesis Apocryphon: A New Text and Translation with Introduction and Special Treatment of Columns 13–17*. Leiden: Brill, 2009.

———. "'Each to His Own Inheritance' Geography as an Evaluative Tool in the Genesis Apocryphon." *Dead Sea Discoveries* 15.1 (2008) 50–66.

———. "Flood." In *The Eerdmans Dictionary of Early Judaism*, edited by John J. Collins and Daniel C. Harlow, 645–46. Grand Rapids, MI: Eerdmans, 2010.

Magness, Jodi. *The Archaeology of Qumran and the Dead Sea Scrolls*. Grand Rapids, MI: Eerdmans, 2002.

Morgenstern, Matthew. "A New Clue to the Original Length of the Genesis Apocryphon." *Journal of Jewish Studies* 47 (1996) 345–47.

Morgenstern, Matthew J., and Michael Segal. "The Genesis Apocryphon." In *Outside the Bible: Ancient Jewish Writings Related to Scripture*. Vol. 1, edited by Louis H. Feldman, James L. Kugel, and Lawrence H. Schiffman, 263–71. Philadelphia: Jewish Publication Society, 2013.

Mulder, Martin Jan, ed. *Mikra: Text, Translation, Reading & Interpretation of the Hebrew Bible in Ancient Judaism & Early Christianity*. Peabody, MA: Hendrickson, 2004.

Muraoka, Takamitsu. "Further Notes on the Aramaic of the *Genesis Apocryphon*." *Revue de Qumran* 61.16 (September 1993) 39–48.
Naveh, Joseph. *Early History of the Alphabet: An Introduction to West Semitic Epigraphy and Palaeography*. 2nd rev. ed. Jerusalem, Israel: The Magnes Press, The Hebrew University, Jerusalem, 1987.
Newsom, Carol A. "4Q370: An Admonition Based on the Flood." *Revue de Qumran* 49–52.13 (October 1988) 23–43.
———. "4QAdmonition Based on the Flood." In *Qumran Cave 4, XIV: Parabiblical Texts, Part 2*, edited by Broshi, M., et al., 85–97. Discoveries in the Judaean Desert XIX. Oxford: Clarendon, 1995.
Nickelsburg, George W. E. *Jewish Literature between the Bible and the Mishnah: A Historical and Literary Introduction*. 2nd ed. Minneapolis, MN: Fortress, 2005.
Oegema, Gerbern S. "Tradition-Historical Studies on 4Q252." In *Qumran-Messianism: Studies on the Messianic Expectations in the Dead Sea Scrolls*, edited by James H. Charlesworth, Hermann Lichtenberger, and Gerbern S. Oegema, 155–74. Tübingen: Mohr Siebeck, 1998.
Peters, Dorothy M. *Noah Traditions in the Dead Sea Scrolls: Conversations and Controversies of Antiquity*. Early Judaism and Its Literature 26. Atlanta, GA: Society of Biblical Literature, 2008.
Pfann, Stephen J., James C. Vanderkam, and M. Brady, consulting editors. *Cryptic Texts; Miscellenea, Part 1: Qumran Cave 4, XXVI*. Discoveries in the Judaean Desert XXXVI. Oxford: Clarendon, 2000.
Puech, E. *Qumran Cave 4, XVIII: Textes hebreux (4Q521–4Q528, 4Q576–4Q579)*. Discoveries in the Judaean Desert XXV. Oxford: Clarendon, 1998.
———. *Qumran Cave 4, XXII: Textes arameens, premiere partie: 4Q529–549*. Discoveries in the Judaean Desert XXXI. Oxford: Clarendon, 2001.
———. *Qumran Cave 4, XXVII: Textes arameens, deuxieme partie: 4Q550–575, 580–582*. Discoveries in the Judaean Desert XXXVII. Oxford: Clarendon, 2009.
Qimron, Elisha. *The Hebrew of the Dead Sea Scrolls*. Harvard Semitic Series 29. Harvard Semitic Museum Publications, 1986; repr., Winona Lake, IN: Eisenbrauns, 2008.
———. "Towards a New Edition of the Genesis Apocryphon." *Journal for the Study of the Pseudepigrapha* 10 (1992) 11–18.
Qimron, E., and J. Strugnell. *Qumran Cave 4, V: Miqsat Ma'ase ha-Torah*. Discoveries in the Judaean Desert X. Oxford: Clarendon, 1994.
Reymond, Eric D. *Qumran Hebrew: An Overview of Orthography, Phonology, and Morphology*. Atlanta, GA: Society of Biblical Literature, 2014.
Roitman, Adolfo D., Lawrence H. Schiffman, and Shani L. Tzoref, eds. *The Dead Sea Scrolls and Contemporary Culture: Proceedings of the International Conference held at the Israel Museum, Jerusalem (July 6-8, 2008)*. Studies on the Texts of the Desert of Judah, 93. Leiden: Brill, 2011.
Sanders, J. A. *The Psalms Scroll of Qumran Cave 11 (11QPs^a)*. Discoveries in the Judaean Desert IV. Oxford: Clarendon, 1965.
Saukkonen, Juhana. *The Story Behind the Text: Scriptural Interpretation in 4Q252*. Helsinki: University of Helsinki Press, 2005.
Scanlin, Harold. *The Dead Sea Scrolls & Modern Translations of the Old Testament*. Wheaton, IL: Tyndale House, 1993.
Schiffman, Lawrence H. *Reclaiming the Dead Sea Scrolls: Their True Meaning for Judaism and Christianity*. New Haven and London: Yale University Press, 2009.

———, ed. *Archaeology and History in the Dead Sea Scrolls*. Sheffield: JSOT, 1990.

Schiffman, Lawrence H. and James C. VanderKam, eds. *Encyclopedia of the Dead Sea Scrolls*. 2 Vols. Oxford: Oxford University Press, 2000.

Segal, Michael. "The Literary Relationship between the Genesis Apocryphon and Jubilees: The Chronology of Abram and Sarai's Descent to Egypt." *Aramaic Studies* 8.1–2 (2010) 71–88.

Shanks, Hershel, ed. *Understanding the Dead Sea Scrolls*. New York, NY: Random House, 1992.

Skehan, Patrick W., Eugene Ulrich, and Judith E. Sanderson. *Qumran Cave 4, IV: Palaeo-Hebrew and Greek Biblical Manuscripts*. Discoveries in the Judaean Desert IX. Oxford: Clarendon, 1992.

Stegemann, Hartmut. *The Library of Qumran: On the Essenes, Qumran, John the Baptist, and Jesus*. Grand Rapids, MI: Eerdmans, 1998.

Steiner, Richard C. "The Heading of the *Book of the Words of Noah* on a Fragment of the Genesis Apocryphon: New Light on a 'Lost' Work." *Dead Sea Discoveries* 2.1 (1995) 66–71.

———. "The Mountains of Ararat, Mount Lubar, and הר הקדם." *Journal of Jewish Studies* 42.2 (1991) 247–49.

Stern, Sacha. "Qumran Calendars and Sectarianism." In *The Oxford Handbook of the Dead Sea Scrolls*, edited by Timothy H. Lim and John J. Collins, 232–53. Oxford: Oxford University Press, 2010.

Talmon, S., J. Ben-Dov, and U. Glessmer. *Qumran Cave 4, XVI: Calendrical Texts*. Discoveries in the Judaean Desert XXI. Oxford: Clarendon, 2001.

Tov, Emanuel. "The Exodus Section of 4Q422." *Dead Sea Discoveries* 1.2 (August, 1994) 197–209.

———. *Scribal Practices and Approaches Reflected in the Texts Found in the Judean Desert*. Leiden: Brill, 2004.

———. *Textual Criticism of the Hebrew Bible*, 2nd rev. ed. Minneapolis, MN: Fortress, 2001.

———, editor. *The Texts from the Judaean Desert: Indices and an Introduction to the Discoveries in the Judaean Desert Series*. Discoveries in the Judaean Desert XXXIX. Oxford: Clarendon, 2002.

Tov, Emanuel with collaboration of R. A. Kraft. *The Greek Minor Prophets Scroll from Nahal Hever (8HevXIIgr)*. Discoveries in the Judaean Desert VIII. Oxford: Clarendon, 1990; reprint with corrections, 1995.

Ulrich, Eugene, ed. *The Biblical Qumran Scrolls: Transcriptions and Textual Variants*. Leiden, Boston: Brill, 2010.

Ulrich, Eugene, Frank Moore Cross, et al. *Qumran Cave 4, VII: Genesis to Numbers*. Discoveries in the Judaean Desert XII. Oxford: Clarendon, 1994; reprint 1999.

Ulrich, Eugene, Frank Moore Cross, Sidnie White Crawford, Julie Ann Duncan, Patrick W. Skehan, Emanuel Tov, and Julio Trebolle Barrera. *Qumran Cave 4, IX: Deuteronomy, Joshua, Judges, Kings*. Discoveries in the Judaean Desert XIV. Oxford: Clarendon, 1995.

Ulrich, Eugene, Frank Moore Cross, Russell E. Fuller, Judith E. Sanderson, Patrick W. Skehan, and Emanuel Tov. *Qumran Cave 4, X: The Prophets*. Discoveries in the Judaean Desert XV. Oxford: Clarendon, 1997.

Ulrich, Eugene, et al. *Qumran Cave 4, XI: Psalms to Chronicles*. Discoveries in the Judaean Desert XVI. Oxford: Clarendon, 2000.

VanderKam, James C. "The Book of Enoch and the Qumran Scrolls." In *The Oxford Handbook of the Dead Sea Scrolls*, edited by Timothy H. Lim and John J. Collins, 254–77. Oxford: Oxford University Press, 2010.

———. *Calendars in the Dead Sea Scrolls: Measuring Time*. New York: Routledge, 1998.

———. "Calendrical Texts and the Origins of the Dead Sea Scroll Community." In *Methods of Investigation of the Dead Sea Scrolls and the Khirbet Qumran Site: Present Realities and Future Prospects*, edited by Michael O. Wise, 371–88. New York: New York Academy of Sciences, 1994.

———. *The Dead Sea Scrolls and the Bible*. Grand Rapids, MI: Eerdmans, 2012.

———. *The Dead Sea Scrolls Today*. 2nd ed. Grand Rapids, MI: Eerdmans, 2010.

———. "The Origin, Character, and Early History of the 364-Day Calendar: A Reassessment of Jaubert's Hypothesis." *The Catholic Biblical Quarterly* 41 (1979) 390–411.

———. "The Textual Affinities of the Biblical Citations in the Genesis Apocryphon." *Journal of Biblical Literature* 97/1 (1978) 45–55.

———, consulting editor. *Qumran Cave 4, VIII: Parabiblical Texts, Part 1*. Discoveries in the Judaean Desert XIII. Oxford: Clarendon, 1994.

VanderKam, James C. and M. Brady (consulting editors). *Qumran Cave 4, VI: Poetical and Liturgical Texts, Part 1*. Discoveries in the Judaean Desert XI. Oxford: Clarendon, 1998.

———, consulting editors. *Qumran Cave 4, XX: Poetical and Liturgical Texts, Part 2*. Discoveries in the Judaean Desert XXIX. Oxford: Clarendon, 1999.

———, consulting editors. *Miscellaneous Texts from the Judaean Desert*. Discoveries in the Judaean Desert XXXVIII. Oxford: Clarendon, 2000.

———, consulting editors. *Qumran Cave 4, XXIII: Unidentified Fragments*. Discoveries in the Judaean Desert XXXIII. Oxford: Clarendon, 2001.

VanderKam, James C., and Peter Flint. *The Meaning of the Dead Sea Scrolls: Their Significance for Understanding the Bible, Judaism, Jesus, and Christianity*. New York, NY: HarperSanFrancisco, 2002.

Vermes, Geza. *The Complete Dead Sea Scrolls in English*. Revised edition. London and New York: Penguin, 2004.

Wacholder, B. Z., and Martin Abegg Jr. *A Preliminary Edition of the Unpublished Dead Sea Scrolls: The Hebrew and Aramaic Texts from Cave Four II*. Washington, DC: Biblical Archaeology Society, 1992.

Wise, Michael, Martin Abegg Jr., and Edward Cook. *The Dead Sea Scrolls: A New Translation*. San Francisco: HarperSanFrancisco, 1996.

Würthwein, Ernst. *The Text of the Old Testament*. 2nd ed. Grand Rapids, MI: Eerdmans, 1995.

Zahn, Molly M. "Rewritten Scripture." In *The Oxford Handbook of the Dead Sea Scrolls*, edited by Timothy H. Lim and John J. Collins, 323–50. Oxford: Oxford University Press, 2010.

Zuckerman, Bruce. "The Dynamics of Change in the Computer Imaging of the Dead Sea Scrolls and Other Ancient Inscriptions." In *Rediscovering the Dead Sea Scrolls: An Assessment of Old and New Approaches and Methods*, edited by Maxine L. Grossman, 69–88. Grand Rapids, MI: Eerdmans, 2010.

Index of Scripture and Second Temple Period Literature

HEBREW BIBLE/OLD TESTAMENT

Genesis

1	130, 136
1–2	123
1–3	127
1:1	128n31, 137n56
1:1—2:4	128
1:2	136, 137n56
1:9	137n56
1:14	137
1:14–15	131
1:14–18	147
1:15	137
1:15, 17	131, 137
1:24–25	137n56
1:26–27	137n56
1:28	66, 128, 137n56
1:28–29	66
1:28–30	65–67, 133, 147
1:29	137n56
1:29–30	66, 108
2:2	128
2:8	65
2:15–16	133
2:16–17	128
2:17	134
3	123, 128n33, 134
3–4	128, 133
3:11	134
5:28–29	43–44
6–9	127
6:1–4	37–38, 40, 42, 47, 79, 83, 142
6:2–4	43–44, 48–49, 62
6:3	75n25, 81–84, 93, 142
6:4	118, 144
6:5	38–39, 109, 111–13, 128–29, 131, 133–34, 143n1, 146
6:5 7	37, 142
6:5–8	37
6:6–12	113
6:7	38
6:8	48
6:8–9	46
6:8–10	112
6:9	129, 131
6:11–13	37, 62, 142
6:12	51n118, 111–12, 146

Genesis (continued)

6:13	38, 51n118, 83–84, 113, 137n56
6:13–22	113
6:17	38, 51n118, 113, 131, 136, 137n56
6:18–22	137n56
6:19	51n118, 131
6:22	129, 131
7:1–10	113
7:1–16	137n56
7:4	131
7:5–6	129, 131
7:7	129, 131
7:10–12	75n25
7:11	85, 90, 112–13, 115–16, 129
7:11–12	84, 115, 131, 143
7:12	85, 87, 90, 116, 130–31
7:13–17	113
7:14	117
7:15–16	51n118
7:16	124, 129, 131
7:17	84–85, 87, 90, 143
7:19	130–31
7:19–20	136, 137n56
7:21	51n118
7:21–23	117–19, 144
7:22	117, 129, 131
7:23	117
7:24	75n25, 84–85, 87, 90, 143
8–9	130
8:2–3	144
8:3	85, 87–88, 90
8:3–6	75n25, 84, 143
8:4	59–60, 85, 87–88, 90, 144–45
8:5	85, 90, 137n56
8:6	85, 90
8:8–14	75n25, 84, 143
8:10	86, 90
8:12	86, 90
8:13	86, 90
8:13–14	63
8:14	86, 90
8:14–19	90
8:17	51n118
8:18	75n25
8:20–21	61
8:21	62, 128
8:22	131, 137
9:1	137n56
9:1–3	65–67, 147
9:2	66
9:2–3	131
9:3	66, 137n56
9:11	51n118
9:11–12	131
9:12	135, 146
9:12–13	131
9:14	62
9:15	131, 136
9:15–17	51n118
9:24–27	75n25
11:31	75n25
13:14–18	63
15:1	63
15:4	34
15:9	75n25
15:17	75n25
18:31–32	75n25
22:10–12	75n25
28:3–4	75n25
35:2	138n57
36:12	75n25
49:3–4	75n25
49:10	75n25, 93n65

Exodus

7:5	135, 146
9:12	124
10:15	124
14:4	135, 146
15:10	116

Leviticus

4:17–18	62n137
4:25	62n137
4:27—5:26	62n137

INDEX OF SCRIPTURE AND SECOND TEMPLE PERIOD LITERATURE

4:30	62n137
5:7-10	62n137
6:15	62n137
11:32	138n57
13:6, 34	138n57
14:8-9	138n57
15:13, 28	138n57
16:30	138n57
17:5	138n57
22:4, 7	138n57
23:33-44	88n56
23:33-35, 39	88n55

Numbers

8:6-7	138n57
19:12, 19	138n57
24:16	131
31:23	138n57

Deuteronomy

1-4	106
8	111, 119, 143
8:10	108-10
8:10-20	110n50
8:11-14	110
8:11-18	110
8:19-20	110

Judges

5:4-5	56

1 Samuel

2:10	114, 148n12

Isaiah

24:18-20	114-15, 119, 148
29:6	114
63:1	56
66:16	52

Jeremiah

13:27	138n57
33:8	138n57

Ezekiel

24:13	138n57
26:3	131
28:13-16	65n147
36:8	107n37
36:25, 33	138n57
37:23	138n57
39:12	131
43:26	138n57

Joel

3:18	107n37
4:15-16 [MT]	114, 148n12

Amos

9:13	107n37

Habakkuk

2:14	131

Malachi

3:3	138n57

Psalms

18:8, 14, 16 [MT]	114, 148n12
29:3	114-15, 148n12
33:6	128nn30-31
68:9 [MT]	114, 148n12
72:16	107n37
78	106, 132n43, 135
105-6	106
105	132n43, 135

Job

4:17	138n57
37:4–5	114, 148n12

Ecclesiastes

11:3	131

Daniel

7:9–14	56
7:11	57
9:24	83

Ezra

6:20	138n57

Nehemiah

9	106
9:25–27	110
12:30	138n57
13:22	138n57

NEW TESTAMENT

Matthew

24:37–39	49–50, 114n56, 147n9

John

1:1, 3	128n30

Romans

5:12–18	128n33

Hebrews

	106

1 Peter

3:19–21	139n60, 145n7
3:20–21	139

2 Peter

3:3–7	49–50, 114n56, 147n9

Jude

6–7	38

Revelation

14:14–20	56
14:17–19	57
14:18	56
20:11–15	57

APOCRYPHA AND PSEUDEPIGRAPHA

1 Enoch	22, 27–28, 33n78, 37–40, 43–44, 47, 139, 142	5:25	90
		5:27–28	90
		5:28	60, 145
1:4	56n127	5:30	90
5–11	37	5:31	90
6–7	42	5:31–32	90
7	55	5:32	89–90
10:1–3	38, 48	6:1	89
10:20–22	138, 145n7	6:2	62
54	37	7:1	60, 145
65–67	37	7:20–25	38
83–84	38		
86–89	38	*3 Maccabees*	106
89:5–6	118–19, 144n5		
90	49–50, 114n56, 147n9	2:4	118–19, 144n5
90:24–27	57		
106	45	*Sibylline Oracles*	49, 114n56, 147n9
106–107	38, 44		
106:15	89		
108	49–50, 114n56, 147n9	1.261–274	60, 145n6

Jubilees	4, 20, 22, 27–28, 33n78, 38, 40, 60, 91, 137, 142	*Sirach (ben Sirach)*	
		16:7	118, 144n5
4–6	42		
4:22	38		
5:6–20	38	*Wisdom of Solomon*	
5:21–32	89		
5:23–25	90	14:6–7	118, 144n5

DEAD SEA SCROLLS

1Q19 (Book of Noah)	4, 7, 9	0:5–6	39, 50
		0:5–11	39
		0:5–13	50
		0:6	52, 57–58
1QapGen (Genesis Apocryphon)		0:8	39–40, 40n92
	2–11, 13–38, 49–50, 57–59, 67–68, 141–43, 145, 147–49	0:10	39
		0:10–11	39, 50
0:4	39	0:11	39
0:5	51, 58	0:12	36n80, 39, 58
		0:13	39, 57–58

207

0:15	36n80	X:12–18	61, 63, 145
0:17	40–42	X:13	61
0:18	39	X:13–17	37n80
I:1	42, 42n97	X:13–18	62
I:2	42	XI:1	62–63, 145
I:2–3	48	XI:9	63
I:22	51	XI:9–15	145
I:25	42, 51, 58	XI:11	37n80, 62–63
II:1	44, 52	XI:11–12	37n80, 65, 67, 147
II:1–7	44	XI:13–15	64
II:5	44, 48	XI:15	63
II:8–18	44, 52	XI:16–17	65–67, 147
II:10	52, 58	XII:13	60–61, 67, 145, 147
II:15	52, 54–55, 58	XII:16–17	37n80
II:18	52, 58	XIII:8	54
II:19–26	44	XIII:8–12	54
III:1–13	44–45	XIII:10–11	54
III:9–12	45	XIII:12	55
IV:11–12	45	XIII:13–14	55
V:2–4	36n80	XIII:16	51
V:3–4	45	XIII:16–17	55, 58
V:9	53	XIV:9	37n80
V:10	45, 53, 58	XIV:9–15	52–55
V:12–13	45	XIV:11–17	55
V:13	58	XIV:12–14	55, 58
V:16–19	45–46	XV:9–15	56
V:28	46	XV:10–12	50, 56
V:29	31–32, 34–35, 46	XV:12	56, 58
VI:1	52, 54–55, 58	XV:21	54
VI:1–6	46–47	XVI:8—XVII:19	37n80
VI:4	36n80	XVI:12, 14	37n80
VI:6	51, 58	XIX:7	37n80
VI:8–9	47, 49, 143	XIX:8	37n80
VI:11	48, 62	XIX:14	37n80
VI:11–15	47	XIX:25	36n80
VI:11—VII:5	47, 49, 53, 143	XX:8–31	36n80
VI:12	48	XX:14	51
VI:13–14	48	XX:18	51
VI:16	48, 62	XXI:8–14	37n80
VI:19	62	XXI:9–14	63, 145
VI:19–20	48	XXI:21–22	37n80
VI:23	48, 54	XXI:23—XXII:11	36n80
VI:25–26	48, 53	XXII:30–31	51
VI:26	54	XXII:31–33	36n80
VII:2	54	XXII:34	37n80
VII:5	47n106		
X:12	34, 60–62, 145		

INDEX OF SCRIPTURE AND SECOND TEMPLE PERIOD LITERATURE

1QH^a (Hodayot)	13n1, 98, 148n12	I:7–9	85–86
		I:7–10	87
		I:8–9	90
VIII:4–14	59n130	I:8–10	88
XI:34–35	114	I:9	87, 90
		I:9–10	85, 87, 90
		I:10	145
1QIsa^a (Isaiah^a)	13n1, 17, 124	I:11–12	85, 90
		I:11–13	87
		I:12	86n52
1QIsa^b (Isaiah^b)	13n1	I:12–13	90
		I:12–14	85, 90
		I:13–14	86n52, 87
		I:15–17	86–87, 90
1QM (War Scroll)	13n1, 21	I:17	86n52
		I:18–20	86–87, 90
		I:19–20	86n52
1QpHab (Habakkuk Pesher)		I:20–22	86–87, 90
		I:21–22	86n52
	13n1, 98	II:1–2	88, 91
VII:10–14	59n130	II:1–3	86, 90
		II:1–5	87–88, 93
1QS (Community Rule)	13n1,	II:2–3	86n52, 91
	21–22, 98	II:4–5	91
		II:5–8	75, 79, 81, 92n64
		II:8–13	79, 81, 92n64
		II:8–14	93n65
4Q185	105–6n33	III	75
		III:1–6	79, 81, 92n64
		III:6–14	79, 81, 92n64
		IV:1–3	81, 92n64, 93n65
4Q244	4, 9	IV:1–7	79
Frag 8, lines 2–3	60, 145	IV:3—VI:2	75, 81, 92n64
		V:1–4	93n65
		V:1–7	93n65
4Q252 (Commentary on Genesis)		V:1—VI:3	79
	2, 4–11, 69–82, 92–94,	V:5	79
	141–44, 147–49		
I:1	72n6, 83	*4Q254a*	
I:1–3	81–84, 92n64, 93, 142	*(Commentary on Genesis D)*	
I:1—II:5	75, 77, 79, 92, 148		
I:3—II:5	81–82, 84, 92n64, 93, 143	Frag 3, line 2	91
I:3–4	142		
I:3–5	85–86, 88, 90		
I:5–7	85–86, 90		
I:6–7	87		

4Q370 (Admonition Based on the Flood)

	2, 4–11, 95–106, 111, 119, 141–44, 146–49
I:1	102, 107–8, 111, 143
I:1–2	101, 110–11, 143, 146
I:1–3	119
I:1–6	101
I:1–9	104
I:1b–2a	108–11, 143
I:2	102, 106, 111–12, 117, 143, 148
I:2–3	112
I:2b	109, 111–113
I:3	101, 110–11, 115, 143, 146
I:3–5	101–2, 112–14, 116–17, 146, 148
I:3–6	119
I:3b–4a	114–15, 117, 119
I:4–5	115–16
I:6	101–2, 117, 119, 144
I:7–8	97
I:8–10	96
II:1	103
II:1–4	105
II:1–9	104–5
II:2	103
II:5	105
II:7	107 (cf. n35)
II:9	103, 105–6, 117, 148
I:10–12	133
I:11–12	134
I:11–13	128
I:12	128, 133–34, 136, 146
II:1	129
II:1–13	131
II:2	129
II:2–5	146
II:2–6	129
II:3	129
II:4	129
II:5	124, 129
II:6	129
II:6–8	129, 138
II:7–8	130
II:8	130, 138
II:8–9	134–35, 138–39, 145
II:8–11	135–36, 140, 146
II:9–13	130, 136, 140, 146–47
II:10	136–37
II:10–12	124
II:11	124
II:12	137
III:1–7	132
III:2	132
III:3	132
III:4	132
III:6	132
III:7	124, 132, 134–36, 139–40, 145–46
III:7–12	132, 134
III:11	124

4Q422 (Paraphrase of Genesis and Exodus)

	2, 4–11, 120–33, 139–41, 145–47, 149
I:6	128
I:6–8	128
I:6–13	122–23, 128
I:7	124, 128
I:8	128
I:8–9	133
I:9–10	128
I:10	134

4Q464

7, 10

4Q577

7, 10

4QInstruction

124

4QJub[a] (Jubilees[a])

137

6Q8	60, 145	*11QT*ᵃ *(Temple Scroll)*	17

11QPsᵃ XXVI:9–15
(Hymn to the Creator)

Damascus Document (CD)

                                    111, 119, 143

XXVI:9–15   107–8
XXVI:13   107–8

                                      4, 77, 98, 106

II:18–21   118–19, 144n5
IV:10–18   59n130

HELLENISTIC JEWISH LITERATURE

Josephus, Antiquities

1.70–71   49–50, 114n56, 147n9
1.92   60, 145n6

www.ingramcontent.com/pod-product-compliance
Lightning Source LLC
Chambersburg PA
CBHW070255230426
43664CB00014B/2544